Triumph Over Turbulence

By
Jim Magoffin

Alaska's Luckiest Bush Pilot

Founder
Chairman Emeritus — Retired
Interior Airways
Alaska International Air
MarkAir

To order, call toll free anytime
1-800-444-2524 EXTENSION 416

At: Air Venture '98

To: Gary and Bonnie

With all good wishes —
Keep on flying!!!

Jim Magoffin

Library of Congress Catalog-in-Publication Data

Magoffin, Jim
    Triumph Over Turbulence / Jim Magoffin — 1st edition
    A. CM.
    ISBN 0-9637806-0-3
    Autobiography

    Library of Congress Catalog Card Number 93-079310

Copyright © 1993 by Jim Magoffin

Printed in Hong Kong.

Front end sheet: Davey Crockett, vice president of sales for Lockheed, delivering a Hercules to Jim and Dot Magoffin.

Back end sheet: Living quarters for seismic crews being delivered to Sagwon, Alaska, by Hercules, Oct. 1968.

Acknowledgments

First, I thank my devoted parents, who lived a frugal life and worked so hard to provide all of their six children with a happy and healthy childhood.

Their efforts, good judgment and sacrifice ensured that each of us gained a complete education in the best schools in the United States, an invaluable asset leading to our many accomplishments.

I thankfully acknowledge the encouragement and suggestions of Alaskan author Cliff Cernick, a major reason that this story has become a book.

The *Fairbanks Daily News-Miner* most graciously allowed the use of news items, clippings and pictures, for which I am very appreciative. The few items from other publications are noted, and I thank them for permitting their reproduction.

Most of all, I thank my beloved wife, Dot, for making my life thoroughly enjoyable and for contributing so much to our story. Dot is the one who put my tape recordings on paper — the hardest part of writing a book.

Contents

Foreword

The Magoffin story is the remarkable saga of an indomitable young Lower 48 couple who gave up the comforts of life after World War II to seek a future in Alaska. The way they met Alaska's challenge while facing the fiercest odds and triumphed at last to achieve the American dream is an exciting success story.

It's the story of how Jim and Dot Magoffin converted hopes and dreams into glowing reality through sheer determination. These pages treat you to a literary feast as you embark on an almost incredible global odyssey. Before the last page is turned, you will have glimpsed the North Pole, skimmed the jungles of darkest Africa, soared over the forbidding wastes of Australia's outback and, most of all, experienced deepest Alaska at its rawest and roughest.

And you will have met two vibrant people with an unusual capacity for struggle. We meet them early in the book as a young honeymoon couple new to Alaska and living, if that's what it can be called, in a frontier-style log cabin at the outskirts of a desolate mining camp shrouded in ice fog. Outside, it's 50 degrees below zero or worse. A merciless, bitter wind is whipping veils of snow around the tiny dwelling's rough-hewn walls, obliterating the surroundings. Is this, as some might consider it, some kind of frozen hell?

Not really. Within these rough, unpainted walls reigns the warmth of love and faith that the good things the future holds are going to materialize if they work hard enough and keep their goals in mind.

Life was never easy for the Magoffins. Often, their situation deteriorated to near-hopelessness so bleak other young couples would have given up. Not the Magoffins. Time and again, circumstances slammed them against the ropes. Time and again the knockout countdown almost had them on the canvas. They never threw in the towel. Persistently, courageously, they kept struggling.

All of us love happy endings and no fictional happy ending can be as spectacular, as triumphant or as deserved as the one the Magoffins celebrated after long terrible cliffhanger years filled with trouble, turmoil and near-failure.

Having said all those good things about the Magoffins, let me point out that Jim Magoffin was no angel (though Dot is). Jim himself admits he "broke every aviation law in the book except the law of gravity." He relished knock-down-and-drag-out battles with bureaucrats. He was mule-stubborn at times. Tell him he can't do something and he'd go right ahead and do it. He cut corners dangerously, usually bringing wolves gnashing at his heels.

A wicked in-fighter when it came to regulation and competition, Jim often skated on extremely thin ice. He admittedly did things that were far from kosher. Yet it should be kept in mind that he was in a desperate struggle for his survival and the survival of his family and, in the final analysis, for Alaska.

When he finally and successfully created an aviation empire in the North that ultimately brought him more wealth than any man needs, the rewards he reaped came as well to Alaska's economy and Alaska's citizens. If for no other reason, Jim should, at this point, be forgiven his considerable sins.

What the Magoffins achieved in Alaska helped — and is helping — the 49th state to grow and prosper. How he parleyed a miserable little one-aircraft charter service into Alaska's dominant intrastate airline — while all around him comfortably certificated firms were biting the dust — testifies once again to his innate business sense and his skill in staying the course no matter how wild the storm.

In this book, Magoffin skillfully reconstructs an Alaskan aviation era largely neglected: the oil boom years. Yet, well before oil was discovered, Magoffin wisely set up an infrastructure designed to be put into play when oil development came. He was unerringly (and to his competitors, exasperatingly) prophetic in going ahead and building his own airport out on the desolate tundra though there was virtually no use for it at the time. And there was really no justification at the time for the navigational aids and sophisticated communications he installed at Sagwon, which was just a chunk of nowhere out on the North Slope of Alaska. All this was part of his vision and foresight and his conviction that the day would come when oil companies would have to move mountains of supplies to hundreds of locations and transport armies of workers to countless sites where there were absolutely no roads.

When that day came, Magoffin vowed, his firm would be right there to provide the transportation. There was no thumb-twiddling while waiting for all that to happen. The Magoffins launched an international air operation breathtaking in its boldness. The bustling enterprise was administered out of offices in London and Johannesburg. This unique, Alaska-owned business steadily piled up the capital that was needed when, inevitably, the oil skyrockets began bursting over Alaska.

Neither overseas nor in Alaska did Jim run his business from a swivel chair. He was out there seven days a week flying with the rest of his pilots and logging an amazing number of hours: 27,729 to this date. Dot, too, pitched in by flying charter trips and regular schedules. In all the millions of miles Jim and Dot Magoffin flew in Alaska, neither has wrecked a single aircraft — a matchless safety record.

In this book, Magoffin tells about the bad times and the good times and pulls no punches. And he doesn't spare himself as he recounts the mistakes he made and the costly wrong decisions that blighted, from time to time, his firm's forward movement.

You can be sure of one thing: What's here is authentic. This book reflects the extensive diaries and notes the Magoffins kept, as well as company records and government documents. Events are presented exactly as they happened. Quotes given are the words people spoke. Expressions cited are those commonly used by the Alaskans the Magoffins knew. Some names used applied at the time but changed later. For example, the Army Air Corps is now the U.S. Air Force and Barter Island is now Kaktovik.

Though they retired in 1982, the Magoffins are still very active pilots. They maintain their home in Fairbanks.

The book you are about to enjoy is a compelling history of their tempestuous times. It's also a solid contribution to Alaska aviation history.

Above all, this remarkable story is a testament to the invincibility of the human spirit. It demonstrates once again how hard work and determination on the part of just a few can make life richer and better for us all.

Cliff Cernick
Public Relations officer — Retired
Federal Aviation Administration

Prologue

For several years, I have been asked by family members, friends, business associates, employees and people who have flown with me to document at least some of my experiences as a civilian and military pilot. The story they thought worth telling was that of a pilot who has flown since 1934, a pilot who, with his wife, started and built, over a 46-year period, what has become one of Alaska's major businesses.

Up to now, I hesitated to undertake this project for many reasons. For one, my story lacks spectacular crashes or the kind of daring adventures that would appeal to modern readers. Practically, since I'm still an active pilot, I wondered about the wisdom of disclosing, with historical accuracy, activities that were then frowned on by the authorities. Let's make no bones about it. During my career I broke every aviation law except the law of gravity.

Even so, now that I'm past my mid-70s, I decided I might as well suffer whatever consequences could ensue from the things I did or didn't do in the past. If nothing else, this book will enlighten my family and other interested persons, since I have no interest in financial gain from what I set down here.

Since retirement, I have had the leisure to read a great deal about Alaska aviation and bush pilots. Much of this material was interesting, informative and accurate. Some of it, however, was written by people who had obviously spent a relatively short time in Alaska, talked to a few pilots and compounded their neglect by writing with shocking inaccuracy. Some of what they wrote was pure imagination — junk.

For example, one author, writing in the October 1952 issue of *Men* magazine, so distorted the facts of my life that his article has to be called utter fiction and nonsense. This book, I hope, will set the record straight. It's based on the facts.

Brevity dictates that I mention just a few of the thousands of flights we made and only a few of our business deals.

Although we started in Alaska we have been able to seize business opportunities worldwide. Our main Alaskan bases were at Fairbanks, Anchorage, Barrow, Barter Island, Umiat and Sagwon. Overseas, we maintained headquarters in London and Johannesburg.

Here, I am attempting to document events experienced by a pilot who was there way back and who, with his wife and associates, was instrumental in bringing Alaskan aviation to where it is today. I want this to stand as a factual record of vital Alaska events in contrast to the scrambled, second-hand stories recounted by writers relying on someone else's memory or, worse, dredging stuff up from their imaginations.

Much has been written about intrepid early bush pilots. A five-foot shelf could be filled with accounts of the exploits of such noted early Alaska pilots as Carl Ben Eielson, the Wiens, Harold Gillam, Bob Reeve, Bob Ellis, Mudhole Smith, Shell Simmons, Art Woodley, Frank Barr and Oscar Winchell, to mention just a few.

These pioneers earned their niche in Alaska aviation history. They risked their lives in primitive aircraft of doubtful reliability and some even managed to survive. Many of them were still active when Dot and I came on the scene in the post-World War II era.

The war's end gave a boost to aviation. Cessation of hostilities released scores of experienced pilots — I was one of them — and made available thousands of surplus military aircraft. Many former military pilots who wanted to continue flying bought aircraft Uncle Sam didn't need anymore and sold at far less than cost. After the war, aviation boomed in the United States, but not without thorny problems.

Many surplus airplanes were not licensed for commercial use and some were poorly maintained. This dramatically increased the accident rate, alarming civil aviation authorities and creating an adversarial relationship between the federal government and the newcomers. Non-scheduled airlines, commonly referred to as "non-skeds," created business by offering inexpensive charters and air freight service to remote areas.

Most non-skeds flourished briefly, usually until their first serious accident, then disappeared from the scene. However some, for very specific reasons, managed to survive. Contributing to the few successes were education, piloting and maintenance efficiency, leadership and personal discipline. Success or failure was also influenced by such things as geographical location, being in the right place at the right time and just plain "who you knew."

"Who we knew" saved our company several times, but our initial advantage was the excellent civilian flying instruction I received at the Fontana Flying Service and the superb training and experience given me by the Army Air Corps, now the U.S. Air Force.

Besides contributing invaluable experience, Air Corps pay bought us our first airplane and Air Corps connections helped save our company at critical times.

Surviving non-skeds in a few cases gradually evolved from "fly-by-night" operations and "gyppos" to efficient, properly certificated legitimate airlines. Some early certificated carriers met their demise for a variety of reasons, including limited education, under-financing, over-expansion and labor turmoil.

In our case, unusually good husband-and-wife teamwork was crucial to our success. I was blessed with a talented, remarkable wife who pitched in to help and support me with incredible skill and devotion.

Dot Magoffin flew commercially for our company, becoming one of our best, safest pilots. For many years, she managed the office with great efficiency. Dot's home has always been — and still is — a center of genuine hospitality. This was invaluable fallout for our business because she helped entertain employees, customers and business associates.

Once, Dot had been visiting for a few minutes over coffee with a group of our pilots. She had just gone back upstairs to her office and I happened to be within earshot of the pilots' ready room. I overheard one of the pilots, Jim Dunlap, remark to the others: "Now, *there's* a lady with real class." How right he was.

Interior Airways, founded in 1946, was one of the fortunate non-sked survivors. While the name "Interior Airways" was appropriate in the early days when most of our flights were to points in interior Alaska, the later change to "Alaska International Air" more properly described our far-flung overseas operations that we pursued while waiting for the Trans-Alaska oil pipeline permit to be issued. The most recent change, to MarkAir, eliminated the confusion between two airlines — Alaska and Alaska International — operating in the same area.

Contrary to some verbal and written pronouncements, Interior Airways and Alaska International Air are not defunct. Both are alive and well. They continue to operate under a different name: MarkAir — and some people we hired in the late '50s are still active with the company.

However, many of those who worked with us in the '40s and early '50s are now either retired or deceased. It gives us pride and satisfaction to be able to say that most of those hired by Interior Airways or Alaska International, who performed well and stayed with the company, benefited both financially and professionally.

We were extremely fortunate in many ways. We founded our airline at just the right time. It was a time of opportunity that gave us important advantages over firms founded at other times by equally determined aviation entrepreneurs. We insisted on dependable engines, efficient instrumentation and proper electronics. Of critical importance, we had access to reliable maintenance even before we could afford our own mechanics. And we were fortunate to come on the scene in Alaska at a time when pilots were enjoying more and better ground facilities and navigational aids.

Another major advantage was our area of operation. The weather in interior Alaska is predominantly good. Though interior winters are bitterly cold, the flying environment in this part of Alaska is generally favorable and manageable if you prepare for it.

Getting piston engine planes ready for flight in winter is tough and time-consuming. Once in the air, however, a normal inversion facilitates flying because of the warmer, moisture-free air aloft. Pilots based in places like Juneau, Ketchikan or Kodiak often negotiate more bad weather in a month than interior pilots have to cope with in an entire year.

Another factor affecting the longevity of our airline was the lower cost element resulting from the length of our flights. Few were under 100 miles and many were 400 miles or more. In some areas, pilots must land every 50 or so miles, spending more non-revenue time loading and unloading than they do flying.

It didn't hurt at all to come on the scene at a time when Alaska's population was booming and big things that boosted the Alaska economy were taking place. We were on-stage for the most important event of all: the oil boom. Our firm was financially blessed by DEW line construction activities, the Ballistic Missile Early Warning System (BMEWS), the Native Land Claims settlement, as well as other developments.

Finally, just plain good luck favored us. In more than 22,000 hours of Alaska flying, for example, I have had only one complete engine failure and in all our Alaska flying, neither Dot nor I has ever wrecked an airplane. I might add, incidentally, that Dot, who has logged more than 3,600 flying hours, holds commercial, multi-engine, instrument and seaplane ratings. So far, neither one of us has had a single CAA or FAA violation.

Since this is a no-holds-barred book, written with candor and sincerity, chips are certainly going to fall. So let me say right at the outset that should any of the statements and disclosures herein be hurtful or painful, it's because I'm telling it like it is and was. Though I'm sympathetic, I make no apologies should what lies ahead offend certain government agencies, politicians, races, religions, industries, corporations, unions or individuals.

So fasten your seat belts. ✝

To dauntless Dottie Magoffin,
without whom this adventure
never would have been possible.

CHAPTER 1

Lucky

My luck, it seems, began when I was born in northern Minnesota in 1917. I had three brothers and two sisters. For some reason my parents called me by my middle name, Shelby, probably because a neighboring family who were our very close friends, the Wilbur Van Everas, had a boy named Jim. However, my nickname was "Cot" — short for cottontail rabbit — a name that stuck with me throughout my school years.

My dad, a member of a large Kentucky family, was an avid outdoorsman. When he finished school, his first job was supplying game to a timber company on the Canadian border. It took a lot of moose and deer meat to keep those lumberjacks happy.

My earliest memories are of my dad teaching us to hunt and fish. Very early, he instructed us on snaring rabbits and trapping muskrats. Later, he showed us the fine points of hunting deer, ducks and grouse.

Dad was a class of 1893 graduate of the Virginia Military Institute in Lexington where, during his senior year, he was captain of the football team. A reserve officer and an engineer, he spent considerable time in Alaska and in the Yukon Territory during the gold rush. He was hired by the U.S. government to survey Alaska's Seward Peninsula, something he did on foot. He later joined Klondike stampeders, settling in a log cabin outside Dawson, where he lived in 1898 and 1899.

Though Dad's prospecting was mildly successful, he needed to raise cash to keep alive. Acquiring a dog team, he began shooting wild game, which he sold to proprietors of Dawson's crowded restaurants.

Though not talkative, Dad occasionally shared with us stories about his Dawson days. His early letters to his sister in Duluth were rich in Klondike sidelights. He told about selling a sled load of moose meat in Dawson for $900. He told about being hired by Dawson merchants to go to Seattle along with several other young fellows to bring

---

Deerwood enterprise - Fri. nov. 16. 1928-

Eleven Year Old Boy Kills Big Deer.

Shelby Magoffin, 11 year-old son of Mr. and Mrs. B. Magoffin, Jr., has the distinction of being the youngest hunter here who has bagged a deer. He with his father and brothers were out south of Kimberly, at sunrise Sunday morning and were getting established on certain lookouts along the deer trails when a big buck came within range of Shelby's shotgun which was loaded with a ball, and he blazed away at it. The deer had eight-prong antlers and weighed 250 pounds dressed.

Shelby, quite naturally, is today the hero of the day, not only among his boy friends, but also among the seasoned hunters who know that killing a big buck is a thrill that does not come to any one very often.

My dad, Beriah Magoffin Jr., during the Klondike Gold Rush, 1898.

north a load of groceries and merchandise to sell in Dawson stores. Bringing these supplies in, they loaded them on a flat barge on Lake Bennett and hired a steamboat to tow it. Everything went okay until a storm arose and the steamship captain, fearing his boat would be lost with the barge in tow, cut it loose. The barge drifted onto the rocks and broke up, and all the cargo was lost.

A very conservative man, Dad raised his children to work, save and invest. He wisely steered us away from bad habits by insisting that deer could smell people who smoked and if we did, we'd never get a shot at one. As soon as I was old enough, I was sent to Boy Scout camp and the following summer to caddie camp near a big golf course where I caddied 18 holes for 50 cents.

The following year, 1934, I was enrolled in the Citizens Military Training Camp at Fort Snelling, Minnesota, an infantry training outfit with rifles and light tanks. Fort Snelling

Hunting and fishing improved the menu at our boarding house in Michigan.

After high school, I enrolled in the Virginia Military Institute in 1935, finishing with a degree in civil engineering in 1939.

was not far from the Minneapolis airport, where the flights quickly caught my interest. The only time I'd ever flown was once during the winter of 1923, when a barnstormer landed an OX-5 Jenny on a frozen lake near our home. At my urging, Dad sent me enough money to start taking flying lessons in Minneapolis.

My first lessons were at the Elmer Hinck Flying Service at Wold-Chamberlain Field. It was before Piper got into the aircraft manufacturing business and we flew Taylor Cubs. The Cubs had no electrical system, no battery, no starter, no lights, no brakes and no tail wheel — only a spring-steel skid hanging down in the rear. Landings had to be judged so the drag of the tail skid would stop the airplane before it ran out of usable space.

After a few lessons at Hinck's, I had just enough money left to take a lesson at the DePonti School of Aviation at Wold-Chamberlain. There we flew a Rearwin Cloudster with a radial engine, a bit more airplane than the Cub.

I took my first airline trip in the summer of 1936, enjoying a flight from Washington to Chicago on Pennsylvania Central Airlines. The plane was the original twin-engine Lockheed 10E Electra, the only airliner I've ever seen with wicker passenger chairs.

After high school, I enrolled in the Virginia Military Institute in 1935, finishing with a degree in civil engineering in 1939. Not too excited about taking an engineering job then, I enrolled at the Michigan College of Mining and Technology, emerging two years later with a degree in mining engineering.

Enrolling at Michigan Tech was a stroke of luck. I got there just when war fever was heating up in Europe. Some far-sighted government officials had seen the need for military pilots and launched the Civilian Pilot Training program. I enrolled immediately, and within two years had a commercial pilot's license and an instructor's rating.

At Michigan Tech I paid $40 a month for room and board at the home of Buck and Marie Vivian, a few blocks from the campus. I was troubled because they served very little meat. When I complained, Mrs. Vivian pointed out that if she served meat the cost of room and board would go up substantially and some of the boarders were having money problems as it was.

My friend Robert C. Weed, a mining engineering student at Michigan Tech, 1940. Weed and I became good friends, and some 36 years later, he played a part in our business efforts in Africa.

That evening, I drove out of town a few miles to where I had seen promising deer sign. I had a flashlight safety-pinned into the right side of my cap, a procedure I learned from northern Minnesota backwoodsmen we called "Jackpine Savages." Walking down an old logging trail, I spotted eyes shining in the light beam. Easing closer, I shot a buck deer standing on top of a beaver dam. I pulled it to dry land, dressed and skinned it and placed it in the trunk of my car.

I flopped the carcass onto the Vivians' kitchen floor and asked them to let me know when that was gone. They were pleased but nervous since deer season still had not opened. From then on, I helped keep the menu interesting by bringing in grouse and northern pike.

I'd go hunting and fishing often with my younger brother, Chick, also a mining engineering student at Michigan Tech, and his fraternity brothers. One of the frat men who went along was Robert C. Weed, a mining engineering student and enthusiastic outdoorsman. Weed and I became good friends, and some 36 years later, he played a part in our business efforts in Africa.

The European situation prompted the U.S. Army Air Corps to activate contract flying schools throughout the country. After graduation from Tech, I got a job training British cadets at the Lakeland School of Aeronautics in Lakeland, Florida. They were easy to teach, knowing their training was not for pleasure but for combat. One young Britisher was so good he embarrassed me. I'd demonstrate a snap roll or slow roll, then let him try it. Darned if he didn't do it better than I could.

At Lakeland, I flew with students most of the winter, every morning one week and every afternoon the next. During free time, I tested Florida's superb hunting and fishing, catching bass and crappies, shooting quail and generally providing for myself, although my cooking wasn't so hot. Each morning I'd aim my .22-caliber rifle out of the window of my shack, shoot a grapefruit off a tree, and my dog would retrieve it. ✛

CHAPTER 2

The Army Air Corps

After Pearl Harbor, I contacted Washington and had my reserve commission changed from the Infantry to the Air Corps. I was ordered to report to Maxwell Field, Alabama, where I was assigned to the Air Inspection Section, a unit that supervised training schools. I went in to see my commanding officer, Lt. Col. Robert A. Breitweiser, a West Point graduate, and explained I had the "red ass," common slang for being burned out as a flight instructor.

"I want to be assigned to a fighter outfit," I told Col. Breitweiser.

The colonel looked me right in the eye and barked, "Magoffin, after me you come first!" Within two weeks, he was gone but I was stuck there.

Then another lucky break: Col. F. H. Robinson, my new commanding officer, was a regular guy, a pilot's pilot. Surmising I wasn't happy riding with students, he ordered me to the Navy's Air Gunnery School at Pensacola. There, we flew North American AT-6s that had a .30-caliber machine gun mounted in each wing. I made good scores because, while duck hunting in Minnesota, I had learned something about leading a moving target.

An experience at Pensacola influenced my later activities in Alaska. One day, during a gunnery session, my ailerons jammed, requiring me to control the aircraft by skidding the turns. I told the control tower operator what was wrong, and he cleared the field so I had no competition on final approach.

When I landed and taxied up to base operations, the operations officer came charging out red hot because I had aborted the mission and disrupted other landing traffic. When I slipped back the canopy he yelled, "What in hell's going on? What's this about jammed ailerons?"

When he grabbed the right aileron and shook it, the hull of a .30-caliber cartridge clattered to the concrete. He picked it up, stared at it, then stopped cussing. We became pretty good friends.

We were to meet again 30 years later in Washington, D.C., when I was chairman of Alaska International Air and he was a high-ranking officer in the Naval Aviation Command Supply section.

No sooner had I returned from gunnery school than Col. Robinson got me enrolled in the Air Corps Instrument Flying School at Bryan, Texas, a great break for me.

I arrived in Bryan the day before my first class. The next morning a January pea soup fog had socked in the field. We were in one of the classrooms waiting to be addressed by the school's commanding officer, Col. Duckworth. He was in Tulsa, so we figured the class would be cancelled until the weather improved. But at a quarter to 8 we heard his airplane taxi up on the ramp, which we couldn't see because it was shrouded in thick fog.

We heard the engine shut down and moments later Col. Duckworth entered the classroom — a mighty impressive way to launch intensive instrument flight training.

I'll never forget Col. Duckworth's remark that morning: "There's no weather you can't fly safely through if you have the proper equipment, a well-trained pilot and know how to handle the situation." My later experiences often demonstrated that he was correct.

I finished the training at Bryan and got the Air Corps "white card" signifying I was proficient in instrument flight. I immediately set out to get the "green card," giving me clearance authority. Pilots with "white cards" had to have their flights approved by operations officers but "green card" holders could clear themselves and proceed where and when desired.

Preparing myself for my "green card" instrument check-ride, I'd fly a P-40 into the worst weather I could find, making as many approaches as I could to get myself feeling as comfortable as possible while flying under instrument conditions.

Next I became an Army check pilot assigned to the primary flying school in Helena, Arkansas. To start with, we flew Boeing PT-17s, changing later to Fairchild PT-19s. The 17s, biplanes with radial engines, were quite good at acrobatics. The PT-19s — low-wing monoplanes with Ranger engines — weren't good for acrobatics but had a wide landing gear and no tendency to ground loop, making them easy to learn on.

There were interesting moments at Helena. Once, I witnessed an argument between a newly arrived Army pilot, a second lieutenant, and an old civilian flight instructor, "Sarg" Madison. The "shavetail" went to great lengths in describing how to execute a slow roll. Old "Sarg" butted in: "Listen, son," he said, "I've got more time on my back than you've got straight and level." That ended the argument.

While flying PT-17s at Helena, one instructor consulted me about a student having trouble making good landings though otherwise he flew the airplane quite well. Reluctant to solo the student, the instructor asked me to ride with him to evaluate his flying.

Watching the student get into the cockpit, I noticed he was quite short. He made a couple of good landings and then botched one badly. I surmised he couldn't see how close to the ground he was, so I had him taxi back to the Ops building and stop the airplane. I went in, got an extra parachute and put it under the student, elevating him about seven inches. We went up again, whereupon he made three good landings, so I soloed him.

I had forgotten the incident until, in 1968, a highly decorated Air Force full colonel walked into my office in Fairbanks and, after introducing himself, asked, "Remember me?"

"I'm sorry, I don't," I told him.

"I'm the cadet you soloed at Helena after you put an extra parachute under me!"

The colonel had come through the war with a good record and wanted to thank me for keeping him from washing out.

Two things bothered me a lot at Helena. Instructors taught students different techniques for the same maneuvers, confusing them since each student might fly with several instructors during the primary course. For example, some instructors taught students to handle crosswind landings by crabbing into the wind until ready to touch the ground, then quickly aligning the airplane with the runway by using downwind rudder pressure. Others were taught to lower a wing and slip into the wind, landing on the upwind wheel first and then easing the downwind wheel onto the ground as the airplane slowed.

The second thing was that too many accidents were occurring during simulated forced landing practice. I wrote a training manual titled "Standardization of Primary Flying Training," setting forth standard procedures for teaching students the various maneuvers, and the manual was accepted by the Eastern Flying Training Command. My manual stipulated that all simulated forced landings should be terminated a minimum of 200 feet above any ground obstacle.

The new procedure went over well with instructors and military authorities alike and cut down on accidents.

The problem was that instructors let the aircraft get too low in an effort to show the student whether he would have hit or missed the chosen landing area. By the time the throttle was advanced, the engine had cooled and often failed to produce power immediately. As a result, the aircraft would end up in the trees.

The 200-foot safety cushion that I stipulated would give ample time for the engine to develop power and clear any obstacles. Actually, engine failures were rare and when they did occur, students usually got the airplane down okay.

Shortly afterward, I was promoted to first lieutenant and assigned as military check pilot at the pre-glider training school at Antigo, Wisconsin. At Antigo, we didn't have gliders, so we used J3 Cubs. Climbing to 2,000 feet, we'd cut the ignition, then glide to a landing on a fairly good-sized grass field, thus preparing students to land without power. Many glider pilots who took part on D-Day in World War II got their training at Antigo.

Hunting there was great. Each afternoon during hunting season, I'd fly low over

My brother "Bear," an Annapolis graduate and commander of the destroyer Preston.

fields near the airport until I flushed a flock of sharp-tailed grouse. I'd watch where they landed, then drive out there with my dog and enjoy a nice grouse hunt before dark. The people I was staying with liked wild game and were always happy to get a mess of grouse.

Next, I became an Army check pilot at the Primary Flying Training School at Lafayette, Louisiana. Here, the routine was the same — flying with students and instructors. The best part of my Lafayette duty was goose hunting in the rice fields and the savory goose gumbo subsequently served at my boarding house table.

I then transferred back to Maxwell Field as a member of a travelling Air Inspection Team. Maxwell Field was a great place to be stationed because a wide variety of aircraft was based there and my commanding officer was the kind of guy who thought airplanes should be flying. I got checked out in virtually everything on the base including:

Cessna UC-78 twin
Beechcraft C-45 twin
Lockheed 10E twin
North American B-25
Boeing B-17
Consolidated B-24
Seversky P-36 Fighter
Bell P-39 Aircobra Fighter
Bell P-63 Super Cobra
Republic P-47
Curtis P-40
Douglas Dive Bomber SE
Vultee BT 13
North American AT-6
Curtis AT-9
Beechcraft AT-10
Douglas C-47 (DC-3)
Noorduyn UC-64 Norseman
Beechcraft Staggerwing D-17

One day, a ferry command pilot flew in a brand new North American P-51 fighter, parked it and turned over the delivery documents to base operations, then left. The P-

My brother "Mort" — a West Pointer and fighter ace — was commander of a P-47 group in England.

51 had just come out and nobody there knew how to fly it. When Col. Robinson told me to check myself out in it, I found it to be the sweetest flying plane I've ever been in. It had a wide landing gear, no ground looping tendencies, was stable in flight and on approach, carried lots of fuel and was long on power and speed.

Late one Saturday night, I flew the P-51 to South Dakota where I was met by my friend, Fred Best. After a great pheasant hunt, I arrived back at Maxwell on Sunday night with the gun compartments stuffed with birds. Our Air Inspection Section enjoyed a grand pheasant feed.

I couldn't shake off a feeling of guilt since my three brothers were all in combat. "Bear," an Annapolis graduate, was commander of the destroyer Preston. "Mort," a West Pointer and fighter ace, was commander of a P-47 group in England. "Chick" was a B-17 bomber pilot stationed in England. In his letters, Chick advised me to stay where I was, stating that combat "wasn't any fun at

My brother "Chick," a B-17 bomber pilot stationed in England.

all." Chick's planes were so shot up that he went through three B-17s to get his required 25 missions before rotating back to the United States. Both Bear and Chick were service casualties. Though shot down and wounded, Mort made it back and is retired in California.

At Maxwell, I built up quite a few hours in Boeing B-17s and Consolidated B-24s. One of my duties was to check out bomber crews for efficiency and compatibility before they were assigned to overseas combat units.

One requirement was that each crew fly a long cross-country and remain overnight. Most crews would head for Los Angeles or Las Vegas and get drunk and do the other things young men do on trips like that. One June day, I suggested to this captain that instead of going out to the West Coast, we take his crew up to Minnesota and go

Army Officers Verify Tales of Arrowhead Angler
Duluth News Tribune June 28, 1944

LEFT TO RIGHT, CAPTS. DAVID L. WILLIS, ROBERT HENNING AND JAMES MAGOFFIN.

3 FLY 1,100 MILES TO FISH HERE

The plane flown from Duluth to Maxwell field, Ala., yesterday by the army air force captains in the above picture, carried four wall-eyed pike instead of bombs. The officers were Capts. David L. Willis, Shelby, N. C., Robert Henning, West Salem, Ohio, and James Magoffin, Deerwood, Minn.

A special flight training course, which they are taking at the Alabama field, requires a training flight to an optional destination which must be at least 1,000 miles away. After listening to Captain Magoffin's tales of Minnesota fishing, the fliers selected Duluth as their flight destination and telegraphed the Duluth Chamber of Commerce to make fishing arrangements for them. They flew here Monday to verify Captain Magoffin's claims.

Allowed a 24-hour lay-over, they spent most of the time in a boat on the St. Louis river near Fond du Lac. Four big wall-eyes, the largest of which weighed four and a half pounds, took their bait. Satisfied, the fishermen threw back a number of smaller fish.

The fliers left the Duluth airport for Alabama yesterday noon, expecting to make the 1,100-mile flight in about five hours. Captain Magoffin, grandson of Beriah Magoffin who was an early Duluth settler, is a flight training officer at the field and left with a promise that the catch would send more fliers to Duluth for their training flight.

fishing. He agreed and other crew members didn't seem to mind.

I called the Duluth Chamber of Commerce to arrange a walleyed pike fishing trip. We flew to Duluth, parked the bomber and enjoyed an afternoon's fishing, leaving the next day with a nice catch. Everything would have been fine had the press stayed away. Before we left, a reporter came out and took a picture of us in front of the B-24 holding a string of fish. When the article appeared in the Duluth newspaper, something hit the fan.

Not long after returning to Maxwell, my commanding officer called me in and told me Washington had complained. Wartime gasoline rationing was in effect and a St. Paul citizen wrote Chester Boles, head of the Office of Price Administration, complaining that while he couldn't get enough gas to go to his cabin a few miles north of St. Paul, this Capt. Magoffin could fly a four-engine bomber a couple of thousand miles just to go fishing.

I figured I was in a pack of trouble but Col. Robinson answered that I had been ordered to make the trip as part of my duty and training command requirements. Though I got out of that one nicely, the local operations officer subsequently got on me because the runway at Duluth wasn't, according to aircraft specifications, long enough for a B-24.

On our inspection trips, my duty was to ride with the school's flight instructors and students to evaluate the efficiency of the training. A maintenance department inspector accompanied us, as well as an officer to check such things as administration and mess halls. One senior administrative inspector was Col. Harmar D. Denny, who flew with me on several inspection trips. Col. Denny and I became good friends and he was to play a very critical role in my business affairs after my Air Force duty.

Following our inspections, we gave school officials the opportunity to explain discrepancies. We tried hard to be helpful in our efforts to increase flight training efficiency and assure that cadets were getting the best training possible.

Among the schools we checked was the one for black cadets at Tuskegee, Alabama. Being a Northerner, it was a new experience for me to glance in the mirror and see this black face partially covered by helmet and goggles in the rear cockpit of the PT-17, with gosport tubes protruding from each earpiece.

I was particularly impressed with the school's commanding officer, Col. Benjamin O. Davis, a West Point graduate, who was as sharp as he could be. Col. Davis was soon to become a general officer and lead his fighter pilots to fame in World War II.

We also monitored training at Beverly Howard's Hawthorne School of Aviation at Orangeburg, South Carolina, where the students were French cadets. Hawthorne was a fine school with good instructors and good management but its cadets were quite a contrast to British students. French cadets were sloppy dressers, lacking the inherent discipline most Britishers display. However, Bevo Howard, a renowned stunt pilot, was an inspiration to his students and his school produced many good pilots. ✝

CHAPTER 3

My New Commanding Officer

Dot Riddle was the daughter of a farmer in north central Alabama. From the first, I knew she was an exceptional girl.

Back at Maxwell, where I wrote up inspection reports, a pretty little secretary who worked in the commanding general's office had attracted my attention. Dot Riddle was the daughter of a farmer in north central Alabama. From the first, I knew she was an exceptional girl. A pretty brunette, she had a wonderful personality, always laughing and smiling and very open and outgoing.

She was never haughty, and after I met her parents in Ashland, I could see why. They were good, genuine people, Southern Baptists, but not overly religious. Dot seemed so happy all the time I nicknamed her "Sunshine" — a name that stuck with those who worked at headquarters.

Dot wasn't the typical, soft Southern belle. She was in as good physical shape as I was. Her strong muscles stood her in good stead in Alaska where, as a bush pilot, she had to lift five-gallon cans of gas over her head and dump them into a funnel on the aircraft wing. Also, she loaded and unloaded cargo and baggage, something bush pilots were expected to do.

It was obvious Dot was no stranger to work. She had finished business college and could take shorthand as fast as I could talk and type just about as fast. A wonderful secretary, Dot has been instrumental in our many business successes. She was always a snappy dresser with a pretty, slim, little figure that accentuated the clothes she made or bought — always in good taste. An outdoor girl, Dot suited me to a T because I lived for hunting and fishing. Social functions were always a pain to me and still are.

When Dot told me there were coveys of quail on her dad's property, the first day we could get off we headed there and hunted quail, ducks and doves.

After Dot transferred to Atlantic City, I just had to visit her. One dark night I was flying up there in a North American AT-6, a single-engine advanced trainer, which required a fueling stop at Charlotte, North Carolina. I was on final approach to Charlotte's airport and had been cleared to land when just as I was about to touch down, the airplane almost went out of control. The left wing tipped down and dragged on the concrete. When I overcorrected, the right wing dragged on the other side.

After parking the plane, I went to the operations office and found out what caused the problem. The crew chief of an A-20 attack bomber had been running up both engines with the tail pointed toward the runway. The AT-6 was caught in the propwash and almost flipped over. Damage wasn't serious, just a few scratches on both wing tips, so I fueled up and continued to Atlantic City with no problems. That was the only time I scratched one of Uncle Sam's aircraft.

1943: I was a training inspector at Maxwell Field. That's where I met Dot, who became my permanent commanding officer.

Shortly afterward, Dot was transferred again, this time to Louisville, cutting the visiting distance in half. One warm, humid Saturday night in April, one of the South's famous spring warm fronts was moving across the country. A B-17 was available, but I had to find a co-pilot. Kyle Sloane, a warrant officer who liked to fly, agreed to join me. He mentioned it might be a bad trip with all the lightning, rain and wind. I explained I was trying to get instrument experience anyway, so off we went. While paralleling the warm front enroute to Louisville, we experienced an unusual amount of St. Elmo's fire — eerie patches of bright light dancing up and down the wings during much of the flight. We landed in heavy rain at Louisville, stayed a few hours and then flew to Maxwell, a rough flight but valuable experience.

At war's end, I was still at Maxwell Field. Training schools were beginning to close, cadets were being dismissed and the Air Inspection Section was being dissolved.

One day the general's aide, a young second lieutenant, came into my office and informed me that "Maj. Magoffin was going to take the general's daughter to the dance at the officer's club this coming Saturday night." I had met the general's daughter and didn't relish the thought of taking her anywhere. I asked Col. Robinson if there was any way I could get out of it.

"Jim," he said, "if you're going to be in the peace time Air Force, you're going to have to put up with this kind of thing." Then he grinned and ordered me to deliver a B-17 to the training school at Sebring, Florida, taking me off the hook.

When Col. Robinson became commanding officer at Moody Field in Valdosta, Georgia, he took me with him as commandant of cadets. The only problem was that there were no cadets there when we arrived. I promptly got orders that stated: "In addition to your other duties, you are hereby appointed Base Game Warden."

When the Valdosta area was taken over for a military reservation, it was inhabited by a number of cows. Over the years, with no human contact, the cattle became as wild as deer.

The colonel suggested I shoot a wild cow for a barbecue. I spent two days trying to find a cow to shoot. I could sometimes hear them splashing through the swamp but couldn't get a shot. Finally, I bagged one by using a headlight at night when I caught one on the edge of the swamp. The colonel sent out a truckload of cooks and helpers who transformed the carcass into prime cuts. A few days later we enjoyed a grand barbecue with the barbecue sauce mixed in a washtub.

After my orders for separation from the Air Force as a lieutenant colonel came through in early April 1946, I drove on to my home in Minnesota. A few days later, Dot came up and we were married with my mother and older sister there. The best man was my former flight instructor, Mario Fontana.

"Rosie," Dot and Terry crossing the Smoky River on a railroad flatcar in Alberta, Canada, April 1946.

Immediately after the marriage we packed up my old Ford, called "Rosie" because of its faded red color, and headed for Alaska.

A job was waiting for me in Fairbanks. The Michigan Tech mining department arranged for me to take a position with the Fairbanks Exploration Co., a division of the U.S. Smelting, Refining and Mining Co.

At that time, the Alaska Highway had just been opened to civilian traffic and fuel stops were few and far between, so I carried an auxiliary supply. At a couple of places, we had trouble getting across rivers. One time we went across on a ferry. At another crossing, we put Rosie on a flatcar and rode across on the railroad.

When we reached the north country, we camped out at night, parking the car on the side of the road, dragging out our sleeping bags and pitching a small tent.

One night in British Columbia, wolves started serenading us right after dark. Dot sat up in her sleeping bag, her hair sticking straight up. She didn't like it at all, but there were no problems. Wolves don't attack humans, but we didn't know that then.

Spring thaw was well along, and in some sections the Alaska Highway almost disappeared into the swamp. At times, our car had to be towed through the muck by Road Commission tractors stationed at bad spots in both Canada and Alaska.

We arrived in Fairbanks in the evening and got a room at the Cheechako Hotel. The next morning, I went to the mining company office and checked in. Charlie Fowler and Al Seeliger were office managers for the firm. I was assigned to a mining engineering job out at the company's placer operation on Ester Creek, 10 miles west of Fairbanks. ✝

CHAPTER 4

Below Zero
Log Cabin Days

Not long after we got to Fairbanks, we were able to buy, for next to nothing, a sad excuse for a log cabin. It was set in a rough clearing not far from Ester's tailing piles. The dilapidated place was in terrible shape. Outside light filtered through the logs where moss chinking had fallen away. Shoving more moss into the cracks didn't help too much; we still shivered.

Our feeble, uncertain heating system was a 50-gallon wood-burning barrel sunk in a hole deep beneath the cabin, reachable only by an eight-foot ladder. This underground contrivance kept balking at keeping us warm until I got the bright idea, after the first big snowfall, of insulating the cabin almost to the vanishing point by covering it up with snow. Only then were we cozy and warm during that blistering cold winter.

But our real problem wasn't cold; it was making ends meet on the $272 a month I earned for a seven-day week. Putting enough food on the table would have been tough had it not been for hunting; that made a tremendous difference.

Shortly after we settled in our cabin, I lost no time in going out to Weeks Field,

1946: Dot with six caribou at our first home in Ester, Alaska. Putting enough food on the table would have been tough had it not been for hunting; that made a tremendous difference.

the town's airport on the south side of the Chena River.

At the Fairbanks Air Service, one of my first stops, I learned that the owners, Bud Seltenreich and Al Lorentzen, were operating a flying school and needed an instructor. Without much delay, I hired on to teach students in the evenings after my day's work at the mine. Dot wasn't too enthusiastic about my doing all that extra work, but we badly needed the money. At $5 an hour, I made as much in two hours of instruction as I could all day at the mine. With the extra income, we managed to save a little each month and began making a few modest investments. At that time the Dow Jones Average had just topped 200 and the volume of shares traded was flirting with the 2 million mark. Those figures changed to an average comfortably over 3,000 and a volume over 200 million shares during the period covered by this writing.

From the day we arrived in Fairbanks, Dot and I retained our avid interest in flying. The Fairbanks area had only a few miles of roads and it became obvious to us that if we were going to see much of Alaska, it would have to be by air. Our basic interest, initially, was flying's recreational rather than commercial potential. We saw aviation as a way to take us into the territory's superb wilderness hunting and fishing areas. So very early, we began to talk about buying our first airplane.

What made it possible was our accumulation of war bonds purchased during World War II. We calculated that by cashing all of them we'd have just about enough to buy a small airplane.

Our first aircraft, a Taylorcraft BC-12D. We paid $3,250 for it, all the money we had, and coincidentally, a tremendous bargain.

I wrote to Mario Fontana of Iron Mountain, Michigan, my former flight instructor. Fontana was an aviation natural. As a boy, he worked in auto repair shops, then became a pilot and subsequently a flight instructor, and then the head of his own flight school.

Fontana's flight school was awarded the federal Civil Pilot Training contract to teach a number of Michigan Tech students. The challenge of introducing youngsters to flight fitted Fontana like a glove; he was tireless in teaching students to handle aircraft safely. Personable and friendly, Mario is blessed with a warm personality and a world of patience, both outstanding attributes for any instructor.

Busy as a one-armed paper hanger during those hectic pre-World War II years, Mario taught both ground school and flying. His nights were spent maintaining his planes and grading student papers. By war's end, more than 4,500 well-trained pilots had passed through Fontana's flight schools. Fontana was honored in 1990 by being installed into Michigan's Aviation Hall of Fame.

Often during training, Fontana would invite me and other students to his home for lunch. He and I enjoyed many hunting trips at his deer camp near Iron Mountain. To this day, the Fontanas are among our closest friends.

It was only natural, then, that we would turn to Fontana for guidance now that we were about to make the important purchase of our first aircraft. As a Taylorcraft dealer and a member of Taylorcraft's board of directors, Fontana was sold, of course, on that type of plane. He offered us a Taylorcraft with floats for just $3,250, all the money we had, and coincidentally a tremendous bargain.

I'm sure he sold us the plane at cost. To top it all off, he personally delivered the plane to us, arriving in Fairbanks on Aug. 10, 1946, with his wife, Audrey.

We were delighted the Fontanas could stay in Alaska a while and arranged a hunting trip that took the four of us down the Alaska Highway to the Little Gerstle River.

Dot and Audrey stayed at the river camp while Mario and I reaped a good crop of blisters scouring higher elevations for sheep. They eluded us, and the black bear we killed wasn't much of a consolation. Even so, we packed out a few bear steaks, which we naively tried to pass off on the girls as sheep meat. When they tried to cook the bear meat, it was tougher than the frying pan and we had to admit we lied.

The Ester mine tailing pile had been bulldozed flat for a roadway and, since it was near our cabin, we used it for a landing strip. Mining personnel helped me build a small hangar out of discarded pipes on which we draped heavy canvas to shield the plane from the weather.

As a reserve officer, I had the privilege of shopping at the commissary at Ladd Field, so it was there that we purchased a ham — the only item of meat that we bought our first year in Alaska. Our meals consisted of a minuscule cube of ham plus generous quantities of duck, rabbit, grouse, ptarmigan, moose or caribou. It was amazing how far one ham could be stretched.

It helped immensely that the date of our arrival in Fairbanks, April 20, 1946, coincided with the annual migration of northbound ducks and geese.

Spring waterfowl shooting wasn't frowned on then as much as it is now. Dot and I took advantage of the plentiful birds that stopped by vacant fields just out of town, at Creamer's Dairy and at the University's Experimental Farm.

Dot, who enjoyed hunting as much as I did, pitched in regularly to help keep the larder stocked. On one occasion that fall, she selected the sprawling dredge pond near our cabin as the scene for one of her solitary hunting trips. Venturing out to the middle of the pond on a huge hydraulic pipe, she sat there waiting for something to fly by that could be combined with ham for the evening meal. The ham supplement arrived promptly and she fired the 12-gauge Winchester shotgun we shared, with splashing results. The gun's perceptible kick dislodged her from the pipe, and she went toppling into the awful gumbo.

Swamp-style mud covered her from head to toe, transforming her into a shapeless apparition as she clambered her way onto the pipe, a scene that was now being observed with great fascination by a couple of F. E. workers who reported to me later. As she made her way back to shore, her footsteps left splotchy mudpies all the way to the car. She opened the car door and suddenly realized what the load of mud she was carrying would do to the interior of the vehicle. The sharp slam of the door echoed over the pond and tailing piles as she turned and headed glumly back to the cabin on foot.

I encountered worse and more odorous mud while hunting out near the University Experimental Farm one day. The big greenhead mallard I dropped plunged right into the thick of the farm's pigpen. There was nothing to do but climb over the fence and plow through the stuff. Falling off the pipe might have been more pleasant. Anyhow, the duck we had for supper that evening was mighty tasty.

In December, our meat supply was replenished and our menu changed for months to come when I managed to bring down six caribou. As I drove home one evening through heavy snowfall, the headlights picked up strings of caribou tracks across the road. On snowshoes the next morning, I followed the tracks to an area bordered by stands of spruce and thickets of willow. Here, I heard branches breaking and animals running. As the caribou approached a narrow opening a hundred yards in front of me, I knelt on my snowshoes to rest my elbow on my knee and get steady shots.

In single file, the caribou moved across the narrow clearing and in the next few moments my six shots rang out over the wilderness. Iver Anderson, a mine foreman at

Ester, helped me load the six carcasses on a low, wooden sled, a "stoneboat." Using a small tractor to pull the sled, we delivered one of the caribou to "Rusty" Heurlin, an artist friend living in a nearby cabin, who himself had experienced lean times. Other carcasses were distributed to a couple of other friends who likewise would probably have had a meatless winter. Getting those caribou was a stroke of luck that came at just the right time in that freezing winter.

Remarkable hunting opportunities like that helped give a warm glow to those tough early days in Fairbanks. It was a time when my F. E. job left much to be desired. I had very little to do and what I did wasn't all that interesting. Generally, mine work halted during the severe, "way below zero" winters. Nobody did much out on the mining grounds until the welcome, long-awaited days of spring and summer returned.

Dot and Terry ready to hunt rabbits in Ester, Alaska, 1946.

Among my limited, strung-out duties was monitoring sections of ground scheduled to be mined the following summer. My temperature recording duties took only a short time each morning. Then I'd drive to F. E.'s Fairbanks headquarters to prepare maps and compute yardages of overburden to be removed prior to dredging.

That work was far from exciting. A little more interesting for me was hobnobbing with the mine's "Bull Gang" in the mine itself. There I learned a lot about placer mining from Phil Schmidt and Clink Wollen who, though not much older than I, had been in the business for a long time. I had never done much real physical labor but the Bull Gang changed all that.

Rabbit hunting near our cabin with Dot was great sport and the rabbits were fine eating. Dot would station herself in a place where she figured she'd get a good shot while I circled the area with our dog and herded rabbits past her gun. Such hunting was zestful for her but since she was now immensely pregnant with our first child, she was beginning to have trouble keeping her balance on snowshoes. Shooting a kicking shotgun was not as easy for her as it had been earlier in the year.

Life in a utility-less log cabin was really difficult for Dot. Gregarious and outgoing by nature, she had to adjust to a virtually non-existent social life and this, for someone who really enjoyed entertaining and meeting people, was tough going.

Just keeping house without a raft of appliances and an endless supply of hot and cold running water, as is true in modern homes, challenged Dot's ingenuity and remarkable ability to cope with difficulties. Getting enough water to drink and cook with was a chore in itself. Drawing our supply from Ready Bullion Creek about a half-mile away wasn't too bad in summer. We'd simply drive Rosie down and fill up a couple of old five-gallon milk cans with sparkling, cool water. Winter water-getting was another matter. Then, in below-zero weather, I had to chop a hole through creek ice to reach the stream below. Ladling dippers of water out of the icehole into the cans was a miserably cold job. Hauling the heavy load of water cans back to the cabin on the sled was tricky, and I had to be careful to keep the cans upright to prevent spilling that precious liquid.

Cooking, even on a modern stove, can be difficult, but on the miserable, old gasoline cook stove in our cabin it was often frustrating and bothersome. The beat-up old stove, which resembled an old cast-iron (and cast-off) kitchen range, was regarded as some kind of booby trap by our commiserating friends who dropped by from time to time.

A bicycle type pump was mounted on the side to force air into a tank filled with white gas. Every time we lit the burners on top of the stove or in the oven, there would be a sudden *whoosh* of blue and white flame. Though ordinarily harmless, such flame bursts aroused trepidation when viewed by a visitor. One friend who saw us fire up our stove remarked, "It'll be a miracle if you two don't blow yourselves up with that thing!"

Dot's condition amidst this Spartan lifestyle generated unending concern. When, weeks later, we told our uneasy friends we were selling our cabin and moving into town, they were relieved almost to the point of celebrating. We had more or less been taking our frontier life style in stride but our Ester friends and neighbors were on pins and needles and were delighted to hear we were leaving the headaches of cabin living behind at a time when a newcomer was about to join our family.

As luck would have it, our first child, Jim Jr., was born on April 19, the day we moved from our whooshing, waterless cabin to the enfolding warmth and unimaginable comfort of our new house on the southern edge of Fairbanks. After the miserable cabin, we felt suddenly ensconced in an oasis of convenience and ease.

Our new home had belonged to Mr. and Mrs. August Thies, grandparents of Harvey and Pat Marlin, our Ester neighbors. The Thieses were leaving Alaska to enjoy a warmer climate. As for our first little home in Alaska, we sold it to an Alaskan artist, Ted Lambert. +

CHAPTER 5

New Home, New Business

Sitting in my first office in our Fairbanks home, April 1947.

So many things pleased us about our new home. For the first time, there was enough space to give me an office of my own. And there was a telephone, so essential to my fledgling flying business and so vital for Dot with our new baby after being isolated and without communications at Ester for so long.

Now, our home became as well an important message and business center. If I happened to be working around the Taylorcraft, which we lost no time in moving to the east end of Weeks Field just a block from our house, and Dot got a business call or a call for a charter, she'd let me know by hoisting a long pole with a red flag on it, clearly visible from the airport. I'd hurry over to the house and check it out.

Now preoccupied with flying, one of the first things put up on the wall in my office was a large chunk of plywood on which I glued Alaska air charts. This familiarized me with the vast bush country around us and helped me memorize names and locations of landmarks and settlements. A mileage scale and a measuring cable with Fairbanks as its hub helped me measure flying distances.

What bothered me, however, was having to fly a plane completely devoid of flight instruments. The Taylorcraft didn't even have a battery. To keep the wings level if I lost sight of the ground or horizon, I inscribed an arc on the instrument panel and hung a .30-.30 cartridge on a string from the top of the panel. All this improvising after years of flying military aircraft with the latest in instruments and electronics was like whistling in the dark, and I had trouble adjusting to the grossly unsatisfactory situation. Without adequate instruments, I knew flights would have to be delayed or cancelled. Even more important, I knew good instruments and flight safety go hand-in-hand.

Shortly after we had moved our plane to Weeks Field, I was approached by two young fellows who needed help, Al Wright, a pilot, and Bruce Ward, a mechanic.

Al, who lived in Nenana, owned a Taylorcraft and was doing some flying to outlying native villages and trapping camps. On one trip he experienced in-flight en-

Gassing the Howard. Al Wright pumped while I held the funnel.

gine failure, forcing him to land his ski-equipped plane on a lake near Bearpaw. He had determined that the engine had to be changed and had already obtained another engine. Bruce Ward had agreed to assist with the engine change, and Al had rented a Stinson to fly the engine out to the lake. His problem was that he needed a pilot who had flown a plane of that size.

I agreed to fly the Stinson SM8A, so we loaded in the engine and tools. Then the three of us flew out to the stranded plane. It was a cold day with blowing snow. The raw, bitter wind made it miserable to work out on the frozen lake. However, we set up a tripod out of spruce poles, unhooked the bad engine and installed the replacement. I brought Bruce and the damaged engine back to Fairbanks, and Al flew his Taylorcraft back.

For several months both Al and Bruce stayed in our spare bedroom and operated with us, until Bruce accepted a good job in a warmer climate. Al pursued his own flying business, which became one of the most durable and successful bush flying services in interior Alaska. Al Wright gained the reputation of being among the best pilots in the state.

There were experiences in bush flying I never encountered in flight instruction. Getting marooned was one of them.

In December 1947, I landed the Taylorcraft on skis at Bettles to pick up a Fairbanks-bound passenger, Pat Murphy, a gold miner. While over the Yukon Valley enroute to Fairbanks, ice kept building up dangerously on the aircraft forcing me to land on a frozen lake. We had to camp in a stand of spruce that night. In better weather the next morning, I got the ice cleared off the plane and then flew to Fairbanks.

Murphy joined Dot and me for lunch. He really must have enjoyed that savory moose stew because, before he left, he presented Dot with a dazzling gold nugget, which she had made into a necklace, still one of her prized possessions.

So-called ladies of the night were occasionally among our flying customers. Despite their profession, Alaska pilots welcomed them as passengers; hookers always paid in cash and were exceptional tippers. Faye High went where the men were. When a Nenana railroad dock reconstruction project brought in a flood of construction workers, she kept a room reserved at the Nenana Hotel and shuttled frequently between Nenana and Fairbanks. Somehow, she settled on me as her pilot of choice.

It was somewhat embarrassing for me and a bit agitating for Dot when the phone rang late at night and Faye's sultry voice would ask, "Is Jimmy there? Tell him I gotta get to Nenana right away!"

Though flying her back and forth between Fairbanks and Nenana was a bit of a nuisance, I wouldn't have felt right about turning her down. Her greenbacks were just as useful to us in paying our bills as anyone else's.

Frank Barr, the local manager for Alaska Airlines, lived right off the end of the runway and just a couple of hundred feet from where we parked our plane. Frank saw that we got trips his firm rejected for one reason or another, and I always gratefully accepted his much-needed assistance.

Never will I forget one of Barr's "gift" trips: a flight to August Lohi's trapping camp on the Chena River. Lohi, who made an unusual request when I reached his camp, subsequently gave me lots of business. About every three weeks, I'd fly in groceries or whatever else the little Finlander needed.

On this occasion, he asked, "Jim, would you turn in a limit of beaver for me?

Engine change on Bear Paw Lake, Alaska, 1947.

We're allowed to catch only 25, but I've got 50 of 'em. I need you to turn in the other 25."

I agreed and we carried bundles of hides out of his log cabin to the airstrip. At the plane, he stopped. Grinning, he told me, "Now, I want you to catch each of these beaver."

He proceeded to toss each of the 25 hides to me, and I caught them one by one, not sure what was going on and wondering if maybe Lohi had been staying by himself in the cabin too long.

Date	1947 Customer	Plane	Trip	Paid	Due
9/22	A.I.A. - Freight	3	Minto-FX		25.00
9/23	Joe Carrol	3	FY-Bear Mt.	40.00	
9/24	" "	3	" "	210.00	
9/24		3	" "		40.00
	(Will Pay in Spring)				
9/25	Joe Carrol	3	FY-FX	15.00	one
9/26	Faye High	3	FX-NG	15.00	
9/27	St. Oil (Mr. Vincent+1)	1	NG-FX		58.10
9/27	Carl Haggstrom	1	6'sthc-NG		40.00
9/29	Arnold Anderson(St.Oil)	1	FX-NG-Ruby-	Paid	232.00
9/30	Weather —				
10/3	W.J. Lynn + 2.	1	FX - Rampart		99.66
10/5	" " " + 2 engineers	1	Ramp-FX		99.66
10/6	Glenn Carrington Co.	1	FX-Healy (G.A. Gustafson)		45.00
10/11	" "	3	HY-FX (Gustafson)		35.00
10/13	Faye High	3	FX-NG	15.00	
10/13	Harry Munroe	3	NG-FX	15.00	
9/15	G.A. Gustafson —	3	FX-NY (Weathered Out)		
9/16	Whitey Hoff +1	5	NG-FX	30.00	

This late September and October flight log in 1947 shows customers who were businessmen, gold miners, sportsmen and Faye High.

"Why am I catching these?" I asked, when the strange ritual was over.

"Jim," he said, "you're catching them to be legal. The law says the beaver have to be caught by the trapper who turns 'em in. Now, you can honestly say you caught every one of them."

I couldn't help but chuckle as we packed them into the plane. I had a hunting, fishing and trapping license and, as Lohi said, I had caught the beaver.

Things didn't seem so funny when I got to the Fish and Game office and was confronted by two of the sharpest federal game wardens in the enforcement business. Ray Woolford and his assistant, Frank Chapados, flew their own observation plane off Weeks Field. There wasn't much they didn't know about what was going on at trapping camps and airports, so I felt a bit uneasy as I handed over the bundle of 25 furs for tagging.

Chapados studied me coldly for what seemed a long time. Then he asked, "You sure you caught these, Jim?"

"Caught every one of 'em," I assured him with a straight face.

Both kept looking at me quizzically and it was obvious that neither believed me.

Chapados tried another tack. "Now, look," he said, "you couldn't possibly have trapped these beavers. Jim, you're out there flying around every day, and when you're not out flying, you're right here on the field fooling around with your plane. We see you every day. How could you possibly have done any trapping?"

"I caught every one of 'em," I insisted.

There really wasn't much they could do. They just shook their heads and began tagging the stack of pelts.

That little episode wouldn't die. It got to be a kind of a joke. For years, every time I ran into Chapados, he'd grin, look me in the eye and declare, "Jim, you can't tell me you caught those beaver."

"I'm sorry you don't believe me, Frank," I'd say, "but I caught every one of them."

And now it can be told! ☩

"Sober" was not always true of bush pilots in 1948.

CHAPTER 6

Cease And Desist

Barr later gave us another "switchover" — a three-day trip flying a wealthy Whitehorse mining man, Pete Versluce, to several locations. The trip generated nothing but trouble for me.

Versluce, who wanted to visit prospectors at points in Canada and Alaska, had been turned down by both Wien Airlines and Alaska Airlines before being referred to us by Barr. I picked the passenger up at the Nordale Hotel and flew him from Fairbanks to Dawson, to Aklavik, back to Dawson and Thistle Creek, then to Whitehorse.

Just after that trip, things hit the fan. Somehow, Wien found out about my international flying and had proof since border crossings were documented when I cleared customs. Wien lodged a complaint with the Civil Aeronautics Board.

Shortly afterward, I received the following registered letter:

Mr. James S. Magoffin
Interior Airways
P.O. Box 438
Fairbanks, Alaska

Dear Mr. Magoffin:

It has come to our attention that you are engaging in commercial aviation without a proper certificate. You are hereby ordered to <u>cease and desist</u> from any further commercial air operation.

> *Alexander Dunham,*
> *Alaska Representative, Civil Aeronautics Board*

I was on the griddle. I had to see Dunham.

The following day, I parked the Taylorcraft at Safeway Airways on Anchorage's Merrill Field and went over to Dunham's office.

For a key federal official, the guy looked slovenly and disheveled. As he slumped in ungainly fashion behind his desk, I noticed that both his shoes were untied and his shoelaces were dragging on the floor. There was no secretary.

"Well?" he asked.

"Mr. Dunham, I came here to discuss your letter," I said after introducing myself.

"Oh, yes," he said. "Magoffin, we had to notify you that you can't fly commercially in Alaska without a Certificate of Convenience and Necessity."

"What's that?"

"That," said Dunham, "is a document issued by the Civil Aeronautics Board. It's supposed to prove you are providing a needed air service to the people of Alaska."

"Okay," I said, "how do I get one?"

"You can't."

"Why can't I?"

"You can't because the CAB has determined that as of the present time there's sufficient air service throughout the territory."

That, of course, was the end of the meeting.

Back at Merrill Field, I talked with Charlie Halleck and Paul Kroening, owners of Safeway Airways, and to pilots Gentry Shuster and Ward Gay. All had received similar letters ordering them to cease and desist.

It was decided the only thing we could do was to try to fight the revolting development in a political way. We gyppos got together a few dollars to hire Wendell Kay, a prominent Anchorage attorney, to represent us.

Kay was willing. He said he'd get the appropriate person in the territorial legislature in Juneau to go to bat for us. Kay succeeded in arranging a hearing. A bill was presented in the legislature and it was debated. But the small operators lost.

"What went wrong?" Kay was asked.

His answer was: "It looks like Wien paid our man in Juneau more than we did."

Nevertheless, there were too many of us gyppos to be ignored completely. In an oblique way, the government apparently relented and began issuing Alaska Pilot Owner Operating Certificates.

Far from helping the small operators, what the certificates amounted to was telling the pilots to drop dead. Operators who thought they had something realized in time they had absolutely nothing. The certificates were so restrictive that they did more harm than good.

The prohibitions were stifling. We could not fly any aircraft weighing more than 12,500 pounds. We could not advertise. We could not parallel a scheduled route. In short, we could not fly for hire.

Virtually any destination requested by our customers was served by a scheduled carrier. An armada of scheduled planes served countless locations. Wien had 247s, the twin-engine Boeings. Alaska Airlines had the Norseman, a Stinson, the Pilgrim and their Bellancas. Wien's fleet also included Norsemans, Bellancas, a Cessna Airmaster and other aircraft flying mail routes throughout interior and northern Alaska.

It seemed hopeless. We were being told, in effect, that if we wanted to fly any-where and stay strictly within the letter of the law, it would have to be to some un-named lake or creek, or maybe a moose pasture out in the wilderness.

We were forced into angry defiance. Most of us decided, sink or swim, to keep flying wherever our customers wanted to go.

I was one of those who kept flying. And, like the others, I had to keep looking over my shoulder to see if something was gaining on me.

Survival was at stake in this risky game. The entrenched bosses of Alaska's cer-tificated scheduled airlines, backed by the might and power of the federal government, were apparently out to wipe us out once and for all. Alaska's small struggling opera-tors, it seemed, were doomed.

The federal government emphasized repeatedly that at all costs their certificated carriers were going to be protected. We were David and they were Goliath. But it didn't look, in this instance, like the biblical story was going to be repeated. There seemed to be too much power against us.

So my mood was glum as I prepared to leave Anchorage. Before flying back, however, I stopped over briefly at Reeve Alaskan Airmotive to make a purchase and for the first time ran into the almost-legendary Bob Reeve himself.

Bob remarked that he had hunted with my brother Mort when Mort was sta-tioned at the Elmendorf airbase in Anchorage a couple of years earlier. It was always good to visit with Bob. I have been grateful for his support and help on several occa-sions to be described later. And until his death, I made it a point to keep in touch with him.

A dark cloud of doubt, worry and concern clung to me as I flew back to Fairbanks. I couldn't shake from my mind Dunham's contention that Alaska already had plenty of air service and we really weren't needed. I found his view hard to dismiss when looked at from all angles. It was hard to argue that the Territory needed more air transportation when there were few people in Alaska at that time and most of them were broke or struggling. The present network of routes looked like a thick spiderweb if you superimposed the routes on Alaska's map. Was there any populated place any-where in this vast land that didn't have access to air transportation when needed?

In my mind, I reviewed the routes and the people flying them. Lon Brennan and Bob Byers were flying out of Manley Hot Springs. Ray Petersen and Nat Browne had the Bethel area sewed up. The crusty Oscar Winchell was flying out of McGrath. Flying out of Fairbanks were Wien, Frank Pollack, Bill Lavery, Alaska Airlines and Jim Dodson.

Jim Dodson's routes took him to destinations along the Yukon and Kuskokwim

Rivers. North and west of Fairbanks was Wien territory. Gene Jack and Archie Ferguson claimed Kotzebue and the Toussaint brothers, Ed and Don, had Fort Yukon. "Mudhole" Smith had his brand on Cordova. Anchorage was home to Bob Reeve, Alaska Airlines, Art Woodley and others; while southeastern belonged to Shell Simmons, Bob Ellis, Tony Schwamm and several more flyboys. Sam White based his Stinson L-5 at Ruby and Tony Shultz manned an Alaska Airlines Norseman at McGrath to give Oscar Winchell competition.

Scanning Alaska from Ketchikan to Barrow, was much left? No. Point to any area on the map, and somebody was serving it with wings. And altogether, several dozen pilots were ready to go anywhere in Alaska where they were needed.

I wondered, "Where does it leave Dot and me?" Had we unwittingly become mixed up in a business that offered virtually no opportunity and no future for little guys like us? Though I struggled to put this despondent train of thought out of my mind, it was hard to find any optimism.

Even so, we were like a bulldog when it came to fighting for a foothold. No matter how dark it seemed, we nourished a fierce determination to fight, to persevere, to hang on, to hold out, no matter what happened. In all the tough blows we had to take in the weeks and months to come, that stubborn feeling wavered a bit from time to time but never left us completely. Damn it, Dot and I were going to prevail! If we didn't, we'd go down fighting.

The jolt that triggered anger and the resolution to keep operating was the realization that my own government was trying to destroy me, a government I'd always been loyal to and proud to serve. Growing up in a conservative atmosphere and having spent four years at the strictest military school in the United States, and another four years in the Army Air Corps, nobody could have been more patriotic than I was. I quickly learned, as many in business do, that the federal government can be enemy No. 1.

In the lean months that fate brought, we had to scratch for every nickel, and some days there were few nickels. It would have been easy those days, to fold our little tent and let our competitors snatch what few crumbs fell from time to time from the tables of the certificated operators. But we refused to give up.

That stubborn attitude merely sentenced me to more tough punishment. There were black days when the bottom seemed to have dropped out. I'd try to generate a commercial trip — any trip — without the slightest success. Listlessly, I'd scout the various mining and trapping camps always hoping — and usually hoping in vain — that I'd be able to turn up some business.

The most discouraging times were those when I realized that more was going out than was coming in. I'd muse, "If only I can make enough to pay for my gas!" Gas, those days, was 28 cents a gallon, but when you weren't bringing in any business, 28 cents seemed sky-high. My plane was chomping up 3.5 gallons an hour. It tormented me frequently to think that 98 cents an hour was being squandered in the sky. The fact that a lot of other pilots were in the same boat with me didn't make my situation any easier. I had the responsibility for finding my own way out.

I guess my worst day — and it was almost like a nightmare — was the day I fought and scrounged and begged for business and flew back home with virtually nothing to show for it. My total take was $10 cash, six whitefish, 12 muskrat pelts and one ratty-looking mink hide.

Telling that sad tale to Dot wasn't pleasant, but she had an even worse shock for me.

"Honey," she said, "a couple of natives came to the door today. They told me they needed money to buy milk for their babies, so I gave them $20."

That revelation, fortunately, left me speechless. But today it signifies to me Dot's basic kindness, good-heartedness and sincere concern for the needs of others, even though I'm sure that hard-earned $20, which seemed like such a huge sum then, went directly to the nearby Nevada Kid liquor store.

In slightly better times months later, while buying liability insurance for the Taylorcraft, I met John Butrovich Jr., one of the owners of the Alaska Insurance Agency. That chance meeting was the beginning of a lifelong friendship. (Butrovich has been a hunting and fishing partner for many years and has helped our company in many ways.)

Very soon after we met we were talking hunting, and the next morning he was riding beside me on a hunting trip to Minto Flats. It was early May and out of season, but spring goose hunting was somewhat accepted then.

I let John off at south Minto Lake to shoot geese while I flew over to Minto Village to deliver a few items the people had ordered from Fairbanks. Taxiing for takeoff from the lake, I spotted a big, black timber wolf hurtling across the ice. Aloft, I quickly assembled my shotgun, then swooped down until the plane was just a few yards off his back. One shot dropped the wolf instantly.

I landed and loaded the monster of a wolf into my plane, then hauled it to Minto Village, where the storekeeper's scales showed it weighed 165 pounds — my weight exactly. I donated the wolf to the natives, who were delighted to get it, even though the fur was not quite prime.

George Titus, a Minto Villager, spotted my threadbare gloves and assured me his wife, Minnie, could make me a better pair. With a pencil, his wife deftly traced around my hand and fingers on a piece of paper. Two weeks later, I was the possessor of the finest pair of cold-weather gloves I've ever owned. Soft and exceedingly sturdy, the moosehide gloves were lined with flannel and had furlined cuffs extending almost to my elbows.

A couple of hours later when I touched down at Minto Lake, Butrovich was waiting for me, proudly displaying a dozen of the tasty, white-fronted geese we call "speckle-bellies."

On our way home, Butrovich pointed out that many travelers came by their office in the Nordale Hotel and suggested the hotel would be a good place to drum up flying business.

I followed up and soon got to know Arne Lee and Frank Nigro, the Nordale desk clerks, as well as the desk manager at the Pioneer Hotel, Dave Davenport.

Butrovich was right. They steered a lot of business our way that we otherwise wouldn't have had. Frequent flyers, like grocery salesmen and fur buyers like "Muskrat" Johnny Schwegler, began showing up on our schedules, keeping us afloat in some of our leanest times. ✝

CHAPTER 7

Struggle And Sacrifice

The years of the late '40s were years of continuing struggle and sacrifice for us. But they were not aimless years, not unproductive and certainly not years of wheel-spinning. Here, in our home in Fairbanks, sat Jim Jr. reading while Dot sewed on her soon-to-be parka. Terrible Terry and Bill are on the floor.

The years of the late '40s, when major Alaska development was still far in the future, were years of continuing struggle and sacrifice for us. But they were not aimless years, not unproductive and certainly not years of wheel-spinning.

It would have been easier for us and lifted our spirits if we had realized we were reaching the periphery of unprecedented progress and development after months of near-stagnation. But we had no crystal ball to tell us golden things were ahead.

What really helped in those years was being able to gradually get a feel for the greatness, the grandeur and the magnificence of this incomparable land. In so many ways, Alaska was communicating to us its subtle, changing moods. We felt the lure of its vast distances, its wilderness lakes and streams. Most important of all, we were getting to know Alaska's wonderful people.

The people we got to know best were those in aviation. How can one characterize or describe Alaskan pilots of that era? They defy description. Or maybe no fancy description is needed. Let's just call them "good guys," "dedicated Alaskans," "hard workers." The best term for most of them, I guess, is just "friends."

Very early I saw, in many Alaskan pilots, the noblest of human traits: a deep concern for one's fellow man. Many of those who shared the skies with me demonstrated an unselfishness and devotion to others that gave a new dimension to what life in Alaska was all about. If a pilot vanished out in the bush or on the merciless tundra, business as usual went out the window. Pilots everywhere pitched in and helped.

That was the magnificent spirit I saw in the winter of 1947-48 when I joined the Civil Air Patrol unit just getting under way in Fairbanks. It was good to be in the

Fairbanks CAP to Expand

1952

Major Jim Magoffin, commanding officer of the Fairbanks Squadron Civil air patrol, and his staff met Tuesday night with Air Rescue and AAC personnel to discuss future CAP plans and problems. During the three hour open forum held in the 74th ARS hangar, Capt. Kester, AAC CAP liaison officer, brought the local representatives up to date on current activities and future plans of the Alaskan wing.

The year 1953 will find an expanding, better-equipped CAP if the plans outlined by Capt. Kester materialize. The Alaska wing is aiming at an enlistment of 500 cadets with approximately 200 of these young air enthusiasts scheduled to come from the Fairbanks area. Aimed at encouraging airmindedness among the youth and citizens of our nation the program covers all age groups and includes topical training on every field of aeronautical endeavor.

The Civil Air Patrol searches for missing aircraft were common when there were few navigational aids and primitive airplanes possessed poor radios — if any.

midst of an astonishing bunch of flyers unconditionally devoted to giving a hand to others. Working with these pilots brought me a much deeper appreciation for essential human considerations too often overlooked. What the CAP stood for, its spirit, the time and energy its members devoted to serving others—all this was interwoven with the strengthening bond Dot and I felt for Alaska itself.

In that fledgling CAP unit, the commander was Frank Barr, one of Alaska's senior pilots. When it was discovered that I had more than a little military experience, I was made Barr's deputy commander. In the ranks of the CAP, I came to realize that there was no higher calling than devoting oneself to helping others in trouble. As I joined with other members in the throes of unraveling life-and-death situations, I became fully aware that there were other things in life far more important than money. The CAP exerted a tremendous influence on all the organizations touched.

I played a major role in only one of the scores of emergencies in which CAP personnel came to the rescue. I like to think my help was instrumental in saving a life, but I'm not sure and it really doesn't matter. What I did gave me a whale of a lot of satisfaction.

When word reached our CAP unit that Andy Anderson, a Bettles pilot, was missing, I lost no time in getting involved. As my plane moved beyond the low-lying barren hills, across the Yukon and into Dall Pass on the search, the incredible vastness of Alaska's expanses moving slowly under my wings was all but overwhelming. Searching for someone in Alaska's outback can be a needle-in-the-haystack affair. Success is often a function of sheer luck. Failure rests on something seemingly insignificant, like a whim of the weather.

As I flew along, it occurred to me that a pilot was terribly vulnerable, especially in winter, as he challenged this trackless, moon-like expanse. Getting lost was easy in these vast distances without navigational aids except for directional radio ranges that were much too far apart. It was easy to become disoriented in this welter of rivers, lakes, trackless vistas of bare tundra and nameless geographical features.

Andy Anderson, waiting for rescue amidst all this nothingness, could testify to that. I soon learned how spotting something down there where you've been seeing nothing up to then can give an incandescent glow to what had been a gloomy, doubt-haunted day.

Suddenly, in the endless whiteness below, I spotted a dark smudge. In moments, that smudge became a plane and then it was clearly a happy pilot waving from the ice on a frozen lake.

Getting to someone trapped in the wilderness brings a burst of satisfaction and a matchless sense of achievement. There's special excitement in discovering that the lost person is still alive, because, early in the search, you can never be sure. So I felt like celebrating when I spotted Andy out on that frozen lake right near the summit of the pass. This was what being in the CAP was all about.

Though it was 40 degrees below zero, Andy might well have survived for several more days, though his chances of walking out were an absolute zero. The engine of his plane was frozen solid. He didn't have a firepot or an engine cover. If a long-lasting storm had socked in that lake, he could have become a tragic statistic.

After landing, I kept my engine running so it wouldn't freeze up and have to be reheated. With my firepot and engine cover, we got his plane

Trouble on the Wire

Toward dusk one day last October, Agent Charles Gray walked into our U. S. Fish and Wildlife Service office at Fairbanks, Alaska. He told me that while flying twenty miles southeast of town he'd spotted an area where the trees and bush were broken and trampled, and in the center of it were two bull moose with locked horns. One was dead. The other, a young bull, stood with his head down, horn to horn with the dead one.

I took off with Charlie at daybreak, and in minutes we were circling the scene. As we flew over the moose, the young bull wagged an ear. He seemed in fair condition, so we returned to Fairbanks to arrange a rescue. Frank S. Glaser, predator control agent, and I, decided to try to free the live bull, and Jim Magoffin agreed to fly us to a landing near the animals.

Next morning Jim dropped me half a mile from the place. Carrying ropes, saw, ax, and camera, I headed through the woods, and soon came on the moose. I got the surprise of my life. The bulls's horns weren't locked together. They were *wired* together with an aircraft-target tow cable.

The cable stretched neck-high for several hundred yards through the brush—a perfect moose trap. The saw and ax I'd brought were useless. What we needed were wire cutters, and when Jim arrived with Frank a short time later, he left at once to get them.

The young bull had worked about two feet of slack into the wire. The hair on his back stood up straight, his ears were back, and his eyes rolled fiercely. He charged when I approached him.

Luckily we'd brought a piece of ⅝-inch rope. We tied a long pole to it and threw it under the neck and in front of the young bull. Then we anchored one end of the rope to a sturdy birch, threw the other end over the animal's back, and started snubbing him toward the tree. When he felt the pull of the rope he began to kick like a Missouri mule. On one charge he snapped off his left antler. But we had him securely roped by the time Jim came back with the wire cutters.

Frank stood guard with his shotgun as I held the bull snubbed to the tree and Jim started cutting the cable. By the time he'd snipped the last strands, both he and I somehow found ourselves standing behind Frank and the gun.

At first the young bull just stood there, an ugly, gruesome sight. He stared at us for a few minutes. Then he started to eat snow, and later he browsed on the tops of some young willows. Finally, with a few kicks, he loosed himself from the rope. Then he sniffed the air, walked sedately to the timber, and disappeared. One more target moose for some lucky hunter.—*Ray Woolford.*

" Out door Life "   SEPTEMBER, 1952   51

Federal game warden Ray Woolford's account of our moose rescue. Published in Outdoor Life magazine, September 1952.

Helicopter Pilot Lost On Journey

Survey Aircraft Vanishes During Flight Yesterday

Four military aircraft and seven Civil Air Patrol planes are searching today for a civilian 2-place Bell helicopter and its pilot which have been missing between Manley Hot Springs and Lake Minchumina since last night.

The helicopter, piloted by a man identified only as a "Mr. Lucy," was expected to arrive at Minchumina from Manley Hot Springs about 6:30 p. m. last night. The route covers a distance of about 90 miles.

Weather Fair

Weather over the route last night was considered fair to good, but fog and ground mist moved in during the night.

Civil Air Patrol pilots participating in the search are Dick McIntyre, Douglas Millard, Bishop Gordon and Mrs. Dorothy Magoffin, all of Fairbanks. Dick Collins and Mrs. Dick Collins of Minchumina are flying, as well as Roy Delaney of Nenana.

There were always emergencies.

warmed up and he was soon happily on his way back to Bettles. Mission completed.

When Frank Barr resigned as CAP commander to run for the legislature, I proudly took his place as commander. To me, Barr always typified the gung-ho, dedicated CAP spirit.

Frank lived just a block from our home and besides being a pillar of the CAP, he was a true friend. Interior Airways may not have survived without his generous assistance. Invariably, he came through for us when things were the toughest, the times when our enterprise was hanging by the thinnest of threads. Most amazing of all, Barr was doing all this for a competitor!

Typical of the numerous times he helped were the mail runs to the Fortymile country he turned over to me when he couldn't take them himself, or when he was short of a pilot or for some other reason couldn't go.

I didn't enjoy flying the Norseman usually assigned to Fortymile mail runs, having flown this type of plane enough to be able to testify that they are not a fun airplane to fly. (However, two of our pilots, Curly Martin and Bob Long, preferred the Norseman over other planes). But, like the Norseman or not, such trips arranged by Barr at a time when we were desperate for funds to keep going, amounted to happy flying for me.

I saw Frank's careful, practical side while I was preparing for a trip in a Gullwing Stinson he owned but was leasing to Alaska Airlines. When I came out to load the airplane, I was startled to find the back end of the plane tightly packed with an incredible mountain of stuff. Aboard was a full-size Yukon stove, box after box of dried foods, a box full of jam and sugar and all kinds of canned goods. Also aboard was a good-sized wall tent, two huge sleeping bags and enough cooking pots and pans for a dozen people.

This incredible conglomeration of stuff just flabbergasted me. I had trouble figuring it out and had to ask Frank about it.

"What's all that stuff you have aboard?" I asked him.

Frank grinned. "Jim," he said, "it *is* a lot of stuff, but it's necessary. That stuff goes everywhere I go."

I was still puzzled. "But why?"

"Well, this is the way it is. If I ever have another forced landing, I don't want to just *survive*. I want to be *comfortable*!"

I learned later that Frank had been far from comfortable on a couple of previous unpleasant occasions, and he was determined that for him there'd be absolutely no suffering if anything like that ever happened again.

* * * * * *

Good mechanics are craftsmen, sculptors and artists. Art Leen was all of those. The work he did in putting new metal on the Norseman's skis was so incredibly artistic and beautiful it should have been framed. Leen skillfully attached a thin sheet of black iron on the bottoms of the skis, then varnished the boards to glistening brilliance. When he got through, those skis were a joy to look at as I set off for a Christmas mail trip to villages in the Fortymile country.

I had more than those beautiful skis to concern me as I began circling Eagle's airstrip. Brisk winds had swept the snow off the runway right down to gravel in many places.

Trying to land there on skis could end in big trouble.

I rolled out the trailing antenna of the T30 Lear radio and contacted Frank Barr in Fairbanks.

"Frank," I told him, "we got problems here at Eagle. I can see rocks and gravel sticking through the snow all over the place. It's…"

Frank interrupted: "You've just *got* to land, Jim! We're 10 days overdue with the Eagle mail as it is. The post office is getting on our tail. You've just got to get in there!"

My stomach felt queasy as I made another pass and saw all those bare spots on the runway. But the urgency in Frank's voice had got to me. I realized how crucial my getting in to Eagle was for his company. If I did it just right… well, maybe. I settled slowly toward the runway.

When the skis hit, it was as if a hundred buzzsaws, sparks and all, had started working on Art Leen's handiwork. The awful racket and ski punishment didn't end until I gradually and thankfully slid to a stop.

Quickly, I got the mail off, the on-going mail loaded and began my takeoff. It was painfully slow going as I accelerated and the gravel ground away at the once-glistening skis. They took tremendous punishment, far more than most skis are designed to take.

When I returned to Fairbanks, poor old Art just about cried when he inspected what I had done to what he had created. The skis were a mess. I couldn't have wrecked them worse if I had set out to do it deliberately. Art had to remove the skis and re-cover them with fresh bottoms.

* * * * * *

They don't make pilots — and human beings — much better than Jim Dodson. It was a pleasure to deal with him and with his pilots, such outstanding men as Alden Williams and Jerry Church.

Dodson arrived in Ketchikan in 1930 to fly for Pioneer Airways. An education graduate of the University of Washington, he taught math and science for a time at Franklin High School in Seattle. And when he founded Dodson Flying service in Fairbanks, it was the start of a first-rate operation. Our dealings with Dodson and his personnel were always in an atmosphere of friendliness and cooperation. There was no dog-eat-dog competition.

When Dodson's company, along with others, merged to form Northern Consolidated Airlines, Inc. Dodson opened the Black Diamond Coal Mine near Healy. His favoring Interior Airways with flying business for the mine was highly important to us.

The way Dodson consistently dealt with us and the way we tried to deal with him had deep significance for me as a basic guideline signifying the way all business ought to be conducted. Thanks to watching Dodson at work, I came to live by this business adage: respect for and friendly relations with your competitors always results in greater dividends for your business than confrontation and hard feelings. I have tried to operate that way. ✝

CHAPTER 8

Flying Characters

There were characters a-plenty on the early aviation stage. Details of their exploits in the sky and on the ground enlivened thousands of story-telling sessions.

Don Emmons qualified for membership in that most-talked-about fraternity. When I got to know him, he was flying for Alaska Airlines and was, reputedly, an excellent pilot.

One of my early passengers, Jim Baker, related the following episode to me: On that occasion a young lady, whose home was in the lower states, had created concern in Kotzebue due to her extensive consumption of strong drink. The decision was made to send her back to her home, though she protested bitterly.

Don Emmons was the pilot of the plane flying her to Fairbanks, along with two male passengers. She was forcefully put aboard the aircraft. As the plane was taking off she fought her way to the door and managed to squeeze through just as the plane was leaving the ground.

Horrified, one of the men snatched her by the ankles and kept attempting to drag her back in. The force of the airflow, however, kept the door pinned back and he was hardly able to keep from losing his grip.

"Don! Don!" he hollered desperately, "she's trying to jump out! Do something!"

"Let 'er go!" Emmons advised as he swooped low over a huge snowbank. The woman tumbled head over heels into the snow.

Incredibly, she survived, though she had to spend several days in the hospital.

Later, Don remarked dryly, "No question about it. She would have been killed if she had been sober!"

Emmons and a partner owned a trading post at Stevens Village and Don would fly merchandise there from Fairbanks. Once, he was taking off from Weeks Field in an intolerably overloaded Gullwing Stinson in mild weather that made the snow very sticky. The heavy, sluggish plane roared down the runway without gaining anywhere near takeoff speed. Don's plane used up the entire runway, then began plowing through thick clumps of willows bordering the far end of the airstrip. The plane was badly damaged before it came to a spectacular stop.

Though unhurt, trouble was just beginning for poor Don. Rushing from the plane with the intent, somehow, of getting his cargo removed from the crash site so there'd be no overloading evidence, Don was foiled. A determined CAA inspector was already speeding to the scene.

Sniffing around the bashed-up plane, the inspector shook his head sadly at a cargo area brimming with canned goods, heavy cases of beer, liquor and other weighty items.

"What you got on board here," he told Emmons, "would have strained a DC-3. You and I've got some talking to do."

With the loss of his license, Emmons was forced to go to work in a southeast Alaska pulp mill where he lost his life in an unfortunate accident.

I had made one flight with Don Emmons when he was "slow-timing" a new engine in an Alaska Airlines Bellanca. I liked the guy and have always felt bad about his untimely demise.

* * * * * *

Government offices were the source of a number of charters and I got a considerable amount of business from the Bureau of Indian Affairs, the Public Health Office, the marshal's office and the Bureau of Land Management.

One trip I made to Stevens Village with Elsie Mae Smith, an Alaska Native Service nurse, was memorable because it briefly brought on stage an unusually enterprising young man whom I didn't know then but who would play a key future role in our business, a real star as far as we were concerned.

There was something compelling about the way this youngster operated after he came on the scene at Stevens Village flying a black, Gullwing Stinson on skis owned by Jim Dodson Air Service. The way the skinny, black-haired kid jumped briskly out of the plane immediately caught my attention while I was chatting with the storekeeper. The pilot was a dervish of activity. Fascinated, I watched him wrestle

Jerry Church, age 18, in flight training at Tulare, California, 1942.

boxes of groceries and a bulging mail sack out of the plane, then rush them into the store. I kept my eyes on him as he swiftly scooted back to the plane with the outgoing mail. He was efficiency personified, a study in superb coordination. As far as I could see, there wasn't any wasted motion anywhere in this kid's operation. I had never seen anything like it.

That skinny pilot, Jerry Church, came to work for our firm years later. A hard-working, trustworthy pilot, Jerry was exceptionally loyal, efficient and chalked up an enviable record with us. He worked his way up to fly all the company airplanes including DC-3s, C-46s, F-27s and even the giant Lockheed Hercules. He reached the top rungs of our firm, becoming the chief pilot and later vice president of operations for Interior Airways and Alaska International Air. Retiring at age 60, Jerry now enjoys his comfortable home on Orcas Island just out of Seattle. Employees like Jerry Church are the very fabric of any firm's success.

In June of '47, we put the Taylorcraft on floats and were chartered by the Bureau of Land Management to make aerial survey flights over forest fires raging in the Fortymile area. At that time, there were no such things as borate bombers, smoke jumpers and sophisticated firefighting equipment. What the entire effort consisted of then was the one BLM official, Robert Bennett, going aloft with me over the fire and pencilling in the boundaries of the burning acreage on a map that was later sent to Washington along with the official report.

On one flight, we landed for lunch on a pretty lake north of Big Delta.

After lunch, I got out a fishing rod and attached a daredevil spoonhook. A 15-pound northern pike grabbed the lure the moment it hit the water. It was like that at every cast. That beautiful lake was teeming with big fish. It occurred to me that the lake would be a good place to bring fishing customers and we made good use of it.

Among those we later brought there was one Cheechako couple who will always remember their seemingly incredible trip. Catching a small northern pike around two feet long brought high excitement to the lady since it was the first fish she had ever caught.

She couldn't get over her excitement and was oohing and aahing over her insignificant catch when I asked her, "Mind if I use your fish for bait?"

Her husband roared with laughter as the woman gave her somewhat reluctant consent.

I worked a big hook under the back fin, tied it on a carpenter's chalk line and let it down over the side of the boat.

Suddenly, the line began feeding out briskly and when I gave it a strong jerk, I knew I had a big one on.

I began pulling in a 27 1/2-pound northern pike, so big I had to shoot it in the head with my rifle before I could lift it into the boat.

I reached down, yanked the smaller pike from its mouth, removed the hook and politely handed the smaller fish back to the lady.

"Thank you," was all I said.

That episode was never forgotten by the couple and they mentioned it often in the letters they wrote us over the years.

* * * * * *

Just about any pilot with a lot of mileage has had close calls. One of my worst brushes with big trouble came while flying Alaska Airlines' Norseman on the Forty-mile mail route.

I was flying without a starter; it had burned out and Alaska Airlines didn't have a spare. Mechanic Leen just bolted a plate over the hole where the starter should have been, and we propped the airplane by hand.

This wasn't easy because the plane had a 650-horsepower engine.

At Chicken, I unloaded mail and cargo, leaving the engine running. But at the next stop, Boundary, I shut the engine off to await improvement in the weather.

When Neil Warren, a Lavery Airways pilot, landed, he swung the prop for me and I went on to Eagle, which had a single strip that ran uphill to the west from the river bank. On skis, it was best to land uphill because the bank plunged about 30 feet to the Yukon River.

While I was taxiing down close to the buildings, a bunch of kids and dogs came running out. I had to cut the engine, afraid the prop might hit one of them.

After unloading freight, I boarded a couple of Fairbanks-bound passengers, then enlisted the help of the customs agent to get me started.

I got him up in the pilot's seat and told him how to work the throttle. I had it cracked just a bit and told him to bring the throttle back to a slow idle when the engine started.

He seemed to understand, so I swung the prop, but it wouldn't start. I cracked the throttle a bit more, then swung the prop again. It didn't start. Afraid I might have flooded the engine, I took a precaution before swinging the prop again. I put a rope around the right ski, wrapping it around as far back on the ski as I could get it so it would catch the snow if the airplane began sliding ahead.

When I propped it the third time, the engine roared away much higher than idle, running very fast. The customs agent got confused and failed to pull the throttle back. The plane began inching forward. Fortunately, the rope caught, stopping the right ski and swinging the aircraft to the right. This allowed me to jump in and pull the throttle back.

I got the guy out of the plane and took the rope off the ski and was ready to go.

I shudder to think of what *could have happened* on that occasion. The plane could have plunged over the embankment and smashed on the river ice some 30 feet below.

* * * * * *

Occasionally sad and strange stories came out of the wilderness. Frank Barr rented my Taylorcraft on skis to go up to the headwaters of the Sheenjek River to determine what happened to an old prospector they'd left in that godforsaken place the season before. An unfortunate — maybe even a tragic — mixup in signals had occurred and for some reason nobody went back to get the poor guy as promised.

Now, when Barr landed the T-craft near the prospector's cabin, it looked deserted. He went in to find that it was empty. Nowhere was there a sign of the prospector. Had he been swallowed up by the wilderness or devoured by animals? There was no way of telling. There was no skeleton, no trace. Countless such riddles are woven into the dark fabric of Alaska.

* * * * * *

In mid-August of the summer of 1947, I flew Ella Vernetti from Fairbanks to Koyukuk, where she and her husband operated a trading post. Coming up the Yukon on the return trip, I was at 2,000 feet between Galena and Ruby when I spotted a flock of Canada geese heading upriver at my altitude. Assembling my shotgun in a hurry, I swung around and flew in close to the formation, getting a shot at the last goose in the flock. I watched the bird plunge 2,000 feet into a mud flat, then landed and picked it up. That high-altitude goose hunt resulted in a delicious dinner.

By the fall of 1947, flying hunters and fishermen had become an important part of our small business.

I dropped Dot off the next day at Minto Flats, where geese and ducks were flocking by the thousands, then went on to Minto Village, returning a couple of hours later to where I had left her.

She was holding up one goose. "Don't tell me that's all you got?" I said.

She explained that she had been in chest-high grass when she knelt down with her little bag of shells and dropped one of a passing flock of geese a couple of hundred feet away. She ran over and found the goose but then couldn't locate her bag of shells in the high grass. Our search finally turned up the missing shells.

The superb hunting at Minto Flats gave me an idea. The following day, I pitched a surplus Army tent near the edge of South Minto Lake. On Sept. 1, when the duck and goose season opened, we were in the hunting business. Shuttling hunters in a tiny plane from Fairbanks to Minto convinced me that if we were going to make any progress in the flying business I'd have to have a bigger aircraft.

Again, I consulted Fontana. He recommended that we try a Howard DGA 15P, a high-wing monoplane with a 450-horsepower Pratt & Whitney Wasp Jr. engine. Fontana had been flying a Howard and found its performance excellent. A fast aircraft, at normal cruise power it would scoot along at about 150 miles per hour, much faster than most bush planes in those days. The cabin was relatively quiet and the plane had a good heater making it ideal for our subzero weather operation.

We promptly made the deal for our first large bush plane, NC5554N. Fontana had given it a new paint job, a pretty bright red with dark blue leading edges. Waxed and polished, it sparkled with eye-catching classiness. When I flew it back to Weeks Field from Michigan, its beauty attracted a lot of attention.

I have always sung the praises of the Howard DGA, which actually stands for "Damn Good Airplane." Occasionally, when Alaska Airlines didn't have any other plane available, they'd let me fly a mail run with my Howard, a fun plane to fly. This remarkable plane was far quieter than either the Stinson or the Norseman. It had a full set of instruments, good radios and an automatic direction finder that was handy for getting back to Fairbanks in bad weather but worthless out in the bush where there were no navigational aids.

Best of all, I got my charter rate on the Howard, which was rewarding financially. I'm convinced Alaska Airlines saved money by hiring me and the Howard considering my charter rate was probably lower than just the cost of operating a Norseman or a Pilgrim. In this instance as well, Frank Barr and Alaska Airlines were giving us a boost when the going was extremely tough.

I should point out that ours was not the first Howard in Alaska. Back in 1941, the Morrison-Knudsen Construction Co. acquired a Howard DGA and was using it as an executive transport in Alaska during the hectic times when Alaska was girding up its weak defenses. The airplane was piloted by early bush pilot Herm Lerdahl, the subject of Cliff Cernick's book, "Skystruck." Lerdahl had high praise for the ruggedness and performance of this "Damn Good Airplane."

* * * * * *

The pilot I met in McGrath in the summer of 1948 was another of Alaska's legendary characters, Oscar Winchell. He had been in the flying business longer than just about anybody in Alaska. Winchell helped found McGee Airways in Anchorage in 1932 and, on June 8 of that year, began regular flights from Anchorage to Seward and Fairbanks. Some sources credit him with beginning the first scheduled passenger flights out of Anchorage and with being Alaska Airlines' first pilot.

I wasn't aware of any of this when I took a party of Standard Oil representatives on a survey trip out of Nenana in response to a phone call from Mrs. Coghill, whose family owned businesses in that river town.

At McGrath, after my passengers and I had lunch at Jack McGuire's Roadhouse, I was crouched under the Howard draining the gas sumps when this character I can only describe as strange-looking began pacing around the plane and scrutinizing it closely.

He remarked, "Boy, that's a mighty fine-looking plane you got there. Bet it's fast, eh?"

"Yes, sir, it moves right along," I told him.

"Bet it's hot to land though?"

"No," I said, "Not too bad. It's got big flaps and lands good in a full stall."

"Where you headed from here, anyway?"

"We're going to Holy Cross," I said.

He started waving his hands and hollering, "You mean to tell me you're gonna try to land this thing at Holy Cross. You won't make it! Ever been there?"

"No, never been there."

"Well, let me tell you," he said, "it's a real, real short strip. I know; I fly my plane in there." He pointed to his plane parked on the ramp, an old, straight-winged Stinson.

"Usually come in there gliding it about 35 or 40 miles an hour. What do you glide at?"

"Oh, about 80."

"Well, let me tell you something, mister. I come in there just hanging on the prop. Soon as I clear the river bank, I cut the engine and hit the brakes. Just before I hit the trees, I ground loop it. That's the only way I'm ever able to land at Holy Cross."

After Winchell introduced himself he asked, "Where you going from Holy Cross?"

"To Marshall, then over to Unalakleet and Nome. Then a stop at Flat on the way home."

He shook his head sadly; "You're gonna have to skip Holy Cross," he warned. "Look, why don't you let me take your passengers to Holy Cross and get their business done there, then I'll bring them back here. You can take them on to where they have some *decent*, some safe airfields."

"Well, I don't think so," I said. "I think we'll just fly on down and get a look at it. Then if I don't like it, I can pass it up and come back here to let you take them in."

He didn't say anything.

I found the field at Holy Cross nowhere as bad as Winchell had described it. We came in on a normal approach and stopped with at least a hundred feet to spare.

That was my somewhat dramatic introduction to the noted Oscar Winchell. I later got to know him quite well and found him to be friendly and interesting. I could sympathize with his propagandizing and fabricating for what little business there was — I knew all about that. Times were such that it was quite common for lean, hungry pilots to "body-snatch" other pilot's passengers. Any ruse or deception was considered fair if it might result in making a dollar or two.

At Holy Cross, the Standard Oil surveyors looked over a possible site for a riverboat refueling depot. At the Catholic Mission, we chatted for a while with the holy fathers, then wandered down to where rows of fish were drying on long racks. The early salmon run had already started that far down the river.

Dark clouds of flies swarmed around the rows of drying salmon, settling and feeding on the fish like churning clusters of thick dark moss. I used to like to chew on dried salmon strips known in Alaska as Squaw Candy, but after seeing what I saw there on the drying racks, I never ate Squaw Candy again.

We flew on to Marshall, where the shape of the airstrip often startled pilots; it was uphill and around a turn. You couldn't see one end of the airport from the other, something that's real disconcerting if you're used to straight airports.

When we reached Marshall, another very odd and incredibly dirty flying character came on stage. He proceeded to give an unrehearsed and unashamed performance such as I had never seen before. Our group was at the Marshall store chatting away when we heard a plane approaching and saw the natives begin crowding around down at the high river bank.

I watched the Waco biplane on floats swing around and glide down to the storefront area from downriver. The plane landed and taxied up to a raft anchored next to the beach. Natives tossed ropes around the tie-down horns on the floats, securing the plane to the raft. The plane was painted Army brown and was streaked with oil from prop to tail.

As the pilot emerged, he looked just as bad as the plane. Bedraggled and unshaven, he wore tattered, oil-slopped clothes. Brazenly, with total unconcern and fully oblivious to the giggles of the young native girls, he proceeded to unbutton his fly, draw out his appendage and send a thick yellow stream arcing out over the water. As I said, it was the first time I'd ever seen a public performance like that.

There was more.

The pilot reached into the plane and brought out two one-gallon cans of oil and a funnel. Crawling up on the cowling, he dumped in all the oil. Next, he yanked an old towel out of his plane, opened a gas drain valve, soaked the towel with gas and proceeded to wipe the oil off his windshield. Oil was so thick on the windshield, I couldn't understand how he had been able to see enough to land.

After he unloaded at Marshall, he pumped many gallons of water out of his leaky floats. Then he got outgoing mail and a couple of native passengers aboard.

It was takeoff time.

Thick clouds of smoke spewed up from the plane as he started the engine. A wide band of spilled oil trailed behind the aircraft for a couple of hundred yards down the river.

We watched as the pilot turned the plane around and began his takeoff run. He was still on the water for almost a mile downstream

None of what I had seen, from start to finish, represented my idea of a good air operation. Yet, surprisingly, that pilot had a pretty good reputation in the Bethel area for being a safe pilot, a snappy dresser and a ladies' man.

We flew from Marshall to Unalakleet and then on to Nome, where I met another very remarkable man, Bill Munz, the local fixed base operator.

Munz, who died in St. George, Utah, at the age of 82 in April 1992, was one of Alaska's toughest pilots in terms of his zest for battling bureaucrats. Dick Galleher, who bought the Munz operation in 1962, says Bill Munz, politically, was "out to the right of Genghis Khan."

For quite a while, Munz wouldn't land at Nome airport because he had to talk to government people there and he wanted absolutely nothing to do with the government.

While Munz was in the territorial legislature, he had the reputation for voting no on everything. He pioneered flying to the raw mining camps on the Seward Peninsula and is fondly remembered by the "little guys" — the miners and workers — in out-of-the-way Alaska places who knew him best as a pilot genuinely concerned with their needs.

I got to look at some of the airplanes Munz had and was very much impressed. All were exceptionally clean. All appeared to be freshly painted and polished. They looked like planes Canadian bush operators have; the Canadians keep their planes looking in top shape.

I visited quite a while with Munz, getting his ideas about the flying situation. He expressed an interest in my Howard and later bought a couple of Howards of his own.

Munz told me about killing wolves by chasing them down with his Stinson on skis and bouncing a ski off their speeding heads. I thought I'd do the same once, later on, but chickened out for fear I'd knock off a landing gear.

One remark Munz made has always stuck with me: "I never buy a plane I can't pay off in 60 days."

Thirteen years later, after Alaska achieved statehood, Munz was named to head the state aviation commission formed to regulate intrastate air commerce.

Shortly after his appointment, he walked into the agency's offices in Anchorage, took one look at his fancy desk, then startled his assistant and his secretary by abruptly turning around and, without a word, walking out — never coming back. There would be no stuffy office job for this bush pilot.

Our last stop was at Flat, where we met the Miscovich family. This large clan, which included a bunch of young boys, had quite a setup at Flat. The whole family was engaged in gold mining. They were hospitable, hard-working people.

Mrs. Miscovich invited us to dinner and served a delicious meal of roast moose, vegetable salad and all the trimmings, topping it off with a delicious apple pie. It was a feast I'll never forget.

Mr. Miscovich arranged ground transportation for us down to Railroad City on the Innoko River, the site the Standard Oil people were interested in surveying with a view to setting up a bulk plant to service mines in that area.

Up to that time, it was the most lucrative charter trip I had flown, thanks to the Coghill family in Nenana who also helped me get several earlier charters. ✝

CHAPTER 9

More Pilots And Planes

During the winter of 1947, we were joined by a young pilot, Lou Soha, who had just received his commercial license and who came to us highly recommended by Fontana. Though our business was poor at the time, I gave him a job and turned the T-craft over to him.

Lou drew a minimum salary plus a percentage of what he took in, the usual way of paying pilots in those days. Soha developed quite a clientele around Fairbanks, Fort Yukon, Beaver and Stevens Village and flew lots of trappers and prospectors. A personable guy, well-liked wherever he went, Lou was able to bring us a lot of business we would never have received had he been of a different disposition. He went on to become an Alaska Airlines captain. Now retired, he lives in Seattle.

Another pilot who helped us on occasion was Dick Ragle, a middle-aged University of Alaska professor. An experienced pilot, he had flown for other outfits and knew his way around Alaska, doing a real good job for us.

Of the early pilots Interior hired — Lou Soha, Dick Ragle and Urban Rahoi — none so much as scratched an airplane, even though they all flew difficult missions.

After the Howard, our next airplane was a Piper Super Cruiser, a P.A. 12. Rahoi, a student at Fontana's school, had earned his commercial license and flew the plane to Fairbanks with the floats already on. He stayed right with the Super Cruiser and always turned in a creditable performance.

One of Rahoi's first Super Cruiser trips for us was to Chandler Lake. Rahoi returned with a native passenger, Elija Kakina, whose home was at Anaktuvuk Pass. He was dazzled by Fairbanks, but complained that he couldn't see anything because too many buildings were in the way.

He mentioned there were a lot of wolves around Anaktuvuk Pass. Bob Hayford, a local guide and hunter, joined me in the Super Cruiser on skis in the spring for a trip to Anaktuvuk. We stopped at Bettles and picked up a box of groceries for the people at the Pass. On arrival at Anaktuvuk we met Simon Paniak, the village chief, a fine, intelligent person who spoke excellent English. Paniak made arrangements for us to stay at Frank Ruland's hut, where we spread our sleeping bags. (Anaktuvuk huts were simply bent-over willows covered with caribou skin.) A tiny Yukon stove kept the hut quite comfortable but there was, of course, no running water or other modern conveniences.

We stayed with the Rulands for four days and hunted along the north slope of the Brooks Range. On each trip I made to Bettles to pick up gas for the plane, I'd bring

One of 17 wolves Bob Hayford and I got at Anaktuvuk Pass, March 1948.

goodies for the Eskimo youngsters, as well as groceries for anyone who needed them.

I did the flying; Bob did the shooting — and he was a good shot. We killed 17 wolves, flying them back to the village where the Eskimos skinned them.

One of the Eskimos, Jesse Ahgook, took charge of the wolves when we brought them in. He and his friends would skin and stretch them. We rewarded them with eight wolf pelts.

Twenty years later, while flying members of the Richfield board of directors to the arctic in a DC-3, we stopped at Anaktuvuk Pass so they could get pictures and purchase some of the famous Eskimo face masks. I was pleased to have brought along two crates of fresh peaches, an unheard of delicacy at the time.

Not having a scheduled operating certificate or a mail route, and with nobody completely depending on us, we were always available to take on odd-ball charters, which are what we usually got. We became experts at flying trips no "respectable" airline cared to fool with.

The first summer the T-craft was on floats, I took a local judge and his partner to the Lake Minchumina area to get a look at a possible rich mineral deposit. Other operators had refused to take them.

I loaded some cans of case gas into the Taylorcraft and flew it to Minchumina while my two passengers came with the mail plane. The place where the judge wanted to land was only a few minutes from Lake Minchumina's airstrip but it was a risky landing place. Nevertheless, we found a low spot about 150 yards long covered with shallow water. Flying the pair in and out of that "pothole" was tricky, and I had to make several trips with their gear.

Picking up the pair was going to be a delicate flying operation as well. At Lake Minchumina, I drained all the gas except for a few gallons to get me up to their "pothole" and back. Fortunately, the day was clear and a strong wind was blowing from the northwest, which put it right down the length of the pond.

I took out everything I could from the plane, including emergency gear, and flew up to the tiny landing area. Then I pulled the heels of the floats up on the downwind

Deplaning at Anaktuvuk Pass. I gave an assist to Harry Jamison, Atlantic Richfield's senior geologist. In the center is Brad Bradshaw, company president. At the right is Alaska's premier geologist, Marvin Mangus, who is generally credited with playing a major role in the discovery of Prudhoe Bay.

end. Using Kleenex, I got every drop of water out of each float compartment — then drained out a little more gas, leaving just enough to barely get me from the pothole back to Minchumina.

The judge got in with me and we tried it, just about brushing the cattails on the far end but making it okay. Then I flew back and picked up the other man and made one further trip to get the remainder of their gear. Though successful, that delicate and hazardous operation was marginal. If better business had been available, I certainly would have refused to land in that miniature lake.

Minchumina residents were very interested in this operation. I talked to Dick Collins, the CAA station manager and some local trappers: Slim Carlson, Kenny Granrath, Fabian Carey and Carl Poorman.

Later I arranged with Poorman and one of his friends, Bill Pinto, to build us a cabin on a lake just northeast of Big Delta on the north side of the Tanana River, where fishing for northern pike was extremely good.

I flew them to the lake, and they lived in a tent and trapped when not working on our cabin. Both were good cabin builders and knew how to peg logs together using wood dowels. I bought them a hand-operated winch, which they used effectively to drag large logs up to the cabin site.

They built us a first-class cabin that winter of 1947-48. A sturdy job, it is still standing in good shape.

That cabin and the nearby lake generated a steady flow of revenue for our company for many years. Our family enjoyed fishing and hunting in the vicinity. Our oldest boy, Jimmy, shot his first moose there when he was just 9. Our youngest son, Billy, got his first moose there when he was only 7.

Our policy was to let our employees use the cabin, and other camps we later acquired, for their own recreation. Often, we furnished free air transportation for employees and their families.

As soon as the ice was safe to land on, I prefabricated a small fish house to set out on the lake ice. About the size of an outhouse, the floor had a two-foot-square hole. An ice hole was cut the same size, and a small wood-burning stove was installed in one corner.

The house was painted black on the inside so fish couldn't see movement but the occupants could see down into the lake's clear water by means of the daylight passing through the ice. I had a spear I'd

My kid sister — Susan Shelby Magoffin — in Minnesota, 1940.

brought from my hometown of Deerwood, Minnesota. It was a reshaped pitchfork with spring steel barbed tines so they wouldn't pull out easily. A steel shaft about three feet long cupped the end of the spear for a wooden handle to fit into.

Fish would be decoyed into the fish hole with a wooden decoy I had learned to make back in Minnesota. It was a replica of a small fish, a portion of which was filled with lead so it would sink. Then we put a little wire hook on top to fasten the line to and attached fins made of tin.

When the line was jerked, the decoy would circle the fish hole, drawing the pike to the fake meal. They'd come up close to the top where they could be speared.

I flew many Fairbanks sportsmen down to that lake about 100 miles from Fairbanks. One of my first customers was Col. Bernt Balchen, the renowned arctic pilot and founder of the military air rescue service.

Though there was no name on the map for the lake, Fairbanksans started calling it Magoffin's Lake, a name that stuck for years. A late map designates the lake as Volkmar Lake. This is a mistake. Volkmar Lake is at the head of the Volkmar River, several miles farther east.

* * * * * *

To this day, mystery surrounds the disappearance of "Shorty" Curtis, proprietor of the pub at Ruby.

The U.S. marshal asked me to land a deputy on the Nowitna River, a few miles upstream from Ruby in the vicinity where the man disappeared.

On our way to Ruby we stopped at Tanana, where we met Deputy U. S. Marshal George Sullivan, who was then based in Nenana but responsible for law and order in Tanana as well as several other villages.

After leaving Tanana, we flew to Ruby where we learned additional details about the missing man. Then we flew to the Nowitna River, locally called the "Novie," and spotted the campsite from which Curtis vanished.

We talked to a couple of native youngsters who had been with Curtis on his ill-fated moose-hunting trip. They had traveled up the river by motorboat and set up their camp. Subsequently, some serious drinking got under way. At one point, according to the boys, Shorty, now roaring drunk, peeled off all his clothes. The last they saw of him, he was running toward the river — stark naked!

We flew up and down the river, but found nothing. Nobody has seen any trace of Shorty since. Thus, in their own silent way, Alaska's waters continue to swallow up people from time to time, leaving little but a memory. ✝

CHAPTER 10

Hutch

One of Alaska's aviation immortals is James T. Hutchison Sr., known simply as "Hutch" to everyone.

Hutch, perhaps the finest aviation mechanic Alaska has seen, came north in 1919 as a GI assigned to the Chilkoot barracks near Haines.

After the war, he drifted into Fairbanks and began working as a mechanic for the Fairbanks Exploration Co., Samson's Hardware and Pollack's Flying Service. After working at the Northern Commercial Co. repairing machinery and outboard motors, his stellar career as an aviation mechanic got under way with that firm's commercial aviation division.

In later years, when the "NC" Co., as we called it, decided to get out of the aviation business, our company, Interior Airways, bought NC's hangar, then situated at Fairbanks International Airport.

Hutch came with the hangar and proved to be the jewel of the purchase. He stayed with us for many years and retired finally at the age of 88. At this writing, he's past 93, still active and still living in Fairbanks.

Hutch's dedication and skill, his competence and tirelessness as a worker, and his superb grasp of everything mechanical, had a lot to do with the success of our company.

Alaska pilots came to know Hutch as a great innovator — a guy who could fix just about anything. If he didn't have a part, he improvised one. He'd make many treks out into the bush — winter and summer — to patch up busted aircraft, and I don't know of any instance in which he didn't succeed in getting the plane back in the air, no matter how hopeless a project it might seem to start with.

Hutch worked on airplanes flown by Alaska's earliest pilots, including those of Carl Ben Eielson, who vanished in the Siberian arctic in 1929 with his mechanic, Earl Borland. Eielson was taking part in the mission of flying out furs from the ice-locked ship Nanuk. Hutch was on a flight to the Nanuk with "Pat" Reid when their plane crash-landed on Jan. 4, 1930, in a creek bottom at the head of the Ungalik River. Hutch patched the plane with the wood from gas boxes and with frozen clothing so the flight could continue.

The times Hutch got us out of jams are too numerous to list, but a typical occasion was in 1955 when we had a DC-3 loaded for a winter trip to Point Barrow. Aboard was a group of VIPS in charge of the DEW line radar project.

The Howard on skis, 1947.

The crew that had brought the DC-3 in the trip before had failed to split the handles. This is an operation that requires the DC-3 landing gear handle to be placed in the down position and the flap handle to be left in the up position to provide open passage for hydraulic fluid to circulate through the system as the engines are being preheated. Otherwise, the hot hydraulic fluid is locked in the system and if it expands sufficiently, it will rupture a line somewhere. That's exactly what happened to us that day. Just about the time we were ready to load the passengers, we heard a loud bang and saw hydraulic fluid flowing over the ramp from a steel hydraulic pipe that had burst.

So there we were at 40 degrees below zero with a grounded airplane.

This proved to be a routine challenge for Hutch. "Give me 30 minutes," he said, "and I'll have it fixed."

This seemed impossible to me, but Hutch had it all figured out. He cut some aeroquip hose to fit the ruptured section and replaced the steel line with it. In the time he'd estimated, we were on our way.

Hutch was still working with NC's aviation division when he gave me some yeoman help in putting the Howard on skis I'd bought from Wien. The skis were a beautiful set made out of solid birch with a Bendix air-oil shock strut pedestal mounted on the top that would just fit the Howard.

Hutch repaired the skis, putting on new metal bottoms with big skags to make them slide straight on the snow instead of sideways.

But that wasn't all. At the same time, Hutch fixed three catches on the side of the Howard, one over each of the Howard's three belly gas tanks. The hook Hutch attached over each tank enabled me to hang my filter funnel on the hook and gas the plane by myself, where before, I had to have someone hold the funnel while I pumped the gas.

Hutch kept studying the situation and said, "You're going to need an oil drain can." So he built one large enough to hold the eight gallons of oil the Howard required. He cut a four-inch hole in the top of the can to facilitate draining the oil from the engine and brazed on a flexible spout over on one side of the top for pouring the oil into the aircraft's tank.

A Howard had never been fitted with skis before and the operation attracted the attention of a new CAA inspector, a real nice young guy, Joe Miraldi. I had the plane in the Fairbanks Aircraft Service hangar with Fred Seltenreich and Jess Bachner, two other crackerjack mechanics, doing the job.

Miraldi watched the ski installation carefully since he was going to be the one who had to approve the job.

"What do you turn up on takeoff?" he asked.

"2,300 rpm," I told him. That was the maximum allowable in the book for the R985 Pratt & Whitney engine.

"You know," he remarked, "for ski operation, if you could get another 50 rpm, it would sure help you out, especially in deep snow or if you're stuck. You'd be surprised at the difference an extra 50 rpm will make, and if you don't use it too long, it won't hurt the engine. I was all for it. Miraldi crawled up on a step-ladder and took the propeller spinner off, working more than an hour.

I'll never forget it because I knew I was exceeding the recommended rpm, and Miraldi was certainly going beyond the call of duty to do the work. Subsequently, in a couple of real tight spots, that extra 50 rpm saved my tail.

The Howard was a particularly good airplane on skis because it had a lot of power for its weight and its tail was light. It was no problem to hold the wheel all the way forward, apply power and lift the tail off the ground if the airplane wasn't loaded too heavily. That facilitated quick turns.

The Norseman had a long fuselage with a heavy tail, making it hard to get the tail off the ground. On any ski-plane, it's frequently necessary to block one ski with a chunk of wood or to put a rope around it to make a quick turn. But with the Howard, I could turn in half the radius required to turn most large planes on skis.

For big game in Alaska or pheasants in South Dakota, Hutch rarely missed a hunting opportunity.

I have digressed a bit from my discussion of one of my favorite Alaskans, Hutch, if only to indicate that all the feds I worked with in those days didn't wear black hats. Maintenance inspector Joe Miraldi was as fine a public servant as they come. Before him, the only CAA agent in Fairbanks was another young official, Don Gretzer, who demonstrated in many ways that he was serious about his mission to foster and promote aviation.

Gretzer was very helpful and friendly to pilots. There were only a handful of airplanes in Fairbanks at the time and he knew every one of them inside out; he knew who flew them and who maintained them. An operations inspector, he was concerned with aircraft operation and pilot qualification.

Those early CAA agents were of an entirely different stripe from some we encountered later, and I got along very well with most of them. But there were times when they were a bit unhappy with me. CAA personnel were housed in a barracks-like building located adjacent to the Weeks Field runway. In winter, when days were short, I'd try to judge my takeoffs so I would get to my destination just at daylight. So my takeoffs were frequently very early. I'd start heating up the plane several hours before dawn and go roaring down the runway on skis well before the normal getting-up time. The propeller noise rattled the windows in the CAA sleeping quarters, prompting some less-than-appreciative remarks.

Getting back to Hutch, he is one of our favorite hunting and fishing companions and has gone with us on numerous trips throughout the interior and arctic Alaska, as well as down the coast. He never missed going on Interior Airways' famous pheasant-

April 1949. Taking delivery of the Aeronca Sedan at Iron Mountain, Michigan. At right is Mario Fontana, my former flight instructor and friend, who secured our first four airplanes for us.

hunting expeditions to South Dakota.

In his long experience as a mechanic in the North, Hutch achieved a precise and comprehensive familiarity with virtually all the planes that were gradually appearing on the scene. I got a big kick out of the old airplanes flying around Fairbanks in those years. I remember Lon Brennan of Manley Hot Springs coming in with his Cunningham Hall, a big, awkward-looking biplane that was awfully slow but a good performer. Orville Tosch flew a Lockheed Vega for Northern Airways. Harry Swanton had a Travelair 6000. From time to time, Alaska Airlines had a Pilgrim based in Fairbanks, which Frank Barr flew.

The Pilgrim's performance was always attention-getting. Barr would make a run to the Fortymile and come back with the plane empty or with a light load. He'd come gliding into Weeks Field, kick the plane sideways and put it into an exaggerated slip which made it look like he was backing into the field. Just before the tires touched ground, he'd straighten it out and grease the plane in smoothly. Frank liked the Pilgrim and knew exactly how to handle it.

The progression of airplanes serving Fairbanks in the '40s, '50s and '60s grew from Wien's Boeing 247s, Northern Airways' Stinson Tri-Motor, Lavery Airways' DC-2 and Pan American's and Alaska's DC-3s, to Pan Am's DC-4. It was quite an occasion when the four-engine DC-4 landed at Weeks Field.

After the opening of Fairbanks International Airport, Pan Am brought in DC-6s, as did Alaska a little later. Pan Am next brought in Boeing Strato-Cruisers, but Alaska Airlines was the first to inaugurate jet service, using a Convair 880. Pan Am soon followed with Boeing 707s. Alaska started Boeing 727 service and Pan Am operated Boeing 747s before its Alaska operation was discontinued.

I'll never forget the two Scandinavian fishermen who boarded the Pan Am Strato-Cruiser at Annette Island near Ketchikan for the Seattle flight. One looked at the spiral staircase and nudged his partner, saying, "By Jesus, dey got a basement in dis ting!"

In the summer of 1948, I got my first glimpse of a Cessna 170. I had stopped at a small landing strip at the head of the Firth River on the American side of the line and watched one of the first Cessna 170s in Alaska (Wien's) come in. It struck me as being a truly beautiful airplane, and at the time, everybody considered it the final word in efficient bush aircraft. However, with the rapid advancement in aircraft development, the Cessna 170 with a 145-horsepower Continental engine was soon considered a ground-loving dog. We purchased a used Cessna 170 in 1949, and it gave us good service as long as we were careful not to get into landing places that were too tight.

Hutch, too, watched with interest as these succeeding generations of aircraft came on the Alaska scene. He got to work on most of them. There was hardly an aircraft that flew in Alaska skies that stumped Hutch so far as getting it fixed was concerned.

On his 90th birthday, to pay tribute to him, I scratched out a poem which seems to have pleased him and called attention to his frequently used expression "ippus pippus" meaning "A-okay"!

> *1900 was the year*
> *That little Hutch did first appear*
> *To live an almost perfect life*
> *With a real productive wife.*
>
> *He was the bugler every morn*
> *who'd wake 'em with his noisy horn*
> *And when they marched off to be fed*

Hutch would crawl back into bed.

The kids were coming mighty fast
He thought each one would be the last
He had to stop his little games
'cause they were running out of names.

He raised them all, though it was tough
To see that each one had enough
Clothes and moose meat by the ton
And guns and rods for everyone.

His trade was fixing things real good
With torch and lathe he always could
Make 'em stronger than when new
And usually run much better, too.

And though he's turned 90 now
He still can show the young guys how
To fish and shoot; oh, what a guy!
His formula is old Ten High.

So here's to Hutch, our lifelong friend
We all will love him 'til the end,
And as long as he is with us
Everything is ippus pippus!!!

✝

CHAPTER 11

Flying Fur

We got involved in flying fur during the winter of 1947-48, a development that introduced me to the fascinating, colorful world of the fur traders.

No fiction writer could do justice to such characters as "Walrus" Jacobson, "Muskrat" Johnny Schwegler, Sam Applebaum, Norman Goldberg and a host of others who moved fast and flew far to get their hands on the glistening pelts that added a touch of luxury to American living.

Among the fur buyers of that era was the madcap Archie Ferguson of Kotzebue, whose antics often made the Marx brothers seem tame in comparison.

These buyers, eager to beat their competition, had to fan out over the width and breadth of Alaska to scramble for furs. Uppermost in their minds was getting swiftly to where the furs were, and that's where we came in.

Air travel was essential in getting fur buyers out to the trapping camps where trappers were still able to make a fairly good living off the land, just as gold prospectors could still keep body and soul together by panning the creeks.

By the late '40s, when we were just beginning to grow, trapping had become one of the territory's most important industries. Each year, fortunes in pelts were flown out of Alaska's trapping camps and native villages.

Since the days when Russia owned Alaska, trappers harvested an annual treasure in natural warmth. Though present "easy living" times have resulted in fewer professional trappers, to this day the fur market counts on Alaska for a steady output of fox, marten, mink, lynx, muskrat, wolf, beaver, otter and other furs.

Before we got into flying fur, we were fairly well entrenched in the growing recreational element of our business. In the winter of 1949-50, our fish-spearing camp at Magoffin Lake was prospering. Out on the lake ice, we had set up two fish houses fully equipped with fish decoys, stoves and spears. The main part of our business, however, was still the charters and the hauling of cargo and passengers, including the most welcome trips Alaska Airlines often diverted to us.

Becoming a part of the often exciting chess game that fur buyers played with their competitors and trappers out in the boondocks added a dash of spice to our sometimes bland flying business.

In Bethel, Christmas and New Year's holidays were prime fur-buying days. The Kuskokwim River town was packed with trappers in from the bush and cash-laden fur buyers fresh from the Lower 48.

The whole cadre of pilots, fur buyers and trappers gathered regularly at the Bethel Roadhouse operated by Ed and Barbara Dimock, an outgoing, congenial couple who later gave up the roadhouse business to open the Labow Haynes Insurance business in Anchorage.

Fur buyers were a motley, colorful lot. Among the most energetic were Sam Applebaum and old "Walrus" Jacobson, whose moustache actually gave him the look of a walrus.

As the saying goes, the "fur would fly" as these two battled each other over the stacks of mink and other pelts brought in by trappers.

"Muskrat" Johnny Schwegler was always right in the fray. Besides buying furs in Bethel, he chartered me to fly him out to bush trapping camps where fur buying competition was far less voracious than in Bethel. Flying the Aeronca Sedan on skis, Schwegler and I combed trapping camps and outlying villages at the mouth of the Kuskokwim and up on the Yukon delta.

On one of our return trips from Bethel, we landed at McGrath at nightfall and stayed overnight at Jack McGuire's Roadhouse. There was, of course, no TV in those days, but Jack did own a radio that produced a lot of static-filled squawking and squeaking. After supper, everybody sat close to the radio to pick up the latest Alaska news and gossip.

On this particular occasion, our attention was captured when we heard the announcer say, "Bulletin! The Alaska Airlines hangar at Merrill Field in Anchorage has just burned down."

The announcement startled and upset Oscar Winchell, part of the roadhouse group. Oscar shook his head sadly, "My Stinson was in that hangar for its annual inspection," he said. "It was worth $5,000. Now it's destroyed!" Poor Oscar meditated awhile about this heavy loss. Then, seeming to brighten up, he reared back and declared, "But I guess I should feel lucky. There's an awful lot of people who don't have $5,000 to lose!"

Walrus Jacobson was a canny trader. He never paid more for mink in Bethel than around $65, the going price for a good pelt. Yet, he gladly shelled out $100 to a trapper for an unusually beautiful mink, a glistening black, silky fur about three feet long and six inches wide.

He was so proud of this exceptional mink pelt that he showed it to everybody in the roadhouse before supper, going into extravagant detail about the mink's unusual luster, its size and its incredible quality. The other fur buyers were beginning to have it up to here about Jake's mink and cooked up a deal with Ed Dimock, who had a pass key to all the rooms. While trappers, traders and pilots were eating supper, Ed surreptitiously sneaked up to Jacobson's room and hid the prize mink pelt.

As the roadhouse bull session was drawing to a close, ol' Jake went up to his room while the others, smiling, waited, casting knowing glances at each other. In a few moments, there was a yell from upstairs and Walrus Jacobson came barrelling down the stairs, his arms waving. "Some bastard stole my mink!" he yelled. "I'd like to get my hands on him. That mink … "

Nobody could keep a straight face. Soon everybody was roaring with laughter and Walrus was blustering in confusion.

"Calm down, Jake," Dimock said. "Just having fun — I 'snitched' your mink." And he returned the pelt to Jake, who was still simmering. He never forgave Dimock for pulling that stunt, hilarious though it was.

* * * * * *

When it came to fur trading, or any other kind of trading for that matter, Archie Ferguson of Kotzebue was certainly no slouch.

I got a first-hand glimpse of Archie's nefarious fur-trading sharpness on one of my first trips over to the west coast with a survey party. After helping the surveyors set up their camp, I flew to Kotzebue to gas up and go back to Fairbanks.

The ice had just gone out of Selawick Lake and when I taxied to the beach at Kotzebue, I saw a guy in a white shirt running down to the landing. It was Archie Ferguson.

As soon as I got stopped, Archie began hollering excitedly, "Jim, I gotta get to Selawick in a hurry. Just got to get there! Can you take me?"

"Okay, Archie," I said, "I still have enough gas to get to Selawick and back."

I wondered what Archie was up to now but didn't ask. Instead, I unloaded the gear I had in the airplane and Archie got in. He was something to see. His pockets were bulging with rolls of money. He was in a high state of excitement and impatience. He just couldn't wait to get to Selawick.

We took off and as we crossed Selawick

Archie Ferguson, Kotzebue, Alaska, businessman, pilot and fur buyer. One of Alaska's most famous "characters."

Lake, we spotted a flotilla of Eskimo boats crammed with natives and dogs.

"Here they come!" Archie yelled shrilly, bursting with excitement. "Land here, Jim, and beach her quick!"

I touched down and taxied to shore. Archie, still wildly steamed up, got out and started hollering and waving to the oncoming boats.

Archie pounced on the native party and their boatloads of muskrat hides like a bird of prey. He began flashing his greenbacks, then proceeded to rake in hundreds of muskrat skins. I was busily stuffing the "rats" into gunny sacks and packing them in the plane.

We finally stuffed the plane from floor to ceiling with fresh-bought Selawick muskrat pelts until there were no more "rats" to buy and no place to put them. I could see that some of Archie's skullduggery had been going on because when the muskrat purchase was over, his face took on a grin of supreme satisfaction mixed with a kind of malicious slyness.

His slick buying operation completed, Archie yelled, "Okay, Jim, let's go!"

Further proof that double-dealing had taken place was the fact that Archie chuckled and laughed all the way back to Kotzebue, repeating triumphantly, "I sure screwed Louie this time!"

None of all this made much sense to me until I learned later that Archie, who was fresh from a vacation trip to the Lower 48, had greedily conspired to undermine, once again, his long-standing Kotzebue competitor, Louie Rotman.

Archie had successfully pulled the rug out from under Rotman, a sharp Kotzebue merchant who had grubstaked a bunch of Eskimo trappers for the cost of their annual spring muskrat expedition. Louie furnished them with traps, groceries, tents and whatever else they needed to carry out a successful trapping season. In exchange, the natives were to repay him in muskrat pelts when they returned from their expedition. Here, Archie's cunning came to the fore and he cleverly maneuvered to intercept the native trappers as they crossed Selawick Lake and well before they got back to Kotzebue.

What really was Rotman's property was shamelessly snatched away by Archie without a qualm. Since Archie paid everybody in cash, there was no way Rotman could collect from the trappers. Archie's meager payments would be spent with lightning speed and in his store as the trappers avoided Louie. Thus Archie had soundly and ruthlessly out-maneuvered his longtime rival. Not only that, he was now the possessor of hundreds of valuable furs that really hadn't been his to buy.

Back in Kotzebue, after Archie stored his furs, he told me, "Jim, I've got to fly over to Sheshalik. Wanna ride over with me?"

"Sure," I said.

At the Kotzebue airstrip which, at that time, was little more than a dirt runway paralleling the ocean beach just behind the village buildings, Archie cranked up his Cessna Airmaster and we taxied to the end of the runway.

I couldn't help studying Archie curiously. He was one of a kind. Real short, it looked like he could hardly see over the instrument panel.

At the end of the runway, Archie failed to run up the engine or check the mags. He didn't do a darn thing, just headed the plane down the runway, slamming the throttle as far as it would go. Clutching the stick in his left hand, he kept pushing on the throttle with his right, fanning the rudders something terrible, kicking them and working the stick around in a circle with his left arm.

All during the takeoff run, he kept his head cocked over to the side, staring over the cowling and hollering as if the plane was some kind of stubborn flying horse. "C'mon, ya sombich! C'mon, ya sombich!"

Despite his unsettling, unsafe pre-takeoff performance, Archie got the plane into the air. At Sheshalik there was no sign of a runway but Archie made an approach and landed in the grass alongside the village. Then, after Archie completed some business, we flew back to Kotzebue.

It was one of the most unusual flights I've ever been on as a passenger, and one I wouldn't want to repeat. And I wasn't too happy about unwittingly getting involved in "screwing Louie."

On another fur-related trip, I just about scared the pants off Norman Goldberg, who did a lot of "fur flying" with me in the interior.

Right after takeoff in the Aeronca Sedan headed for Tanacross almost directly east of Fairbanks, I could see that something about the flight was upsetting Goldberg. He kept staring at the instrument panel and getting more nervous as we went along. Goldberg was squirming in his seat as I ducked into a small lake where I'd left a cache of gasoline. After we landed, he stared at the instrument panel, then started to laugh.

"You know, Jim," he said, "you had me real worried. I kept looking at your compass thinking it was the gas gauge. It scared hell out of me because the pointer was on 'E' all the way from Fairbanks!"

Those fur-buying trips were not without their memorable moments. During the winter of 1948, I had a small mishap with the Howard on skis while on a two-day fur trip with "Muskrat" Johnny Schwegler.

We stopped at Big Delta, Tanacross, Nebesna, Boundary and Eagle and were coming into Fort Yukon's airstrip with a nasty north wind blowing, which meant I had to land in a 90-degree crosswind. It was a marginal situation, but since Johnny was eager to get into Fort Yukon, I decided to go in.

The airstrip was not a good one. It had been cut out of a dense stand of tall spruce

The Howard down at Fort Yukon, December 1948.
No damage, but a 12-hour delay.

trees paralleling the river bank in an east-west direction.

When we hit the snow, severe side stress on the gear fractured a support strut dropping one side of the aircraft down of top of the ski. Fortunately, everything else held and the aircraft slid to a stop with the wing tip just barely brushing the soft snow without damaging the wing.

I got word to Fairbanks Aircraft Service, and the next morning mechanic Jess Bachner came flying in with a stout piece of oak and lots of wire and strong tape. Bachner performed a field fix that held fine throughout the return to Fairbanks where Hutch made me two new struts out of wing struts from a wrecked plane. Hutch removed fittings from the old struts and welded them on the new ones he had cut out, remarking, "These will be three times as strong as your original ones." I flew the aircraft for years, even bouncing over hard snowdrifts on the Arctic Ocean. Once again, Hutch had done his job well. I never had any more gear trouble with that aircraft.

On several occasions, flying the fur buyers pointed the way to other badly needed business for us. While flying "Muskrat" Johnny Schwegler around the territory, I got acquainted with all the traders in the interior as well as those up and down the Kuskokwim and Yukon rivers. One trader, Ira Weisner, who ran the Rampart trading post, wanted me to come back during the king salmon run and haul fresh Yukon salmon to Fairbanks, assuming there was a market for them. The owner of Lindy's grocery told me he'd buy all the fresh kings I could bring in.

Thus, our first small scale fish haul business got under way. I made many trips to Rampart during the king salmon season and Weisner had plenty of fresh-caught salmon to supply a waiting market.

Sometimes we had to get a dogteam to haul the fish out to the Rampart airport, with yelping dogs pulling along the fish-loaded sled on wheels. Occasionally, I had to haul the fish out myself in a big wagon, load them into the airplane and fly them to Fairbanks, where Lindy's grocery lost no time in selling them down to the last fish.

That was a fish haul in miniature. We later hauled 12,000 pounds of salmon per load in C-46s and now haul 50,000 pounds of salmon in the Hercules.

In hauling fish, one can never lose sight of how perishable the cargo is. One Bristol Bay fisherman suffered a terrible loss when he was late, and perhaps negligent, in getting his fish to the airplane. They were so badly spoiled, the cannery at Kodiak refused to accept them. They had to be discarded. ✛

Dot with one of her favorite planes, a Piper Tri-Pacer.
Interior Airways was the Piper dealer in Fairbanks, 1952.

CHAPTER 12

Counting The Ways

Life with Dot has taught me that such words as love, caring, sharing and sacrificing are not platitudes but symbols of powerful forces that can move mountains.

Without her love, encouragement, sacrifice and understanding, the things that we achieved could not have been possible. It would indeed be hard to count the ways in which Dot has made my life richer and more fulfilling. Together, all the problems, discouragements and disappointments life handed us didn't seem to matter. Her deep-rooted, positive faith buoyed me up in the darkest of times.

Dot has excelled in so many ways. She has succeeded as a wife, mother, pilot, entrepreneur, cub scout den mother, trouble-shooter, confidante, friend and hunting and fishing companion, to name a few.

Among the many things she contributed to our relationship were her unceasing efforts to make the challenge of building our future a true partnership.

She demonstrated this very early during the worst of the rough times by getting fully involved in our aviation enterprise. With remarkable determination, step by steady step, she became a private pilot, then acquired her commercial license, her multi-engine rating, her seaplane rating, and ultimately, her instrument rating.

Not content to watch from the sidelines, she became one of our company's most valuable pilots and flew commercially for us for years at a time when there were very few women in the left-hand seat, either in Alaska or elsewhere.

She was able to thoroughly demolish the prejudice that questioned the capability of women as pilots. She clung steadfastly to her self-confidence and her well-honed skills at a time when some male passengers weren't quite sure that she could get them there safely. She never dented a plane. We did note that she changed the landing checklist in the Twin Bonanza, a plane that she flew often. In addition to the usual

Dottie Magoffin sat in the cockpit of one of the planes she flies in Alaska.

Lady Bush Pilot

By DOLLY CONNELLY

IF a queen contest were to be held in Interior Alaska, the choice very well could be a pert, small brunette named Dottie Magoffin, one of the few women bush pilots in the new state.

Fourteen years ago, Dottie went to an isolated gold camp called Ester, north of Fairbanks, as the bride of a Minnesota flyer of the Second World War. Jim Magoffin had a job as a mining engineer with a gold-dredging outfit. They had nothing but each other and boundless enthusiasm for Alaska.

In the first year, they lived in a log cabin, ate ducks that Dottie shot, and saved Jim's salary to purchase a small float plane for moose-hunting and fishing. The Magoffins learned early in their Alaskan life that the huge area has twice as many miles of certified air lanes—8,000—as all-weather highways.

Soon the Magoffins were spending so much of their time flying engineers around to mines and dredges and on sports week-ends that Jim dropped mining engineering and went into the charter-flying business.

Dottie and Jim now own Interior Airways (23 planes, 30 employes and 19 pilots). The backbone of the business is the flying of materials to the distant-early-warning line (D. E. W. Line), White Alice, a communications network, and the vast Air Force missile-detection base taking form in the wilderness southwest of Nenana. Dottie's special chore is flying company officials.

Dot was undaunted by the prejudice against women pilots that occasionally raised its ugly head.

"GUMP" (gasoline, undercarriage, mixture and prop-pitch), Dot added an "L" for "lipstick on."

While flying regular schedules to the Ballistic Missile Early Warning Site (BMEWS) at Clear, she'd be at the Fairbanks ticket counter by 5:30 a.m., check in passengers, announce the flight on the P.A. system, get passengers out of the bar or coffee shop and then fly the trip.

She was undaunted by the prejudice against women pilots that occasionally raised its ugly head. On one flight to Clear, a burly construction worker looked over the slim, young woman who was about to get into the pilot's seat and demanded, "Where's the pilot?"

"I'm the pilot," Dot told him forthrightly. "Slide over and let me lock the door."

The passenger turned pale. He was so shook up, he had to bolster his courage by repeatedly nipping at a whiskey bottle hidden in a paper sack, all the way to Clear.

She took on with ease missions so difficult that amazement was expressed that she was doing the flying. She was not only doing the flying but doing it superbly on one of a whole string of challenging flights she made in the late '50s.

On one occasion, all of our male pilots were out of town on jobs and I was at Umiat when our Fairbanks office got word that the Shell Oil geology crew at Lake Peters was in a fix; their small generator had failed and they desperately needed a replacement.

Our Fairbanks general manager, Roy Isackson, promptly purchased a 250-pound generator and loaded it aboard our Cessna 180 on floats. It was up to Dot, the only seaplane pilot available in Fairbanks, to make the 330-mile flight to Lake Peters on the north side of the Brooks Range.

Getting into the lake with a float plane would challenge the skills of the finest of pilots because, though it was early July, the lake was still frozen over except for a narrow strip of open water near the shore.

The geologists scooted out of their tents and watched with trepidation as the Cessna 180 approached the lake. Dot settled the floats precisely on the slim section of open water available, then taxied over to the beach.

A camera close-up of their faces would have been interesting at the moment a pert, slender little brunette wearing hip boots stepped out of the float plane.

I was told later that the geologists experienced something close to shock when Dot made her appearance. While a couple of men unloaded the new generator and invited her in for lunch, a third hustled into the dining tent which was also the kitchen area. Apparently the guy was too flustered to remove the cardboard sign in plain sight on the tent wall. It admonished: "No Farting in the Kitchen."

* * * * * *

Among the many unofficial hats Dot wore while rendering yeoman service to our struggling firm were those of goodwill ambassador and public relations director.

Dot's hospitality was extended frequently to customers, business associates and our employees. She has flown many, many trips with dignitaries and prospective cus-

Not only does Dot share my love for flying, she also shares my love for hunting and fishing. Here, Dot and B.B. Dean, an American Airlines stewardess and friend, return from a combined hunting and fishing trip.

tomers to various points in northern Alaska and the interior.

It was Dot who piloted U.S. Sen. Ernest Gruening and Dr. John Weston on an outing to a remote lake where they enjoyed fishing and a picnic lunch. The senator told me that expedition had been one of the most pleasant days of his life.

There was always a special, extra-friendly dimension to Dot's hospitality. When we took parties of guests to various lakes throughout the interior and in the Brooks Range, Dot wasn't content with serving the usual cold sandwiches for lunch. Instead, she added such extra touches as several kinds of bread, baked corn pudding and vegetables, none of it cold. As soon as a few fish were landed, she'd get the frying pan on and soon, sizzling in the pan, would be a golden arrangement of fresh lake trout, pike or grayling. Her care and forethought gave a unique gourmet touch to those wilderness lunches.

She took in stride even VIP guests, some of whom were reputed to be difficult. On one occasion, we got word that the chairman of the board of British Petroleum, Sir Maurice Bridgeman, and his wife, Lady Bridgeman, were coming over from England to tour northern Alaska and visit British Petroleum North Slope geology crews. The Alaska BP office suggested we take them to our beautiful, scenic camp at Schrader Lake so they could enjoy the superb fishing there.

British Petroleum's chairman, Sir Maurice Bridgeman, and his wife, Lady Bridgeman, visit with B.P. Geology Party Chief Geof. Larminie on Alaska's North Slope.

I flew Lord and Lady Bridgeman and their aide, Mike Savage, to the geology camps on the slope in a Grumman Widgeon, then brought them to Sagwon before proceeding to Schrader Lake for several days of fishing.

Meanwhile, Dot loaded up the Cessna 180 seaplane with groceries and supplies for the Schrader Lake outing. She was careful to include things she was told the chairman liked, such as Glenlivet Scotch whiskey. We were also cautioned that Bridgeman had a finicky stomach and couldn't eat just anything. There were all kinds of things he "simply couldn't have."

Knowing that Sir Maurice wanted to see our Sagwon base, Dot flew out of her way to land at Sag Lake and deliver some items that would make Lady Bridgeman feel at home as she enjoyed "tea time" there. These included bone china tea cups and saucers, and a silver tea set. Thus, Lady Bridgeman wouldn't have to suffer the heavy crockery used by the pilots and geologists. Dot also instructed Suzie Eaves (the cook's wife) on how to make tea as the British do, using the tea leaves rather than tea bags.

I arrived at our scheduled time with the Bridgemans, and we eventually settled down in the dining area. Suzie, as rehearsed in her mind several times, came to the table and politely asked, "Lady Bridgeman, would you like a cup of tea?" Her answer was, "No, thank you, I'll just have coffee."

By the time we landed at Schrader Lake, several hours after Dot had arrived, she had a lovely meal cooked and the VIP couple thoroughly enjoyed it.

I wondered how things would go the following day in view of the chairman's extremely sensitive diet. I came upon him the next morning happily seated in the bright sunshine on a wooden gas box devouring a huge stack of hotcakes topped with lots of butter and syrup and drinking coffee — virtually all the things he wasn't supposed to have. It was obvious he was savoring it all.

Lady Bridgeman was from Scotland and apparently had done a lot of fishing. She enjoyed teaching Dot the precise and correct method of using a fly rod. "It's aaaall in the wrist, my dear," she instructed, as she gracefully swung the line out over the water.

* * * * * *

Among the many refreshing, charming things about Dot is the way she always looks on the bright side of life and has something positive and good to say about everybody and everything. I thought she might be stymied in this regard the day she accompanied me out to the Fairbanks landfill to get rid of a load of trash. Dot was standing by the car as I unloaded the garbage when the door to the dumpmaster's little shack popped open and the dumpmaster, a truly horrible-looking individual, emerged.

His bloodshot eyes indicated he'd been drunk for several days. He hadn't shaved for weeks. Ugly rivulets of chewing tobacco had trickled down to stain his beard and once-white shirt, converting it into irregular yellow swatches.

This revolting apparition staggered toward our car and stopped about 10 feet from Dot. The two looked at each other. All was silent, and I was wondering what favorable remark Dot could possibly come up with for this poor creature.

She was not found wanting. "My," she said at last, "you certainly have a pretty dump here."

The poor fellow absolutely beamed and a lively, friendly conversation was kindled that lasted until we were ready to go.

* * * * * *

Besides being a wonderful wife and mother, besides being a good helpmate all through our business career, besides being a marvelous, meticulous pilot, Dot also remains my favorite hunting and fishing partner.

But it's a wonder to me occasionally how she can hunt at all the way she loves animals and, in fact, all living things. Out in the hunting camp or at home, the dogs must always be fed first. They must have a comfortable place to sleep, preferably our bed.

On one September duck hunt, ice had fringed the lake shore during the night and Dot refused to take our dogs along on the morning hunt because the water and air would be too cold for them. Therefore, we had no dog to retrieve a beautiful drake Widgeon that Dot, herself, had downed. It lay belly up and seemingly inaccessible some 200 feet from shore. I was resigned to leaving it, saying it would make a good meal for a mink, but Dot was determined to get that beautiful bird.

She peeled off her clothes and swam out to the Widgeon. On the way back she held its neck in her mouth so both hands would be free for swimming.

Oh, I thought, my kingdom for a movie camera. Imagine the scene as she crawled onto shore, the duck still dangling from her mouth!

Scenes like that, fortunately, happen only once in a lifetime. That unusual episode, incidentally, inspired a famous poem by Dr. William R. Wood, president of the University of Alaska. He entitled it "The Minto Streaker."

* * * * * *

Dot always cheerfully pitched in to help out when there was a special assignment or extra work to do.

In the spring of 1960, I thought we might be able to save a few bucks by having her ferry a new twin-engine Beech Travelaire from the factory at Wichita to Fairbanks.

Dot was enthusiastic about this assignment and looked forward to it. She invited her good friend, Rachel Henry, wife of the commanding officer of Eielson Air Force Base, to come along on the trip.

The two girls rode the airline to Wichita, and everything seemed fairly routine until several days passed and I got no word from Wichita.

Somewhat concerned, I phoned Beech flight operations. "Can you tell me," I asked, "if Mrs. Magoffin has left for Alaska in our new Travelaire?"

The male voice on the other end asked, "Who?"

"Mrs. Magoffin. Dot."

"Oh," the voice came back as if a light bulb had been turned on, "You mean Dottie. She just took off!"

Rachel Henry and Dot Magoffin (right) departing Wichita, Kansas, for Fairbanks, Alaska, March 1960.

"Then she'll probably be in Fairbanks some time tomorrow," I remarked.

"Oh, no, not at all," the voice replied. "She and Rach, and two of our people flew over to Tulsa for lunch."

Nothing wrong with that, I thought, but in a couple of days I got a telegram from Dot informing me that she and Rachel were "shopping in Edmonton due to weather."

After they got back to Fairbanks, I tallied up the bills and found I could've saved several hundred dollars by sending a hired pilot to get the plane. But I was glad she and Rachel had taken advantage of the ferry trip to do some shopping in much larger stores than we then had in Fairbanks.

* * * * * *

As a hunter, Dot is cool and doesn't get rattled, and once she possibly saved us both from getting finished off by a huge, raging Montague Island bear.

As Dot sat on a cedar snag in an open meadow on the island, I circled around with the aim of chasing a deer to her. When I approached her stand, a monster of a brown bear suddenly appeared over the crest of a hill and began barrelling straight toward me. I shot the bear three times before he fell. Just as he did, a second bear popped up from the same direction. I used my remaining two cartridges to down that one and had started toward the two bear carcasses when a third bear came over the hill and started toward me.

The wind was from the bear to me, and I could hear the animal popping its jaws. I was out of shells now and in big trouble because the bear was heading straight toward me — and fast. I yelled at Dot, who witnessed the whole episode from her position off to the side.

"Shoot it, Honey!" I hollered, my adrenaline reaching a peak.

She had her rifle pointed toward the bear but didn't shoot, so I shouted again as the situation got more dangerous by the moment. "Shoot! Shoot!" I yelled.

Still no gunshot. I felt real terror as I shouted, "For Christ's sakes — shoot!"

Only a moment or two passed before Dot's rifle cracked and the bear collapsed.

Dot met me halfway to the third bear, and I congratulated her on her good shooting, but asked why she had waited so long at a time when I was in real danger.

She said, "Some patches of brush were in the way. I wanted to get a good, clear shot. I got him right through the heart."

Dot's bullet, however, had entered the bear's eye, killing it instantly. She was a little embarrassed and vowed she'd never again confess to where she'd aimed until *after* she'd examined the carcass.

* * * * * *

A subsequent Montague Island deer hunt was far less exciting, but another success for Dot.

While Dot took a stand at the end of a wooded ridge, I drove the ridge from the opposite end, zig-zagging repeatedly to chase deer to her.

I had progressed half way through the drive when I heard three shots in rapid succession and a fourth shot several seconds later. When I walked up to Dot at the end of the drive, she was excited but quite dejected as she described how a big buck deer had come along and stopped behind a tree just as she was about to shoot. All she could see was the deer's head sticking out. She shot at it three times but missed. The deer turned and bounded away from her. She got in a final shot as it jumped over some low bushes.

"Did you go over to see if you hit it?" I asked.

"My first three shots hit that tree," she answered, pointing to the plainly visible bullet holes, "and I didn't stand a chance on that last one. It was just a snap shot as it was going out of sight."

She showed me where the deer was when she last saw it. The buck lay dead just a few yards farther on. The last shot had entered just below the buck's tail, exiting through the back a few inches in front of the base of the tail, severing the main artery — a lucky, deadly shot. That episode prompted one of my infamous poems…

DOTTIE, THE DEERSLAYER

She takes her stand with rightful pride,
The drive is to begin.
She is well hid and has rest aim
With rifle sighted in.

Her part is well rehearsed, you see,
She's practiced it for weeks.
She knows exactly what to do
When venison she seeks.

She'll let him come to open ground,
With nothing in the way.
Then knock him dead
With one good shot.
Today will be her day.

Then out he comes with flashing horns,
She stops him with a yell.
But all at once her mind is blank,
Her plan has gone to hell.

Three times she shoots right at his head,
Three times he fails to flee.
He simply switches end for end,
No danger does he see.

Dot calms herself and checks her scope,
And quickly cleans the glass.
"If I can't hit his head," said she,
"I'll shoot him in the ass!"

* * * * * *

Serious hunters sometimes brave horrible weather conditions to pursue their sport.

It was mid-November when I received a phone call from Jack Moul, manager of Hercules operations for Pacific Western Airlines in Vancouver, Canada.

What's up, Jack?" I asked.

"Well, Jim, I just got back from a terrific goose hunt at Scandia, Alberta. I'm calling to see if you are going to attend the international air cargo conference in Calgary next week."

"Sure am," I advised.

"Well, you better bring your shotgun. I can show you some good shooting."

Dot accompanied me to Calgary, but Jack was enmeshed in a business deal and couldn't go hunting. However, on the morning following the final meeting, I awoke at 4 a.m. to a howling wind. I turned on the radio and heard the announcer describe how Calgary was engulfed in a blizzard with a freezing wind and blowing snow, and he was advising motorists to stay off the roads.

I woke Dot.

"C 'mon, Honey, we're going duck hunting!"

After a hurried breakfast, we drove our rented car to a lake between Taber and Purple Springs, Alberta. The lake was covered with four inches of ice, except for about 10 acres in the center that was so filled with ducks and geese that they kept it open. The north wind was fully 30 miles per hour, blowing clouds of snow, and every few minutes a flock would depart — flying south of the lake to feed in corn fields. When they returned to the lake they were very low and bucking that strong wind. It was a duck hunter's dream.

I left Dot crouched in a patch of willows on the south shore and I walked over the ice to another patch 200 yards away. The wind was so strong I couldn't hear the gunshots, but I regularly saw big greenhead mallards spill out of flocks passing over Dot.

I was enjoying some of the best duck shooting of my life when I suddenly realized that several flocks had passed over Dot and no ducks had dropped. The flocks didn't even flare.

Concerned, I hustled over to Dot's position and found her crouched down, blowing her breath on her hands, her face plastered with snow and her eyelashes about frozen shut.

"What's the matter?" I asked.

"Mmmy fffingers are so cccold I cccan't pull the trigger," she complained.

"Put 'em in your armpits," I yelled above the howling wind.

"There's *ice* in my armpits," she replied.

"Okay, Honey," I said, "We've probably got enough ducks. We'll head on in."

We picked up our ducks and felt very happy to have our legal possession limits.

In spite of a valid export permit, an over-eager customs agent at Seattle tried to take them away from us, saying, "You can't bring Canadian ducks into the U.S."

I protested, "Thousands fly across the border very day!"

Fortunately, the guy's supervisor showed up and waved us through, ducks and all.

* * * * * *

This chapter on Dot would not be complete without citing the outstanding job she did managing the flying school we operated through 1953. She would come to the office regularly and take care of the paperwork, keeping the school running smoothly. In the years we operated the school, no student ever wrecked an airplane and nobody got hurt, though a few students did some wild things.

We were training many students under the GI Bill of Rights, as well as others who wanted to learn to fly. As our flight instruction business increased, we had to buy several extra small airplanes, mostly Cessna 140s, though we did have an Aeronca Chief, a J-3 Cub and a Luscombe.

Our flying service operated at Weeks Field until the International Airport was completed and we moved there.

One of our students, Ray Loesche, scheduled himself for a cross-country trip in a Piper Pacer as part of his commercial course. He was to fly to Northway and return. When he failed to return in the allotted time, I contacted the CAA at Northway and was told the plane had been in and out several times that day.

On checking further, I discovered that Loesche had scheduled a party of sheep hunters to go into the Alaska Range. They had driven to Northway, and he was picking them up and flying them to a sheep camp, landing on the river bars.

Here he was, just a student who set up his own little charter business with a school airplane, attempting flights experienced bush pilots have to be mighty careful doing. Fortunately, he got away with it, but we immediately put a stop to that kind of foolishness.

Some of our students became prominent professional pilots. Among those who graduated from our school were Frank Gregory, Bob Shinn and Ray Tremblay (the flying game warden).

Throughout, Dot's efforts were invaluable in this successful operation as well as in the numerous other developments that followed over the years and ultimately brought us success. ✝

CHAPTER 13

The Great
Fishwheel Gold Rush

There's a little bit of the treasure hunter in just about all of us, and throughout history, great masses of otherwise sensible people have demonstrated incredible eagerness to abandon their life's work and everything else to answer the almost irresistible call of gold.

Over the years, stampedes to Sutter's Mill in California, to the Klondike, to Nome, to countless creeks in the Yukon and in Alaska have uprooted people and impelled them to respond to whatever bonanza story happened to be stirring people's blood at the time.

Though much tinier in its impact, the October 1949 gold rush to an unpopulated spot on the Yukon that came to be known as Fishwheel had all the elements of the sometimes senseless scrambles for bonanzas that preceded it. This gold rush was far different in many respects, especially because a lot of people believed it was manufactured and shouldn't have taken place at all.

In fact, I was wrongfully branded as the culprit who had a hand in generating it merely because I happened to have stopped off in Fort Yukon at a time when the innkeeper there, Gilbert Lord, was excitedly displaying a vial full of glittering metal that could have been gold. According to him, the dust and nuggets in the bottle had just been taken from the bottom of a native boy's fishwheel at his fishing site not far upriver from Fort Yukon. Lord himself had much to gain from the influx of people into Fort Yukon.

The entire village of Fort Yukon was in a frenzy when the news of the "strike" got out and soon the raging fever began infecting people over a far wider area.

I had been flying in Canada and had stopped in Fort Yukon to clear customs when I learned about the so-called gold strike. I didn't think much about all the up-roar and commotion at the time, but when I got to Fairbanks, I found that town also was seething with excitement fed by announcements on the local radio station.

The news caused great excitement among old-time prospectors in Fairbanks, many of them veterans of several earlier strikes that left them empty-handed, disappointed and disillusioned but still hoping for that fortune that was just around the corner. Few of them had relinquished their dream that in the next gold rush, a bonanza was await-ing them. All they needed was a packsack full of grub, a pick and shovel and, of course, a gold pan. And they needed to get there. This was probably the first gold rush in Alaska and Yukon history where stampeders were airlifted.

Among old-timers caught up in the Fishwheel excitement were Sam Gamblin and Earl Hurst, as well as several other old sourdoughs I'd flown out into the bush before.

At our office, the telephone began ringing off the hook. All kinds of people just had to get to Fishwheel as fast as possible to stake a claim. I made the first landing at Fishwheel where I picked out a frozen lagoon that appeared to have ice thick enough to land on. Even so, I rolled up onto a gravel bar before stopping. It was late in Octo-ber, and the ice at Fishwheel was barely thick enough to permit safe landings. This required use of a lighter plane, and I was flying the Aeronca Sedan, taking no chances until I was certain the ice would support the Howard.

Other airlines were also in the act, and the sky began buzzing with planes shut-tling in and out of the remote, forlorn spot on the Yukon. For just about everybody in the flying business in Fairbanks, but only for a few days, charters began skyrocketing. As the fever began to reach its peak, I made four round trips each day just as fast as I could gas and load, and hardly made a dent in the line of people waiting impatiently to board our next flight.

The day after news of the so-called gold strike got out, virtually all the flying outfits in the Fairbanks area joined the Fishwheel fly-in. While I was getting ready to taxi out in the Howard, I saw Bill Lavery warming up his Norseman at the end of the runway. I noted that Lavery, who took off just before I did, used up almost all the 5,200-foot runway to get airborne, so he wasn't flying light. I was sure he was heading for Fishwheel.

Lavery headed down the Chena River, then up the Alaska Railroad toward what is now Murphy Dome. He should have arrived at Fishwheel well ahead of me, but I saw no sign of his Norseman when I reached there a short time later and circled for a landing. I landed, taxied up on the gravel bar and unloaded, wondering all the time what had happed to Lavery.

I soon got the answer. In about 20 minutes, I spotted the Norseman coming upriver then dropping down for a landing. It was a landing with sound effects. As he set down on the ice, it began cracking and booming under the heavy pressure it was taking. "Man, oh man," I thought, "Bill sure has a heavy load in that airplane."

Lavery taxied the Norseman up on the gravel bar, and I helped him unload. His plane was packed to the ceiling with cases of beer. I estimated he was carrying well over 3,000 pounds of cargo — a 1,000-pound overload, at least.

"What took you so long to get here?" I asked Bill.

"Heavy load," he replied. "After I took off, I couldn't get 'er high enough to get over the hills up ahead. To make it here, I had to go clear around by the Tolovana River and up through the Livengood Pass. Then I hit the Yukon Valley and flew upriver."

It had been a tough, maybe even a risky trip for Lavery, but it illustrated the atmosphere of "get it while you can" that prevailed during the rush.

All along the desolate section of the Yukon River, a remarkable tent community was beginning to sprout and spread. If there was going to be a gold rush, Fairbanks merchants weren't going to miss out on it, and many of them moved in their tents and merchandise even before the dust settled.

One Fairbanks surplus store owner lost no time in setting up his tent and selling stampeders gold pans, picks and shovels, tents, axes and outdoor clothing.

Just about everything a prospector might need, even companionship, was on sale. One entrepreneur saw in the influx of gold-seeking men the need to supply something rarely lacking in any gold rush worthy of the name — girls.

There was merchandise, there was booze and there were girls, so, as expected, a few of the prospectors very early began to whoop it up and cavort. But after a couple of days, the steam began running out of all the feverish activity. Saner heads were starting to prevail.

Experienced miners began throwing a damper on the whole business. Many of them were familiar with the geology of the Fishwheel area and were convinced from the start that this couldn't possibly be a legitimate gold strike.

They pointed out, to the dismay of many of the hopeful prospectors, that bedrock, on top of which placer gold deposits usually collect, was situated more than 50 feet below the bottom of the river in the Fishwheel area.

Even then, diehard miners persisted in believing that the gold was there. One hopeful version bandied about was that a closer-to-the-surface dike of rock traversed the Yukon valley at that very spot, putting the gold just under the surface. It was along this geologic exception, they claimed, that the native boy discovered the nuggets captured by his fishwheel.

No further gold came into evidence, however. In little more than a week, sanity and common sense began to set in. Tents began coming down. Air traffic was abruptly reversed. Passengers and cargo began to be flown out with nobody coming in. It was over, and now only a barren riverbank remains of that hectic, short-lived frenzy at Fishwheel. The University of Alaska finally obtained a sample of the fishwheel "gold" and promptly pronounced that it consisted of brass shavings from the bearings the native boy used to support his fishwheel's axle.

Again, I plead absolutely not guilty to having anything at all to do with instigating the Great Fishwheel Gold Rush. However, considering how the stampede helped our flying business for a few days, I sure didn't do anything to stop it. +

CHAPTER 14

"Emerg Land Here"

The huge letters stamped in the snow on the frozen wilderness lake looked like big trouble below.

"EMERG LAND HERE" was the message surveyors of the Ryal Engineering Co. of Tulsa, Oklahoma, painstakingly stamped out on the surface of the lake.

When I spotted the letters, I was flying a Super Cub on skis. It was October 1951, when we had a contract with Ryal to fly air support for them while they surveyed the road from Cantwell eastward across the south slope of the Alaska Range to the Richardson Highway near Paxon Lake — a road now known as the Denali Highway.

We had been supplying the surveyors by float plane until freezeup. After that, and until the winter ice was safe to land on, we air-dropped the camp's groceries and other supplies and their mail.

Now, it was late October, but on the south slope of the Alaska Range, it hadn't been very cold.

Studying the massive letters below, I circled along one side of the lake where the engineering crew had set up a small tent camp. Spruce boughs on the lake marked out a "runway," and I figured since civil engineers were in the group, they should know whether or not the lake ice was safe to land on. With this in mind, I decided to go in. I glided down to the "runway," and the plane slid to a smooth stop. Just after I cut the engine, the ice collapsed under the skis and the plane started to sink gradually.

I whipped open the door, and within a split second, was rolling out onto the ice, having no idea how deep the water was underneath or how far the plane would sink.

Fortunately, the plane stopped sinking when it was only half-submerged. This allowed me to get out the camp's freight, my sleeping bag and emergency gear. Now, the only problem was getting the plane out of this precarious ice-trap.

When I didn't come home that evening, Dot got Fairbanks pilot Dick McIntyre to fly down to the lake to look for me. He circled the lake a couple of times, sizing up the situation, then returned to Fairbanks. When he flew back to the lake again, he air-dropped a block and tackle, plenty of rope, a couple of axes and a come-along.

Using a pole, we hooked the rope onto the ski pedestals. Then we cut around the airplane and allowed it to sink to the bottom of the lake. The next step in retrieving the plane was to cut a trench to lead the rope through so we could drag the airplane to shore along the bottom of the lake and under the ice, using the block and tackle attached to stout bushes on the beach.

Gradually, we dragged the plane to shallow water until the top of the wings began touching the bottom of the ice. Then we cut another big hole in the ice and slowly dragged the airplane right up on shore.

Surprisingly, though the plane was thoroughly soaked, it showed no signs of damage. We dried it out the best we could, drained the gas tanks, and dried out the magnetos. Incredibly, very little water had seeped into the tanks, and when I cranked the plane up, it ran okay.

That three-day operation required a lot of manual labor with everybody pitching in. When it was all over, I flew the airplane back to Fairbanks without incident and put it into the Fairbanks Aircraft Service hangar for a thorough inspection.

It turned out that the only real damage was the residual water retained in two of the steel longerons. When the water froze, it split the tubing. Mechanics had to cut away the fabric and replace the damaged pieces.

That unfortunate episode taught me a lesson that stayed with me. After that, whenever I harbored any doubt about the safety of the ice I was landing on, I'd slide the airplane right up on, or as near as possible, to the beach before I stopped and cut the engine.

What about the sign out on the lake: "EMERG LAND HERE"? It turned out that the emergency that prompted the sign involved one of the men at a camp who, at the time the sign was stamped into the snow, appeared to be developing a mental problem. When the plane plunged through the ice, however, this young man turned out not to be too disturbed, because he had cheerfully pitched in on the job of saving the plane, working as diligently as the rest of the men. After three days of hard work crowned by success, the man apparently was back to normal and no evacuation was necessary. ✝

CHAPTER 15

Bears

My charter customers enjoyed spotting game from the air, especially the big grizzlies we flew over from time to time. Seeing them from the air was exciting and harmless but encountering these big creatures on the ground can be a life-shattering experience.

One of my early passengers, A.C. Johnson, an aspiring prospector, didn't run into a bear on the ground, but did see enough signs that one was roaming around the area he planned to camp in. This led him to make an abrupt change in his plans.

Johnson chartered me to fly him to Wild Horse Lake, situated about 4,000 feet above sea level in the Alaska Range.

The weather was beautiful when we arrived. I taxied up to a sandy beach on the lake's north side, cut the engine and jumped out, then pulled the heels of the floats up on the sand.

I helped Johnson out of the airplane and was unloading his stuff while he wandered about 50 feet up the beach.

"Come on over here, Jim," he yelled to me, pointing at something in the sand. That "something" was a huge set of fresh grizzly bear tracks. They were wicked looking, about a foot long and five inches wide with clearly discernible claw marks sprouting from the ends of the huge bear's toe.

I remarked, "Well, that's just a grizzly bear."

A look of apprehension and concern suddenly crossed Johnson's face. You could see that the more he studied those big tracks the less he was interested in prospecting in this neck of the woods.

"Grizzly bear!" he said, shaking his head in awe. "You know, Jim, I think I'll go back to Fairbanks with you!"

I put Johnson's supplies back on the plane and we both flew back to Fairbanks. I suspect that was the last of this young man's ventures into the North's wilderness.

* * * * * *

Some of the people I flew obviously lacked a healthy respect for the speed, power, ferocity and deadliness of Alaska's bears.

I was concerned with the attitude of one prospector, Harry Townsend, a mining engineer with the Anaconda Copper Co., whom I flew to a place called Twin Lakes on the south slope of the Brooks Range.

We landed on one of the lakes, and he told me the spot he wanted to explore was several miles from the lake, so we'd have to hike.

I tied the airplane down and got our gear out. I had a .30-.06 rifle with me acquired from a second-hand gun dealer in Fairbanks. Because the gun had a broken stock, I paid only $11 for it, then got a carpenter to drill the stock and insert a wooden dowel that made it as good as new.

As I was throwing the gun over my shoulder, Harry said, "Hey, you don't need that thing. We've got enough to pack without that."

"Well, Harry," I asked him, "what do we do if a bear comes along?"

"No big deal, he said. "See this pick and shovel? If we see a bear, I just beat them together and sing at the top of my voice, 'O solo mio.' When he hears that, the bear is going to turn around and go the other way."

Knowing what I knew about bears, I wasn't impressed and took my rifle anyway.

We had gone only about a mile, when up on the side of the mountain, we spotted a good-sized grizzly busily engaged in digging out ground squirrels. I don't think that big, ferocious-looking bear was paying any particular attention to us and had apparently not noticed us up to that point. But he was gradually working his way down the side of the mountain getting closer to us by the minute, and I was watching him cautiously.

I turned to say something to Harry only to discover he was nowhere to be seen. He had taken one look at that big bear and was already half way back to the airplane.

Apparently, on seeing the bear, Harry had forgotten all about beating his tools together and delivering a wilderness aria. I've never seen anyone disappear so fast.

I shot into the rocks near the bear, and he spun around and sped off in the other direction. After I shot, Harry came back and we proceeded on up to take some samples of an outcrop he was interested in.

I can testify that when it comes to meeting a grizzly face to face, one's bravery can disappear awfully fast whether or not one knows how to sing opera.

* * * * * *

In the late fall of 1950, hunting and fishing charters made up a major part of our business. To get more revenue from big game hunting trips, I got a guide's license and was hired by a Pennsylvania hunter who wanted to bag a black bear, a brown bear and a moose.

He appeared to be a fine gentleman and a good sport, but was noticeably cross-eyed. I was concerned that his shooting might leave much to be desired — and it did.

We flew from Fairbanks to a lodge on Caribou Lake, a few miles north of Homer.

Operated by Jess Willard, the lodge, called Willard's Moose Ranch, was set in the midst of good moose country.

Willard rented us a boat and horses. My Pennsylvania "dude" collected a black bear and a fine bull moose shooting from the prone position and using my packsack as a gun rest.

We couldn't locate any brown bears there so we flew over to the west side of Cook Inlet. While flying across the

The birth of my second son, William David, came as I was out in the Kenai Peninsula on a chartered trip with a Pennsylvania hunter.

Inlet, Kenai radio called and asked, "Is this Aeronca 06H from Fairbanks?"

"Affirmative," I said.

"You've just become the father of a baby boy! Mother and son are doing fine at the Fairbanks hospital."

Savoring happiness and pride at being a new dad, I thanked the Kenai operator and we flew on to a large lake where we set up our camp.

This was bear country. Hundreds of dead and dying salmon coated the lakeshore and numerous bear tracks traversed our camp area.

With several hours of daylight remaining, we hiked along the shore looking for a brown bear that would make a good rug in a Pennsylvania office.

As we were rounding a point, a huge brownie emerged from the alders and began walking along the beach in our direction.

We quickly slipped into the woods and crouched down about 30 yards from the shoreline.

The bear stopped directly opposite from us. Preoccupied with sniffing a dying salmon, it set up a perfect broadside shot at close range.

"Shoot! Shoot now!" I whispered.

The rifle cracked, but the bullet missed the bear completely and the unharmed bear spun and vanished into the thick alders.

The guy was a good sport about it. "Jim," he said, "if I can't hit a bear that's big as a cow at 30 paces, he deserves to live. I'm happy with my moose and a black bear rug in my office will suit me just fine. Let's go back to Willard's."

We arrived back in Fairbanks just in time to beat freeze-up and to greet my newborn son, William David. Jess Bachner, our mechanic friend, had picked up Dot and "Billy" at the hospital and had driven them to our home.

* * * * * *

Bears have been known to whisk in and out of wilderness camps like phantoms.

In 1961, a four-man hunting party at Montague Island was fast asleep when one of the island's huge bears stole silently in and out of their cabin. On the trip were Ward Gay of Sea Airmotive, Anchorage bank president Dan Cuddy and oil company executives Bill Bishop and Ross Craig.

Assistant Secretary of the Air Force James Douglas (left), Charlie Hubbs (pilot), Gen. Jimmy Doolittle and his aide, on the DEW line. 1955.

I dropped the party off at our San Juan camp, and then I flew over to Stump Lake to hunt with Tom Culhane. When I picked them up three days later, they told me about their phantom bear.

The day they arrived, they killed a deer on a hill near camp just before dark. They dressed it out and dragged it back to camp, hanging the carcass on the deer pole. That evening at bedtime, Ward washed off the heart and liver, which he planned as a breakfast treat, and left them on a plate on the table.

They slept with the door open and the next morning the deer's heart and liver were gone — snatched up by the bear. Wet bear tracks made a messy trail from the door to the table.

Without anyone hearing a thing, the bear had silently slipped in and made off with the hunters' breakfast delicacies.

* * * * * *

I often think back to the bear stories and other stories associated with one of the finest and most interesting characters I've ever known — Charlie Hubbs. He came to Alaska from Wyoming and became an instructor at our flying school.

Charlie, a very young fellow at the time, told me he learned to fly in a place where the wind blew so hard they used a logging chain for a windsock. "When that chain stuck straight out, it was too windy to fly," Charlie said.

After bumming his way to Alaska from the states, Charlie began teaching our students and also flew a lot of charters for us. He became an expert float plane pilot — probably as good as any airplane pilot in Alaska — and he excelled at getting airplanes off the water under the most difficult conditions.

"If she'll float, she'll fly" was one of his mottos.

That was pretty much true. Charlie seemed to be able to get planes off the water heavier — much heavier — than the average pilot. In the many years he stayed with the company, he went on to get his Airline Transport Rating, then progressed to flying a DC-3 for Interior Airways on the DEW line. He was one of our best-liked employees and was popular as well with the people of Fairbanks.

As the DC-3 captain on one VIP DEW line trip, Charlie's passengers included James H. Douglas Jr., under secretary of the Air Force, and Gen. Jimmy Doolittle along with other dignitaries. I was Charlie's co-pilot on that particular flight. This really tickled him because, though I had thousands of flying hours more than he did, I didn't have an Airline Transport Rating at the time and was therefore barred from being a captain.

Charlie continued to fly for us until his hearing deteriorated and he couldn't pass his flight physical, so he was grounded. He remained in Fairbanks and found his niche in the right-of-way section of the State Department of Highways, becoming a valued employee until his retirement. Charlie passed away in December 1990 at his home in Columbus, New Mexico

* * * * * *

But getting back to bears. One day, Charlie flew my brother Mort, a retired military officer, out into the bush on a moose- hunting trip. They were staying overnight in a wilderness log cabin. It was a warm night and to get ventilation, they propped open the cabin door part way with a water bucket.

Both Charlie and Mort were in their bunks when, early in the morning, a loud racket awoke Charlie. He saw that the door had been pushed open and the water bucket had been turned over. Worse, a huge bear was standing upright in the doorway. Charlie jumped out of his sleeping bag, grabbed his rifle and ran to the door as the bear retreated into the woods.

All the commotion woke Mort, who asked, "Why didn't you shoot?"

"Well, Mort," Charlie explained, "My eyeballs wuz open but nothin' behind 'em wuz workin'!"

Pilot Charlie Hubbs with his prize polar bear.

While Charlie was based at Barter Island, he was always eager to go polar bear hunting. So on one of my trips there, I told him, "Come on, Charlie, we're going polar bear hunting."

I was flying a Barter-based Super Cub on skis, and as we skimmed out over the ice, we spotted several bears. Flying on, we spotted a huge set of bear tracks, which we followed until we came upon a big male.

"That's the bear for you, Charlie," I shouted.

"You bet," he said as I located a smooth spot and landed.

"Now, Charlie," I said, "You go after the bear and I'll fly top cover for you."

"Like hell you will!" he protested. "I'm not getting out on the ocean all by myself with that monster. You've got to hunt with me."

"Okay," I said casually, going through the motions of unfastening my seat belt.

When Charlie grabbed his rifle and jumped out, I hit the throttle and before he could get back to the plane the Super Cub was soaring into the air.

Leaning over and looking down, I could see Charlie standing forlornly on the ice and probably cussing a blue streak. I'm sure that at that moment he could've happily shot me for having deserted him. But he very promptly had other things to think about. I had no sooner cleared the ice when the huge polar bear made his way to the top of a pressure ridge less than 200 yards from Charlie.

The bear stood outlined against the arctic sky just looking at Charlie, and I'm sure the last thing Charlie wanted was for that ferocious creature to get any closer to him.

I saw him get down on one knee and aim at the animal. Charlie got off a beautiful shot, striking the bear in the neck and killing it instantly.

I circled around and landed close to where Charlie was standing near the trophy. He was as white as the bear and so excited he couldn't talk for about five minutes.

We skinned the bear and flew the hide back to Barter Island. There, Eskimo women fleshed it out, cutting all the fat off. It was interesting to see how they put the bear on the snow with the skin side down and stomped on it to clean it of blood, then took it to patch after patch of clean snow until the hide was bright and clean. Charlie sent it off to be made into a beautiful rug that became one of his prized possessions. He called the rug "Beady Eyes," and for the rest of his life, wherever Charlie went, Beady Eyes had to go.

Another time while flying an Aeronca Sedan from Barter Island to Point Barrow, Charlie found himself in what he considered to be a tight spot. I had just made the trip in the opposite direction and was listening in on Charlie's transmissions. On my flight from Point Barrow to Barter Island, the weather was fine except for one section of the route experiencing low clouds and light snow — not good but plenty safe to fly through.

After flying about a hundred miles west from Barter Island, Charlie hit the bad weather area. He radioed back to Barter, "The weather's getting bad, gas is siphoning out of my tanks and the blankety-blank Russians are jamming my ADF!"

I picked up the mike in the Barter radio room (Charlie thought I was in Fairbanks) and told him, "Keep going, Charlie. The weather's fine."

He never forgot that. Later, he wrote in his memoirs: "That G.D. Magoffin could read my mind from 400 miles away!"

* * * * * *

Bears, always pesky and sometimes ferocious and dangerous, roamed at will on the tundra. Their unexpected appearance at camp often stimulated the adrenaline of stateside geologists. A rampaging grizzly was an annoying regular visitor to the garbage pit at Richfield Oil's camp. The wild animal insisted on rummaging around in the camp's trash, setting up a frightful racket as it dug out cans and bottles in its scavenging search for tidbits. This unsettling marauding went on night after night until drastic measures had to be taken.

One of the crew members placed a lighted candle on top of a sealed five-gallon can of gasoline located at one corner of the garbage pit. Then the worker waited for the pest to show up. As expected, the big grizzly made its nightly appearance and headed for the garbage. As the bear was passing the candle-lit can, the man shot into the can with his rifle.

The startled bear was engulfed in a huge ball of fire and took off at unaccustomed speed. Though plenty scared, the flaming experience apparently did no serious harm to the bear, which was spotted several times afterward showing just a bit of scorching. However, the bear never again approached the Richfield Oil camp. ✝

CHAPTER 16

Charters: Good, Bad And Awful

Charters into remote country gradually became the backbone of our business. Some charters, such as those into hunting and fishing country, were enjoyable; others were awful and, a time or two, hair-raising.

In the Army Air Corps I was used to parking the airplane and having a gas truck roll up and gas it. Somebody else would check the oil and other things. Having flown airplanes equipped with the finest instrumentation and electronics spoiled me rotten for the planes I had to fly when we were getting started: no radio, no battery, no electrical system and absolutely nobody but me to service the plane. Getting the plane fueled was a job in itself; I had to pump gas out of 55-gallon drums or pour it out of five-gallon cans.

I had been used to going where I wanted to go almost regardless of the weather. I had to adjust to flying without instruments, without radio, without de-icing capability and the sophisticated navigational capability I earlier took for granted.

Flying strictly VFR was frustrating for me. It was especially tough on those days when I couldn't get where I wanted to go. And there were the times when I flew but probably shouldn't have.

Much of our early flying business came to us from other carriers and from customers dissatisfied by the service being provided them.

For example, we picked up some of Wien's customers who claimed they weren't getting good service. No airline can please everybody, but in Wien's extensive operation there was an unusual number of irritated, angry customers who were glad to switch to outfits like ours.

A good example was Wien's service to Bill Allen's trading post at Alatna on the west side of the Koyukuk River. Allen complained that Wien had carelessly let his perishables freeze. Jim Crouder, operator of the Bettles Trading Post below the confluence of the Koyukuk and John rivers, also was unhappy with Wien. Crouder's gripe was that Wien kept losing his freight and was failing to get his cargo to him in a timely fashion.

I got to know the Bettles and Alatna people well. They chartered me to fly more than 1,000 pounds of merchandise a week to their trading posts.

I had disconcerting trouble on one freight run for Allen in the blistering cold of mid-January. To keep a load of groceries — including potatoes and onions — from freezing, I had to store them in my house overnight. The following morning, I loaded the groceries on a toboggan and bundled an eiderdown robe over them, then pulled

FAIRBANKS DAILY NEWS-MINER   SEPTEMBER 23, 1954

(News-Miner photo by Jim Douthit)

REPUBLICANS TRAVEL—About to board Interior Airways planes for a campaign tour around the Fourth division are Republican candidates for the territorial house of representatives. Shown from left to right are: Charles Hubbs, pilot; Aldine Fowler, stewardess; Alden L. Wilbur, George M. Sullivan, John B. Coghill, Sylvia Ringstad, Dr. James C. Ryan and Phil Gray, pilot. The candidates took-off from the International airport for their first stop at McGrath.

them down to the airport by hand, hustling to get them inside the plane as quickly as possible. Then I covered them again with the robe.

I got a shock when I landed on the river and slid to a stop in front of the trading post. Eight inches of water lay on top of the ice under about 16 inches of snow.

It was so cold I didn't dare shut the engine off and let it idle while Allen and a couple of natives rushed down with sleds, loaded their groceries, then hustled back to the trading post. I was eager to get going before the water soaked up to my skis and they froze in it, trapping me on the river.

When I tried to apply power, I found the throttle was frozen tight in the idle position. I gave a strong shove on the push-pull type throttle with my knee, and it broke loose all at once. In just a split second the engine went from idle to full power.

Since it was 48 degrees below zero, the strain on the cylinders must have been tremendous. The worst part was that when I tried to pull the throttle back, it wouldn't budge. By that time, however, I was tearing down the river and into the air. I was able to work the throttle back as soon as I got up a couple of hundred feet and proceeded into normal flight. But what a wild takeoff! I was worried that I had over-boosted the engine, but it was okay.

A Wien pilot caused a rather harrowing incident that happened at Bettles. I had landed there to visit the CAA station and check the weather. Fairbanks was fogged in, so I decided to stay overnight at Bettles. The next morning, I set the firepot under the Howard's engine cover several hours before daylight. I was working in bitter, 45 degree below-zero cold as I tended the firepot. When I saw that the firepot was functioning normally, I went inside the weather office to talk to the operators, then in a few minutes came back and crawled beneath the engine cover made of heavy, waterproof canvas doubled across the top and with a canvas skirt weighted with lead sinkers to hold it to the ground.

Just after daylight, as I was sitting there waiting for the engine to heat up, I heard a plane approaching. It landed at Bettles and taxied in close to where I was parked. Suddenly, the engine cover blew against me violently. I had to grab it and struggle hard to keep it from blowing into the firepot and starting a fire. The propeller blast continued, forcing me to shut off the firepot and scoot out from beneath the cover.

Only a short distance away was a Wien Norseman on skis parked with its tail pointing directly toward my plane with the pilot revving up the engine.

That lack of airport etiquette — impolite and dangerous — made me mad as hell, though I couldn't be sure he was doing it on purpose. If I hadn't been under the engine tent at the time, it surely would have blown into the firepot and set the plane on fire. The loss of that airplane probably would have been the end of Interior Airways, because we didn't carry hull insurance, only liability.

Generally, I got along well with one of the Wien brothers, Fritz, a real nice guy. Sometimes, when we needed an aircraft part, we'd get word to Fritz, and invariably he came up with something that would keep us going. Noel Wien was a quiet person and I never got to know him too well. In spite of recurring friction with Wien management, we knew and liked many of the Wien pilots. These included outstanding professionals like Bob Rice, Bill English, Randy Acord, Don Hulshizer, Dick King, Don Gilbertson, Fred Goodwin, Bob Murphy and Cliff Everts, to name just a few. I flew with many of them during the DEW line construction. Later, several of them came to work for our company.

In later years, there were several occasions when Wien needed an engine or a propeller or some other part we had, and we were pleased to return the favor to Fritz Wien. ✝

CHAPTER 17

The Pot Of Gold That Got Away

One of our customers dealt us a bitter, heart-breaking blow at a time when we badly needed the income we were expecting. Dick Sellers chartered us to haul personnel, equipment and supplies to his gold mining operation on Big Creek near Chandalar Lake.

At Sellers' request, I didn't submit any bills until after his placer operation cleanup in the fall. Late in August, he shut down his mine and I flew his workmen to town first. On the last trip, I flew in to

The Aeronca Sedan used on the ill-fated Dick Sellers operation.

get Sellers. I hiked up to the mine site with my packsack, and Sellers loaded me with a tightly taped pressure cooker filled with gold. It weighed 48 pounds, but as I headed back to the plane parked on the lake shore, the pack seemed to weigh a ton and the cooker poked into my back with every step.

When we got to Fairbanks that night, I drove Sellers down to the Nordale Hotel and let him out with his gear and the gold-filled pressure cooker.

"First thing in the morning," he told me, "I'll go to the bank and cash in my gold. Then I'll come out to the airport and pay the flying bill."

That sizeable bill represented a major part of my summer's work. I badly needed that income.

When Sellers didn't show up the next day, I called Frank Nigro, the desk clerk at the Nordale.

"Let me talk to Dick Sellers," I said.

"He isn't staying here at the hotel," Nigro said.

"But I let him out right in front of the hotel last night."

"He never checked in, Jim."

Sellers had skipped town with the gold, leaving me and his workers unpaid. Nor did he pay the Northern Commercial Co. for the tractors, groceries and other items they'd given him on credit.

The last I heard of Sellers, he was well out of the law's reach in Argentina with an Alaskan friend who himself had absconded a few years before with a large sum of money from the Alaska Railroad. ✝

CHAPTER 18

A Sportsman's Paradise

Like his dad, Billy Heath, son of Financial Vice President Bob Heath, loved to fish.

Some of my best Alaska memories are associated with Schrader Lake, and it was through a charter there that I discovered its matchless beauty and wealth of fish.

In mid-July of 1949, I got a request to fly two prospectors to the lake on the north slope of the Brooks Range. I first hauled a load of gasoline to cache along the route so I'd have plenty to make the trip with the prospectors and get back to Fairbanks. In Fort Yukon, I talked with Ed Toussaint, the local pilot, about going through the Brooks Range. I had never been through it that far east and he told me he hadn't either.

"I've been up to the head of the Chandalar River," he said, "and there's a pass, but I've never been on the north side."

At a lake beyond Arctic Village, I cached part of my gas, using only enough to get me back to Fairbanks. The next morning, I loaded the two prospectors and their gear and away we went.

Our arrival at Schrader Lake was on a beautiful, sunny day without a breath of wind to wrinkle the lake. The lake's waters were crystal clear. As we flew over at 1,000 feet, we could see fish everywhere. It looked like one huge aquarium just teeming with thousands of good-sized fish.

When we pulled into the beach the prospectors picked for their campsite, one of them put together a fishing rod and threw out an imitation mouse. The water boiled with activity where the lure touched water. Each cast produced a trout weighing anywhere from four to 15 pounds. Every time the lure hit water, a big trout would grab it and a bunch of other trout would churn around the lure, trying to take it away from the "winner."

And it wasn't only the fishing that was fabulous. As I flew around the area I could see incomparable wilderness vistas populated with caribou, mountain sheep and grizzlies. In November 1953, we built a camp on Schrader Lake that still stands.

Fred Benninger — former Flying Tigers chief executive who sold us three large airplanes and who is now chairman of the MGM Grand Hotel in Las Vegas — joined us for a few days of hunting and fishing.

Schrader Lake proved to be a dream site for our operation. It became a headquarters for our recreational flights catering to hunters and fishermen, and it was also used by geology parties working for several different oil companies and for U. S. Geological Survey teams.

By the time I returned to Fairbanks from dropping the prospectors off at Schrader Lake, I had been flying for two days without sleep and I was thoroughly bushed.

After tying the plane down on the Chena River, I headed for our airport office, reaching there about 11:30 p.m. Waiting there for me were Dick Collins, the CAA manager at Minchumina, and his family.

"We need to get to Minchumina tonight," he said.

I couldn't have been less enthusiastic about flying him anywhere, the way I felt. "Geez, Dick," I said wearily, "I'm just pooped. I haven't been to bed for two days and I don't know if I'll be able to stay awake."

Collins didn't give up. "I'll keep you awake," he assured me.

Worn down, I finally — and reluctantly — agreed to make the trip, something I certainly shouldn't have done. All the way to Minchumina, Dick kept chattering like a magpie and, as he promised, it kept me awake. Going back alone was the problem.

On that unforgettable return trip, I was headed toward Fairbanks when fatigue took over while I was cruising along at 5,500 feet.

The noise that woke me up was the plane nicking the tree tops. That horrible racket alerted me to the danger just in time to allow me to pull up and avoid what could have been disaster. That grim episode taught me a lesson about flying without at least minimal sleep. ✝

CHAPTER 19

Charters With Headaches

Many an Alaska pilot has learned to his sorrow that there are times when one shouldn't put too much faith and confidence in what the customers say about the suitability of landing areas and, like so many other things, I had to learn the hard way.

My caution stems from back in the summer of 1948 when I got involved in supplying the Philpott family prospecting camp near the mouth of the Firth River close to the Arctic Ocean on the Canadian side of the border.

When I questioned the Philpotts about landing conditions, I was assured: "We've got a runway marked out with white flags. You'll see it when you get over our camp."

I had no reason to question that and set out in the Super Cruiser on wheels, landing on a sandbar at Old Crow to gas up at what I considered the outrageous price of $1.50 a gallon. In Fairbanks, we were paying 30 cents a gallon for gas — up from 28 cents in 1947.

From Old Crow, I flew up to the Firth River and had no trouble spotting the Philpotts' camp, but got a shock when I saw their proposed "runway." This was nothing more than a bunch of white rags tied to the tops of the niggerheads (the common Alaskan term in those times for grass humps), and though the rags roughly outlined what the Philpotts thought was a good landing area, it most certainly wasn't. If I'd have tried to go in there, I would have smashed up the airplane or worse.

I cruised around the area until I located a barren hill about a mile from the camp that seemed smooth enough to land on and got in there okay.

Members of the Philpott clan walked over to the plane, but were obviously not too happy about having to pack their freight back to camp for such a long distance.

I helped them pack their stuff to camp not regretting one bit my prudent decision. One compensation was the fishing I did in the nearby Firth River. I brought in several arctic char weighing from two to four pounds and was able to bring home a mess of these beautiful firm, silver-sided, green-backed fish, which proved to be wonderful eating.

* * * * * *

Right in the midst of the waterfowl hunting season, on Sept. 23, I had to interrupt flying hunters back and forth to our Minto camp to fulfill a promise I'd made earlier to Jimmy Carroll, who ran a store at Fort Yukon.

Carroll had asked me to fly two of his sons to their trapping camp at the head of

Black River. They told me there was a lake suitable for landing just a couple of hundred yards from their main cabin.

I promised Carroll I'd pick the boys up and take them to their camp. Fairbanks was still enjoying mild weather when I left, but when I reached Fort Yukon, a strong, bitterly cold north wind was blowing, and I was concerned about getting the job done before freezeup.

I shuttled supplies up to the boys' camp, but night closed in and there were still many more loads to go. I tied up to the beach at Fort Yukon and the next morning the temperature was below freezing. The plane was frosted over and ice formed where waves were lapping at the floats.

I got the frost roped off the wings, loaded the airplane and managed to take off, but the water rudders froze up on takeoff. I had to kick the rudder pedals hard to break them loose.

Getting the two boys, their dogs, groceries, traps and other stuff from Fort Yukon to the Black River camp required nine miserable trips. It was one of the most risky operations I've ever been involved in. Water would slosh up on the floats and freeze, icing them to a slipperiness that made it almost impossible to stand on them, much less get a foothold to load cargo or heave up gas cans to fill the tank.

Flying under these conditions was miserable, too, and far from safe. Takeoffs were an ordeal. Water would splash up onto the tail surfaces and freeze, disrupting the air flow.

I was sure glad when that operation was over. After that, I vowed never to promise anyone to do any float flying above the Arctic Circle after the first part of September. ✝

CHAPTER 20

A Tribute To Roy

Roy Isackson, longtime company vice president. Roy loved to fish and hunt.

Seemingly insignificant events often take on tremendous importance. This is true of the day back in 1951 when Roy Isackson, who worked for the Alaska Railroad's freight department in Fairbanks, visited our office.

Exactly my age, Roy felt a job change was in order and he wanted to discuss it. What he told us captured our interest and he was hired.

Originally from Minnesota, Isackson had been a logger in Oregon before heading north. A real outdoorsman, the striking thing about Roy was his remarkable versatility, something he demonstrated every day he worked for us.

He was a jack-of-all trades. He could load an airplane by himself efficiently, speedily and correctly, whether he was loading barrels of fuel, construction steel or heavy pipe. He had the ability to repair just about anything — fishing tackle, guns, you name it. On top of all that, he was a whiz in the office, handling our payroll and flight records for years.

Roy was well-liked by all of our personnel and by all Fairbanksans who knew him. He was especially helpful to our younger employees who frequently came to him with their problems. Roy always took time to assist them.

A man possessing a wide range of skills and abilities, Roy worked his way up to become senior vice president and general manager of our firm.

Sadly, Roy smoked and developed lung cancer, requiring the removal of one lung. He didn't make it. His death in 1975 was a blow to us and all of Fairbanks.

Among my prized possessions is a tribute to him that appeared in the August 1975 issue of our quarterly *Journal*. It was illustrated with a color picture showing Roy out there fishing and displaying a nice string of fish. Every time I look at that smiling photo of Roy, it brings him back.

The tribute that appeared in the *Journal* sums up what he meant to us so well that it's worth repeating here:

ROY ISACKSON — A TRIBUTE

Roy L. Isackson was a man who loved the outdoors. He grew up near Bemidji, Minn., in the hunting and fishing part of the country. In his younger years, he hunted and trapped, living the life of an outdoorsman.

After coming to Alaska in the '40s, he worked for the Alaska Railroad until meeting a fellow named Jim Magoffin. Magoffin was head of a company called Interior Airways. Interior ran eight small airplanes throughout interior Alaska.

Magoffin, out of a growing friendship for Isackson, offered him a job as general manager of the 12 employees who worked for the airline at the time.

In 1953, a lasting relationship started between Isackson and Magoffin and Interior Airways, which grew into Alaska International Industries with his help.

Roy L. Isackson died this spring of cancer. He was 60.

Magoffin in describing him says: 'The most wonderful thing about Roy was his personality. Isackson brought humanity and fair-mindedness to his job; his personality was perfect.'

The outdoor life never left Roy. He often organized and established fishing camps around Alaska, as well as "instigating" out-of-state pheasant-hunting trips to South Dakota.

But besides being a nice guy and a good manager, Isackson

showed streaks of genius during his tenure with Interior and later AIA. Under his guidance, the first camp and airstrip on the North Slope was established in 1963.

The camp, named Sagwon, was used by the original British Petroleum and Richfield exploration teams. This single stroke gave Interior Airways a strong foothold in arctic oil exploration and later supplying the camps that sprang up like tundra flowers after the oil rush of the late '60s and early '70s.

Now, seven giant Hercules cargo planes fly around-the-clock shuttles between Fairbanks and the North Slope, supplying the camps on the pipeline route and the base camps at Prudhoe Bay with life-giving supplies.

Though he never learned to fly, Roy was usually one of the first to head for the plane at the beginning of one of his well-known fishing or hunting expeditions.

"Roy repaired everything from airplanes to fishing rods, whatever was needed," Magoffin recalled.

In his last few years, Isackson bought a condominium in Hawaii, where he and his wife spent the coldest parts of the Alaskan winters.

Roy died away from the Alaskan wilderness he thrived on, but his heart was probably out fishing for one of those jumbo trout that inhabit the crystal-clear streams of the Brooks Range where he and Frances spent so many happy days with the Magoffins, Jim and Dot. ☨

CHAPTER 21

Kongakut Wildlife Drama

My flights to Alaska's out-of-the-way places often treat me to unforgettable glimpses of wildlife, but nothing to match what I saw when I flew to the wild and lonely Kongakut River in the spring of 1952, when I witnessed the aftermath of a savage life-and-death wilderness drama. The bloody and spectacular struggle itself, I could capture only in my imagination.

I was chartered by Warren Taylor, a prominent Fairbanks attorney, to fly him and two other men out to that isolated, wild river.

Taylor, along with Dick Merideth, an engineer, and Earl Hurst, an experienced prospector, had me fly them to the headwaters of the Kongakut, a river that flows northward into the Arctic Ocean through the eastern section of the Brooks Range.

For the month-long trip, starting March 15, they had amassed a whole lot of supplies, including mining gear, a gas stove, a wood stove, gasoline, a windlass, picks and shovels, ropes and ample food. All this required two trips and on the first, which I made alone, I loaded on as much of their stuff as I figured I could get off with as well as some five-gallon tins of aviation gasoline.

After reaching the Kongakut and skimming downriver fairly low, I spotted three wolves clustered on the ice just ahead of the plane.

A closer look showed the wolves had a mountain sheep down and were apparently starting to eat it. Flying on downriver less than a half mile, I located a smooth spot and landed. After putting the engine cover on the plane, I grabbed my rifle and headed back up the river just about sure I was going to get a wolf or two. Each wolf would be worth $100 — $50 bounty and $50 for the pelt.

It was not to be. The wind was blowing upriver, so the wolves could smell me coming, and by the time I got to where the dead sheep was, they were gone.

However, studying the tracks in the snow and other indications, I was able to reconstruct, with fair certainty, what had been an exciting and savage wilderness drama.

I discerned that the wolves had not killed the sheep at all. It was clear the sheep had come down the side of the mountain at a time when a wolverine had been positioned above it.

Tracks in the snow proved that the wolverine had bounded swiftly down the mountain after the sheep in a series of huge leaps, then chased the ram out onto the bare river ice. The sheep, with its hoofed feet, was no match in that arena for the deadly wolverine with its ice-clutching claws. Promptly, after a frantic struggle, the wolverine killed the sheep and was about to dine on it when the wolves reached the scene. They, in turn, were preparing to devour the animal when my arrival scared them off. This was the kind of savage contest that takes place all the time in the Alaska wilds, where the rule of survival of the fittest is demonstrated countless times.

I didn't get the wolverine or the wolves, but I did carve out the hind quarters of the sheep. This proved to be good eating, although spring sheep is nowhere as tasty as sheep brought down in the fall.

* * * * * *

On a somewhat similar occasion, I was flying the Taylorcraft on floats through Anaktuvuk Pass early in the morning headed for Umiat on the North Slope when, just ahead of me, I spotted a band of sheep fleeing across the valley from one mountain to another. Trailing them in hot pursuit was a good-sized wolf. As the sheep moved up the opposite side of the valley, I saw the wolf grab one of the stragglers, and in moments the sheep was dead. I was able to swing around, aim my shotgun at the wolf and kill it. When I told Anaktuvuk Pass villagers about it shortly afterward, they organized a little party to go up and salvage the wolf and the sheep. I flew on to Umiat, but the Eskimos told me later that they easily found both the sheep and the wolf and were happy to get them.

* * * * * *

Another time I was returning to Fairbanks from the west just before dark, flying a Cessna 180. As I passed over the Minto flats, I spotted a cow moose in a clearing, surrounded by wolves — a sight not too unusual. But this was different because there was a trail of blood through the deep snow for several hundred feet and part of the cow's entrails were dragging behind her. How she could still stand up was a mystery, as she was severely wounded and had lost a lot of blood.

I counted 17 wolves and more could have been hidden by spruce trees. On the edge of the clearing I saw the remains of the cow's two calves, now just some hair and bloody snow.

The next morning I returned with a Super Cub and a gunner, but the wolves were gone and the cow, like her calves, was reduced to a dark, bloody splotch in the snow.

* * * * * *

On the Kongakut River trip, I cached the men's belongings in a fairly good stand of aspen, an ideal camp site in an area where there's seldom any timber to be found. Two days later, I flew the prospectors up in the Howard on skis. I suggested to them that if they had time before I came back, they might snowshoe out a runway. I pointed out that although the snow was only about two feet deep, it was soft and packing it down a bit would be helpful to me in getting off with a loaded aircraft.

When I returned for them on April 15, I was amazed to see a runway not much smaller than the Fairbanks airport. At first, the men had tried to prospect, sinking several holes about 15 feet down. Here, however, they encountered a strata of swiftly running water that kept them from reaching bedrock. So they threw in the towel on prospecting and, besides having a carefree outing, they spent much of their ample free time on snowshoes tramping down a runway. They were quick to notice that we didn't utilize more than about a quarter of their "airport" for takeoff.

Although the prospecting part of their trip was a washout, the trip was very significant for me because I got to know Dick Merideth. The following spring, he introduced me to Mike Hamilton and George Wizer of Puget Sound & Drake, a prominent Seattle construction firm. They, in turn, hired me to do some flying for them out of Barter Island on the Arctic Coast, using the Howard which Dick Merideth had informed them was a "Damn Good Airplane."

Even more significant was the fact that this introduction got us lined up for several years of intensive flying during the construction of the Distant Early Warning Line — the DEW line. ✝

CHAPTER 22

A Shield For America

Construction in the arctic of America's Distant Early Warning system — the DEW line — in the mid-1950s held greater significance for Dot and me than any balance sheet could reflect.

It gave us both great satisfaction to be pitching in to help build a 3,000-mile protective radar fence across the trackless top of the continent. It was a time when the Cold War was raging, a time when the Soviet Union was in the relentless grip of a brutal Stalinist dictatorship, alien to everything we stood for. Military and political experts believed there was a real possibility that Soviet bombers might surge over the North Pole to attack the United States and Canada without warning in an attempt to conquer America by force. The Communists knew very well that freedom could never be vanquished in any other way.

Now that the Cold War is over and the communist ideology has crumbled almost everywhere in the world, some raise the question of whether the DEW line was really necessary. We are convinced it *was* necessary. We believe that without this strong deterrence of the DEW line and America's powerful retaliatory capability, the Soviets might have plunged the world into a devastating war.

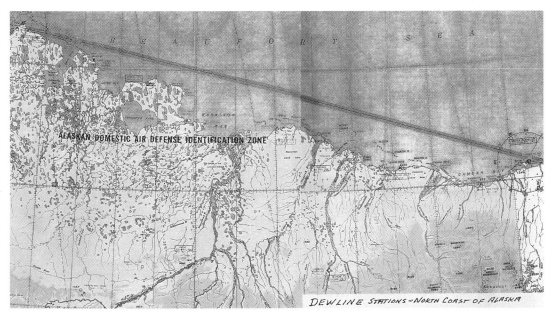

DEW line stations — north coast of Alaska.

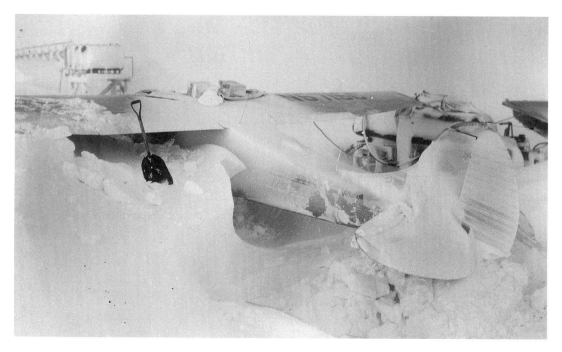

1953: Winter operation at Barter Island. Our planes would have snow packed inside the wings, fuselage and tail. Hours of work and heating were needed to make them safe to fly. Arctic Coast winds can last several days.

In those early years of uncertainty, it made a lot of sense to join with our Canadian neighbors in a program that offered preparedness in the event of an attack. In a few short years, a string of electronic sentinels were scanning the arctic skies to give the nation at least a three-hour warning that Soviet bombers were on the way. Getting that shield constructed during one of the most militarily dangerous periods in American history turned out to be the most ambitious, sophisticated and costly construction undertaking ever attempted by the military. And apart from any economic gain, we were proud and enthusiastic that we could contribute in some small measure to the alertness and readiness of a free nation.

What was in store for our personnel can only be described as a gruelling struggle. Pilots had to become accustomed to almost impossible demands on human endurance and stamina. They were faced with endless, exhausting hours in the cockpit. They had to challenge incredibly bitter weather and blistering cold. They had to put up with often-deplorable living conditions. They had to deal with isolation and being away from their families for long periods of time.

Their story is one of toughness, courage, determination and inner strength. And it was good to be there with them through the worst of it.

Our little outfit became part of one of the greatest construction-oriented arma-
das in history, an incredible accumulation of air support ranging all the way from
Piper Cubs to giant Globemasters. Before the DEW line was completed, several hundred civilian and military aircraft of virtually all types were participating. These included York bombers, 35 C-46s, 19 DC-4s, 18 C-124s, six C-119s, 10 DC-3s, three
PBYs, Bristol Freighters, a B-17, dozens of small single- and twin-engine aircraft and
some helicopters.

Mobilizing this massive airlift under the most rugged of conditions was a triumph of orchestration on the part of the U.S. Air Force and the Royal Canadian Air
Force.

The DEW line job gave strength and hope to our fledgling company and in many
respects it was tailor-made for the kind of operation we had assembled. And best of
all, contract carriage operation for the Air Force came well within the very tight limits
of our operating authority. Being thrust into a vast new flying terrain — the Arctic
Coast — put us hundreds of miles away from civilization and effectively insulated and
isolated us from the sometimes stifling interference of the CAA. It was refreshing for
us to operate within this military-protected cocoon. I can't recall a single time that we
saw anybody from the CAA at either Barter Island or Point Barrow. We didn't miss
them at all. ✛

CHAPTER 23

Forty-One Days
Without A Bath

My first confrontation with the raw arctic was a dismal stretch of 41 days straight with virtually none of the comforts of home. Having to live and work without the luxury of a bathtub or shower was a real nightmare in a world of hellish white, but I tried to adjust to it; just about everything was riding on our DEW line contract.

After landing on the ocean ice at Barter Island, I cut deep holes in the ice with an ax, making "dead-man" tie-downs to secure the airplane in a wind that was howling and blowing strong.

Trying to sleep in our dreary quonset living quarters was difficult. The wind moaned and buffeted the little building all night. When we got up in the morning, the water bucket was frozen solid and the ceaseless winds had created miniature snow drifts all across the floor, having blown the snow through a half-inch crack under the door. It was the first time I'd ever seen indoor snowdrifts, but that was typical Barter Island weather. On several occasions the strong wind drove the blowing snow through every tiny opening in our unhangared planes — filling wings, fuselage and tail surfaces with hard-packed snow. The only way to remove it was to cover the planes with huge sheets of canvas and melt the snow. This was a cold, time-consuming job, but had to be accomplished to make them safe to fly.

When we arrived at Barter Island, I was surprised to see a Wien Norseman parked on the ice. Mike Hamilton said it hadn't been doing much flying, and they were behind in their work. I was informed it was against Wien's company policy to fly single-engine aircraft on instruments. In the winter in that country, if you don't fly on instruments, you don't fly very often.

The next morning we climbed back in the Howard and flew to Herschel Island, Canada, and got permission from the Royal Canadian Mounted Police who were stationed there to make an unlimited number of cross-border flights without clearing customs.

On that first stretch at Barter Island, I flew almost every day in horrible weather. We were using military aerial photos to pick out, from the air, sites for the original DEW line stations. Flying over that desolate landscape, it was just plain hell trying to distinguish the ocean from the land.

Walt McAdam, a Western Electric engineer, rode up front with me, and the only clue we had that we were flying over the land would be occasional spots of black where a little tundra would show up.

We got the job done, but most of the flying was accomplished sitting on the edge of our seats.

For me, flying in this land of howling winds and numbing cold wasn't easy to get used to. There were no prepared strips and snowdrifts were frozen hard. Fortunately, the Howard had a good, strong, spongy gear but even so, it took a pounding. When the ground blow was strong, I could make full stall landings and only slide a few feet to a stop.

The ground facilities took some getting used to. Mike Hamilton and his crew quickly converted a Barter Island quonset hut into a mess hall that served good, wholesome food. To start with, we had no shower. All we could do was melt buckets of snow on top of our oil stove and use the warm water to sponge ourselves off.

It was essential to dress warmly to be able to work in the punishing cold. I wore two sets of heavy, long-handled underwear and the heaviest Woolrich pants and shirts I could buy. My feet were protected by layers of socks inside my knee-high Eskimo mukluks made of caribou hide with the fur side in. A heavy parka topped off my arctic gear.

By the time I got the plane gassed and oiled, the battery installed and the wing and engine covers removed, I'd be so hot that the warm moisture from my body and breath would fog up the inside of the windshield. I solved this by swabbing the inside of the windshield with alcohol before takeoff. Hot air from the plane's heater kept the windshield clear for the rest of the flight.

In the morning, I'd have to climb up on the aircraft and pour the hot oil into the tank on top behind the engine. And I'd have to carry the plane's 62-pound battery inside at night to keep it from freezing. Simple tasks like this were essential to keeping the airplane operating and required a lot of exertion.

Within a few days, an Air Force C-47 brought in a Herman Nelson heater for me to use. Gas was hauled in by the Air Force, so eventually we had a fairly good operating setup.

Arctic takeoffs and landings required a bit of preparation. If there was blowing snow keeping me from seeing more than a few yards ahead of the plane, I'd stick out a line of lath with black flagging stapled to it to mark off the smoothest takeoff path.

Snowdrifts were hazardous because they froze rock-hard. Hitting too many of them on landing or takeoff could raise hell with the landing gear. Yet I never had any real trouble, thanks to the super-strong landing gear struts ol' Hutch constructed for me.

Within a few days, Wien's Norseman was dismissed, leaving Interior Airways solidly involved in a flying contract that was to last several years. This was a high-priority job. The Air Force was eager to get the DEW line test section constructed and tested within a single season.

Another problem with our Arctic Coast operation was that we had to filter aircraft gasoline through chamois-covered funnels locked into the filler caps on top of the wings. Frequently, the icy wind was so strong it would blow much of the gas out of the funnel before it had time to filter through. Roy Isackson, our Fairbanks manager, solved that problem by covering the tops of the funnels with heavy canvas, leaving a hole in the middle just large enough for a gas nozzle to hook into. Our star mechanic, Hutch, brazed hooked extensions onto the gas nozzles so that it was not necessary for anyone to hold the nozzles in place while the planes were being fueled.

Keeping the Howard going under arctic conditions was an eye-opener for me. First, I had to heat the airplane with a firepot I'd bought from Sears Roebuck. It was really a small stove with a 14-inch circular burner that used white gas and put out lots of heat.

At night, I'd have to drain the oil, pack it into the quonset hut and set it on the stove. Hutch made the can for me out of black iron. It weighed 18 pounds empty, so when it was filled with the eight gallons of oil my engine held, it was about all I could do to lift it.

Everything was under close and strict Air Force surveillance. It was only a few days after I got to Barter that an Air Force plane touched down bringing an impressive bunch of high-powered brass. Included was Vern Bagnall, Western Electric's project manager. Bagnall, a vice president, was a sharp electrical engineer, undoubtedly a genius. He conceived the idea for and helped develop the Automatic Direction Finder (ADF), so essential to navigation. He also came up with the idea for interlocking radars that could detect enemy aircraft that might approach from the north and northwest, the primary mission of the DEW line.

In his late '40s, Bagnall was a nice guy but nervous as a cat, with a thousand things constantly on his mind. His chain-smoking had stained his fingers brown. He was dedicated to making sure the DEW line was constructed on time and that it functioned with optimum efficiency.

We became good friends. The day we met, he stressed how important the DEW line was to the nation's defense. He wanted to know what could be done to ensure dependable air service to the project.

"What we need most," I told him, "is a homing beacon at each construction site." With visibility bad, we often found it hard to pinpoint our destinations in the arctic's unrelieved expanse of white.

Bagnall wasted no time in getting problems solved. Within a few days the beacons, a godsend, were installed and operating at all the sites.

Bagnall was a good flying companion. On one occasion, I flew him over the Canadian sector during the early construction phase. We landed at Nicholson Point, where the job was barely getting started. The camp consisted of a couple of sleeping wanigans, a mess hall, a small office building and a tractor.

The meat served us at lunch was real tough. While we were eating, the construction foreman remarked that while digging up some gravel that morning they had run across a frozen, prehistoric mastodon. Bagnall, struggling to chew the tough meat, remarked glumly without looking up, "Yeah, and we know exactly what you did with it!"

On another occasion, the Air Force sent in a C-54 (a DC-4) to pick up a party of inspecting Air Force officers and officials of Western Electric and Puget Sound & Drake. We were operating a Piper Pacer on floats at Barter Island at the time, and I was preparing to fly it to Fairbanks for its annual inspection.

As the others were climbing aboard the C-54, Bagnall kept holding back until one of the officials asked him if he wasn't going along.

"No," he said, "I think I'll ride to Fairbanks with Jim."

So we took off in our little Pacer on floats and landed at Schrader Lake, a beautiful big mountain lake with sparkling clear water and loaded with lake trout. I had a fishing rod and a few lures, so Bagnall was able to stand on shore and fish, catching a beautiful trout at every cast. Even though clouds of mosquitoes were swarming around him, he ignored them and I've never seen a happier man. He kept yanking out big trout after big trout, turning each of them back except for a couple we brought to Fairbanks. Dot cooked us a delicious trout supper that evening.

Bagnall's hectic life style made it obvious to me that he was a prime candidate for a heart attack. Nervous, grossly overworked, badly addicted to smoking, he was courting tragedy. And it happened. The poor man dropped dead of a massive heart attack on a New York street at a relatively young age. ✝

CHAPTER 24

Beehive At Barter Island

In the summer of 1953, there was just no end to the cargo that had to be hauled from Barter to the DEW line sites. As fast as we cleaned out one load, Air Force C-124s shuttled in another. In August, the Sealift brought in a mountain of construction materials, electronics components and other cargo, all of which had to be moved — and quickly. The tempo of moving this material hardly ever eased, and we were flying day and night, amassing a tremendous amount of flying time.

The arrival of the Sealift gave me an unexpected thrill and a scare. I was on an instrument approach (ADF) when the landing craft nosed into the beach at Barter Island, something I hadn't been told about when I radioed Barter for traffic information and an altimeter setting.

I was groping along through thick fog after descending to about 50 feet with the gear and flaps down when suddenly a welter of masts and antennas materialized just scant yards in front of me. Fortunately, I missed them, but being surprised by all these obstacles was more than startling, and they were far too close for comfort.

Getting qualified pilots and suitable aircraft throughout the crash construction phase of the DEW line was always a problem. This was especially true at Barter Island, a desolate, windswept place just off Alaska's northeast coast, but vital nevertheless as part of the DEW line.

Mike Hamilton, the project manager for the construction contractor, Puget Sound & Drake, kept asking for more planes almost every week and I would oblige. The big problem was the absence of airstrips, so we had to land on sandbars and ocean beaches. We fitted airplanes with large tires to give them enough flotation so they wouldn't sink in the soft beach sand. Oversized tires were installed on our Cessnas, tandem wheels on a Piper Pacer and large tires on our Cubs. In this way, for the most part, we mastered the problem of landing on soft sand, but even so, we had our share of noseups and bent props but, thankfully, no passenger injuries or fatalities.

We had to scrounge for planes the best we could to provide aircraft to haul huge tonnages of freight. We had a standing order with Bill Blake of Washington Aircraft in Seattle to supply us with suitable planes, and he was able to come up with several Cessna 180s and one Cessna 170.

We bought a Travelair 6000 from Harry Swanton of Fairbanks and a Stinson SRJR from Gren Collins, who had used the plane for several years in the Bristol Bay fishing industry. Both those planes came equipped with big tires, just what we needed for getting into and out of the Arctic Coast's soft beaches. Cy Hetherington, our maintenance superintendent at the time, named the old Stinson "The Spirit of Barter Island" and painted the name on both sides of the plane. Thereafter, our pilots fondly referred to the Stinson as "The Spirit." After we obtained more modern bush planes, we donated "The Spirit" and a Norseman to the Pioneer Air Museum in Fairbanks.

In the spring of 1952, we got a good break when we acquired a Grumman Widgeon from Chuck Evans, one of the owners of Golden North Airways of Seattle. Getting checked out in the plane by Lana Kurtzer at Seattle's Lake Union provided me with many good pointers concerning its operation, and he signed my log book to signify my proficiency as an amphibian pilot. While at Boeing Field in Seattle, I got to fly a Grumman Goose owned by Nick Bez, a well-known Seattle tycoon. It was a fine plane and a real pleasure to fly.

The Widgeon always served us well and was usually flown by either Curly Martin, Phil Gray or me.

By late fall, the test section of the DEW line was completed and proved successful. Immediately, the push began to complete the line, and we were proud to be right in the thick of the accelerated activity. Most of the workmen at Barter Island belonged to unions, and contractors lost no time in rushing them out of there as soon as they completed a job. This called for frequent flights to Fairbanks.

I soon found myself making dozens of flights in the Howard between Barter Island and Fairbanks, usually carrying four workmen, their tools and personal baggage. Although I never had any serious problem, I was concerned because I sometimes encountered icing conditions while clearing the Brooks Range and the Howard had no de-icing capability.

It became clear that we needed a larger plane, preferably one with two engines and prop alcohol at a minimum, and hopefully, wing and stabilizer de-icer boots.

The airplane that we chose was a type that I'd flown for hundreds of hours in the military and knew it to be a dependable aircraft: a Model 18 twin-engine Beechcraft. Bill Steiner, a Los Angeles aircraft broker, located the plane in Dallas, and he and a friend flew it to Fairbanks for us.

The plane was put to work immediately, and I was the only pilot flying it. A fine aircraft with good engines, it came with a full set of instruments, prop alcohol for anti-icing and wing and horizontal stabilizer de-icer boots. It was equipped with a complete set of radios and a good Automatic Direction Finder (ADF).

I repeatedly flew the Twin Beech from Barter Island to Fairbanks, making as many as four round trips in 24 hours.

An unforgettable trip in the Twin Beech occurred at the early edge of winter with half-snow and half-rain pelting the little camp at Barter Island where the contractor

Interior Airways' first Twin Beechcraft C-18 at Barter Island, September 1953. Jim Magoffin (center) with mechanics.

had five iron workers to send to Fairbanks.

After supper, my passengers started partying and it was hard to get them ready to go, but I rounded them up that sorry night at about 9:30. I started the engines and warmed them to takeoff temperature and then got the five workmen aboard. Just before taking off, I mopped down the wings, props and tail surfaces with alcohol, then hurried into the cockpit, taking off immediately before ice and slush could accumulate on the plane.

After takeoff, I hit the gear-up switch, but nothing happened. The gear wouldn't retract. Flying on a black night in such lousy weather, I was on solid instruments as soon as we left the ground and heavily preoccupied with flying the plane when it happened.

Suddenly, a burly hand reached past the bulkhead and settled heavily on my right arm, the arm I was using to hold the throttles at climb power.

Half-turning, I saw behind me a roaring drunk with slobber trailing down his red beard. He was yelling and jerking at my right arm. "Goddammit," he hollered. "I gotta piss!"

The Twin Beech's throttle quadrant was just about at the height of his face. Releasing my right hand from the throttles for an instant, I swung my elbow back into the drunk's face as violently as I could. The blow toppled the guy backward on his rear end. Then his buddies, a couple of whom were less seriously drunk, pounced on him and pinned him down. They made sure I had no further trouble with him the rest of the way to Fairbanks.

Though I always try to be polite to even the raunchiest of passengers — and he was one of the raunchiest I ever had to deal with — he picked absolutely the wrong moment to consult me about his personal needs.

There wasn't supposed to be any liquor anywhere on the DEW line, but as they always do, some workers found ways to smuggle the stuff in. It is, of course, illegal to fly drunks, but pilots who refused to fly drunks in Alaska at that time would certainly have left a lot of passengers behind.

I was able to crank up the landing gear by hand and went on with the flight with no further problems. The next morning, I brought the plane to Freddy Seltenreich's hangar and told him about the difficulty. Freddy and Jess Bachner got right on it. All that was required was the repair of a broken wire. After that, the landing gear worked okay. ✝

CHAPTER 25

Full Steam Ahead

After the test of the initial segment of the DEW line proved successful, we then had to locate the sites for the extension of the radar chain on west to Point Barrow and then southwest along the Alaska coastline to Cape Lisburne. For that mission, I flew a Cessna 170 with oversized tires. Jim Brannian, a Western Electric engineer, was with me.

That was during warm weather, and it was far simpler trying to pinpoint landmarks than in the winter when everything was white. We completed that summer reconnaissance for site location in just a couple of days. We had a little spare time and picked up some interesting artifacts from the remains of an old campsite used by Eskimos generations before.

DEW line flying, like most flying, was humdrum and boring. Day and night, we traced and retraced the same closely structured flight routes. Only occasionally would the droning routine be spiced with anything memorable.

A somewhat typical journey was the trip I made in a Cessna 180 on skis during the construction heyday. I was flying a group of three Western Electric executives on

The Beechcraft Travel Air 6000 served us well on the DEW line. Shown here departing Point Barrow, April 1955.

Chuck Lawson (center with cigarette) and Vern Bagnall (right, with hands in parka pockets) visiting with Eskimo children at Barter Island. Lawson was the resident construction boss for Western Electric.

an inspection trip of construction sites in the Canadian sector.

On landing at Tuktoyaktuk, I parked alongside a Canadian Norseman. Its pilot, Ernie Boffa, provided me with some much-appreciated information on landing conditions at DEW line stations farther east.

On the first day of our trip, we had made it from Barter Island to Cambridge Bay. The second day, we flew 300 miles farther east, stopping at each station along the way and staying overnight at the easternmost station. There I got my first look at a Bristol Freighter, a large twin-engine cargo plane somewhat resembling our American Fairchild C-82 (the flying boxcar). It had been parked there several days with engine trouble, and water vapor from an open lead in the ocean had covered it with three inches of frost. It didn't look like it would ever fly again.

The third night, we stopped at Cambridge Bay for supper and to fill up with gas, then headed west to Barter Island, cruising at 4,500 feet, enjoying a brisk tail wind and reasonably warm air — only 10 degrees below zero.

When I radioed our position to Cape Parry, the Canadian operator informed us it was 38 degrees below zero with a northeast wind of 30 knots.

Then, unexpectedly, the operator topped off his weather report in this way: "I say, old chap, won't you stop in for a spot of tea and a crumpet?" I had the cabin speaker on so the passengers got a chuckle at the invitation and heard me politely decline. I wasn't about to sacrifice my altitude, warm air and tail wind to land in a near blizzard at 38 degrees below zero just to have tea and a cookie.

There was nothing routine about the DEW line trip I made in the Beechcraft Bonanza with engineers Jim Dalton and Chuck Lawson. They were scheduled to meet with construction bosses from the Canadian sector at Cambridge Bay, where we stayed overnight. When my passengers added Yellowknife, Northwest Territories, to their schedule, it gave me two problems. I had to refuel at Cambridge Bay, where gasoline supplies were nearly exhausted and the only avgas available was military 115/145 — loaded with lead. The Bonanza's engine required lead-free or only lightly leaded gas.

Second, I didn't have an air chart of the route from Cambridge Bay to Yellowknife and couldn't buy or borrow one at Cambridge Bay.

The best I could do was a small-scale map of North America I ripped out of a *National Geographic* magazine. A Pacific Western Airlines pilot informed me of a homing beacon that his company had installed about half way to Yellowknife at Contwoyto Lake, and he gave me the beacon frequency. My ADF needle picked it up solidly when we were an hour out of Cambridge Bay and, after passing Contwoyto, I was able to track out on that beacon until I could pick up Yellowknife.

After passing Contwoyto Lake, the Bonanza's engine began running rough. It got progressively worse as we proceeded toward Yellowknife, where it was pitch dark and snowing hard.

I radioed for permission to make a straight-in approach. By that time, the engine had lost much of its power and was terribly rough as a result of the heavily leaded gas I had filled with at Cambridge Bay.

The next morning, one of Max Ward's mechanics assisted me in removing the spark plugs and shaving off the accumulated lead from the terminals. After Dalton and Lawson concluded their Yellowknife business, I fueled up with the correct gasoline and went on to Fairbanks with no further difficulty. Among my possessions is a knife made of pure native copper purchased at Yellowknife. It was fitted with a unique caribou horn handle. The clerk who sold me the knife told me the yellow copper of the area was the source of the name given the Yellowknife Indians by surrounding tribes.

* * * * * *

After the frantic, hectic pace of air activity out of Barter Island, the emphasis

A "Cat Train" traversing the tundra. Thousands of tons of freight were hauled to DEW line sites by tractors pulling heavy steel sleds.

shifted abruptly to a new area of the DEW line — Point Barrow. If pressure at Barter Island was hot, Barrow was white hot.

At Point Barrow, Jim Dalton and Chuck Lawson were the efficient, driving honchos for the construction companies. Working under heavy pressure and rigid time constraints, the pair organized cat trains to haul living quarters, generator buildings and the like to various sites where construction was beginning. Heavily loaded cat trains pulled by one or more D-8 or D-9 Caterpillar tractors began moving huge sleds across the vast tundra or across areas of sea ice when that was deemed safe for such operations. Occasionally, tractors and sleds plunged through the ice with their precious cargos, most of which were extracted, but with great difficulty.

Bob Long, one of our very experienced arctic pilots, flew a Norseman between DEW line stations, dropping flags to mark cat train routes. A significant improvement in this aerial trail-blazing took place when we cut a hole in the belly of our DC-3, installed a chute made of stovepipe and began dropping weighted flags as the pilot held a straight course across trackless tundra or sea ice.

When word got out about our expanding operation on the North Coast, we began to get job applications from pilots and were glad to hire such experienced men as Bob Savaria, Bob Long, Bob Sholton and Tommy Thompson. Thompson, however, didn't work out for us so wasn't with us very long.

His departure dated from the day I arrived at Barrow in bright sunshine and was dismayed to see a loaded Norseman parked on the ramp.

"How come the Norseman isn't flying?" I asked in the operations office.

"Well," said the man on duty, "we've had a little problem with one of the pilots. He went back to his quonset hut."

I wasn't sure what was going on, but I was going to find out. I drove the weasel — a small-tracked vehicle — over to the hut and went in to find Thompson sitting on his bunk reading a magazine.

"What's the problem, Tommy?" I asked.

"When I turned on the ADF, some smoke came out of the junction box. After that, the ADF wouldn't work."

"But you don't need an ADF today," I told him. "It's clear all the way from here to Moscow."

Thompson didn't answer. "You can pick up your check in Fairbanks," I told him.

I flew the Norseman trip in good weather, and that night we repaired the ADF.

On one of my trips to Fairbanks, I was visiting with Fairbanks attorney Chuck Clasby, who was in our airport office making arrangements to be taken to our Minto hunting camp when hunting season opened Sept. 1.

Clasby was aware of our rapid expansion and suggested that since our net worth was now well over $1 million, it was time to incorporate. He did the legal work on forming Interior Airways, Inc. and Interior Enterprises, Inc., the parent for the airline, the flying school, the hunting camp operation and other businesses in which we were involved or might become involved.

The name Interior Airways, Inc. didn't fit our later operations, which had expanded overseas, so we changed it to Alaska International Air. We also changed the name of the parent company to Alaska International Industries, Inc., as it is today.

Some time later, the airline name was changed to MarkAir. ✝

CHAPTER 26

When Things Get Tough, Go To Washington

There's an old saying: When things get tough, the tough get going.

In our case, there was a dismal time when things got real tough and the fate of our firm — everything we'd worked so hard for — was hanging in the balance. And I had to get going fast to where the power was so far as our particular problem was concerned: to Washington.

As the tempo of work on the DEW line heated up, the pressure on our flying capacity got almost unbearable at times. Air Force C-124s were shuttling mountains of cargo into Point Barrow. It all had to be dispersed — and fast — to outlying construction sites. It was worrisome, and even frightening at times, to be confronted with the surging river of supplies descending on Point Barrow for "instant dispersal." Huge piles of timbers, pilings, steel, crates filled with electronics equipment and an incredible mass of other supplies kept pouring out of the seemingly endless stream of incoming Air Force C-124s, Wien C-46s and other aircraft that immediately turned around and went back for more.

It quickly became obvious that there was no way we could put a dent in all that cargo with the small planes we were using up to then. Very desperately, we needed at least one large aircraft.

I remembered that in the summer of 1952, we had a contract with Williams Brothers Pipeline Co. of Tulsa, Oklahoma, who were building a pipeline from Haines through Canada and Alaska.

They had a DC-3 that I figured might be surplus to their needs since they had completed the pipeline. We learned the plane was for sale and we bought it.

The airplane was a surplus Air Force C-47 (the same as a civilian DC-3) with bucket seats. It was still painted Air Force brown. It had been used for the frequent trips made back to the firm's Tulsa headquarters and to transport large loads and groups of workers to pipeline construction sites.

Buying that aircraft in the spring of 1954 paid off handsomely and took the pressure off us. Our association with Williams Brothers was a solid one, and several years later we landed another flying contact with them on another pipeline project.

Incidentally, while on the subject of Williams Brothers, I'll never forget the trip Buzz Barker (Williams' Alaska manager) and I made for them in a Grumman Widgeon. We were in Tok when word came that the company urgently needed chainsaws to cut the pipeline right-of-way, and we were told to go down to Juneau and buy all the chainsaws we could. At Juneau, we landed in the channel, taxied up to Alaska Coastal

Airlines' dock and went downtown on a chainsaw buying spree, picking up every new saw in town — 22 of them. They completely filled the Widgeon. We headed right back and dropped the chainsaws off along the pipeline route.

Things improved after we bought the Williams Brothers DC-3, and we had no hint trouble was brewing. We made flight after flight out of Point Barrow to Fairbanks, as well as flying frequently to coastal sites. In a very short time, we completed 72 flights and were pretty well getting the cargo problem under control when the blow struck.

Unexpectedly, we were advised by the CAA to cease our DC-3 operation. They pointed out that we had no certificate authorizing us to operate an aircraft weighing more than 12,500 pounds and, therefore, must stop flying immediately. They warned us that we were subject to a $1,000 fine for each flight that we had already made.

Bad. I had to move fast or everything we struggled for over the years could go down the drain. Moreover, the national interest was something that had to be considered here. The DEW line badly needed that DC-3 to keep cargo and personnel moving to the bustling sites. Contractors and the Air Force would be up in arms if that airplane was yanked off the job at this critical time.

There was no way we could solve the problem in Alaska since the CAA would merely move forward with their enforcement action and we'd be through. So there was no time to be lost; I had to go straight to the top and try to get somebody in the nation's capital to overrule the CAA's Alaska regional office.

I had one splendid contact in Washington and lost no time in using it — Harmar D. Denny with the Civil Aeronautics Board. Denny had been an Air Force colonel in the same Air Inspection outfit I'd been assigned to at the time our inspection team was flying around the country inspecting flying schools.

Now, fortunately for us, Denny was a member of the CAB, right up in the top echelon of the agency. I called Denny in Washington, explaining our situation in detail. I pointed out that we were in the throes of a vital DEW line transportation job for the Air Force that was essential to national security. I told him that even though we were not engaged in common carriage, the CAA was doing everything it could to torpedo us.

Denny listened carefully, then when I was through, he said, "Just stand by, Jim. I'll see what I can do, and I'll call you back just as soon as possible."

You can be sure I didn't get far from that telephone. When it rang a couple hours later, it was Col. Denny.

"Jim," he said, "I've set up a meeting for you with the CAA administrator, Fred Lee, for 2 p.m. tomorrow. Can you be there?"

"You bet!" I said.

When I walked into the administrator's office in one of the buildings on Independence Avenue the next afternoon, I sensed the atmosphere was friendly, so there was hope. With the administrator was his chief counsel, and from the start, both were perfect gentlemen.

The officials showed a keen and genuine interest in our Alaska operation and in the problem now confronting our firm. The administrator asked a lot of questions, wanting to know, for example, how long we had been in Alaska and how we happened to be on the DEW line. I did the best I could to answer all of the questions as fully as possible.

After further discussion, the administrator smiled and said, "Well, Jim, when you get back to Fairbanks, I think you'll find that everything will be okay."

And it was.

CAA headquarters had swiftly given the word to the regional director, and Dot was promptly notified that certification would be moved along as fast as possible.

While I was traveling home, Dot was busily typing the application required for our certificate. We had a minimal fine to pay so the violation could be wiped off the books. A few days later, the government granted us a limited operating certificate. This certificate permitted the operation of aircraft weighing over 12,500 pounds — but only on charter and contract — and it had to be renewed every year. Our battle for a full-fledged permanent certificate that included scheduled airline operations was to continue for many years.

Possession of an operating certificate brought with it a whole new set of complications and problems. Now, in a very short period of time, we had to develop operations, maintenance and training manuals, and these had to be approved by the CAA.

Word had leaked out about our problem and the fact that we were now the possessors of a certificate, and once again, Bob Reeve pitched in to help us at a time when we badly

Reeve Aleutian Airways Capt. Gene Strause was loaned to Interior Airways by Bob Reeve to help get the large aircraft operation going — legally.

needed help. He phoned to say he'd be glad to lend us one of his senior pilots to help prepare our manuals.

Bob loaned us Capt. Gene Strause. In addition to writing our operations manuals for us — patterned on the ones in effect at Reeve Aleutian Airways — Capt. Strause flew many flights for us between Fairbanks and the North Slope.

It would be misleading to leave the impression that our hard-won operating certificate solved all our problems with the bureaucrats. If anything, their surveillance of our operation now intensified. Quite frequently, CAA edicts generated heartburn for our people. Particularly maddening were the hard-nosed regulations that, in my opinion, actually resulted in accidents and near-accidents.

For example, our supervising CAA agent insisted that we keep our flight logs current when flying the large aircraft, no matter what the circumstances. We were told we had to write down every landing time, every takeoff time, every radio contact, and to keep everything scrupulously up to date. To do that in the cockpit of a DC-3 that frequently stopped every 50 miles was a real pain in the rear and actually a menace. The emphasis seemed to be on paper shuffling rather than safe flying. Trying to fulfill these requirements was bad for safety, and this made my blood boil. To do their paperwork at night, our pilots had to keep bright cockpit lights on, just about wiping out visibility of the terrain ahead. This precipitated a very close call on one night flight.

On that particular night, Capt. Earl Cassellius and co-pilot Roy Morgan were westbound in our DC-3 (No. 391), the Dewbird, on the Canadian side of the line near Shingle Point.

Interior DC-3 Crashes; Two Aboard Safe

Two crew members aboard an Interior Airways DC-3 airplane which crash landed late last night on the Canadian Arctic coast were alive and unhurt, James Magoffin, president of Interior Enterprises, said here this morning.

The plane made a forced landing about 10 p.m. some 15 miles south of Herschel Island while on its way back to Alaska after flying freight to a Canadian DEW Line site. Magoffin said he had no information on extent of damage to the aircraft.

Earl Casellius, pilot, and Roy Morgan, co-pilot, were spotted at 9:20 a.m. today by an Interior Airways search plane which left Fairbanks at 4 a.m. to hunt for them. Paul Palmer was pilot and Bob Dyment co-pilot of the search plane. Also aboard were Charles Hubbs, chief pilot; Cy Hetherington, maintenance boss, and Bill Casey, mechanic.

Hubbs was evacuating the downed crew members by small plane today.

Magoffin said the last report from the plane was received about ten minutes before the mishap. Cause of the crash is unknown here.

An accident caused by too much emphasis on paper work — rather than safe flying.

In a hair-raising brush with possible tragedy, the plane drifted a bit south of course and, in doing so, scraped the top of a snow-covered ridge. The plane came to a spectacular sliding stop that bent the props and put indentations on the skin of the plane's belly. Luckily, the pilots were uninjured. There were no passengers.

Getting the plane off the ridge was no snap. The following morning, Charlie Hubbs made two hazardous flights in a ski-equipped Super Cub to the site to pick up the pilots. We were able to subsequently repair the DC-3 with much difficulty and put it back on the job.

It was my contention that the bright lights in the pilot's compartment required for in-flight record keeping prevented the pilots from seeing the ridge and contributed directly to the accident.

After that, we called a halt to all in-flight record keeping. All paper work had to be done after the completion of flights. Whether the CAA liked it or not, we felt flying safety was much more important than timely completion of a stack of papers that would probably never be looked at again.

In this and other respects, we always stressed safe operations. I'm proud of our safety record during all the years our pilots flew under the challenging conditions facing them in the arctic. They had to contend with dense coastal fog in the summertime and incessantly blowing snow in the winter that created the dreaded whiteouts. Despite this, though we had mishaps like the one with the DC-3, our worst accident during those initial years was the result of a pilot disobeying company rules.

It happened when Bill Nugent, a cocky young pilot, flatly disobeyed company regulations and attempted to fly a Norseman along the Arctic Slope VFR at night in foggy weather — an absolute no-no.

Nugent strayed too far inland, rolled his wheels along the tundra and the plane crashed. It ended up inverted with the nose pointing back the way he had come and the tail pointing the way he was going.

"He slopped over," was the way the accident would be described by Ward Gay, the owner of Sea Airmotive in Anchorage.

Fortunately, neither Nugent nor his passenger was injured in the accident. Had Nugent made a normal instrument flight, he would have been okay since the layer of coastal fog was very thin and the weather at his destination was clear.

Despite a number of mishaps like this, we took real pride in the fact that in all the several years Interior Airways flew on the DEW line with multiple aircraft operating under the toughest arctic conditions, we came through without a single passenger fatality or even a serious injury.

As the safety slogans put it, a safety record like that is no accident. +

CHAPTER 27

An Accident Worth Celebrating

Maybe it's going a bit too far to label what happened to our DC-3 at Point Barrow as an "incredibly wonderful" accident, but looking back at it now, it's clear that it was truly one of the best things that ever happened to our company.

Yes, it was costly; yes, it put a serious, temporary crimp in our overheated DEW line flying schedule; and yes, it was absolutely the finest, most "beneficial" accident we ever had. What was so great about it was that it brought to our firm a remarkably competent fellow named Bob Rice, who was literally worth his weight in gold. One of the finest pilots I've ever known, Rice made a tremendous contribution to the growth and prosperity of our company.

Rice was our extremely fortunate replace-

Bob Rice, one of the best pilots I've ever known. His flying for Interior Airways allowed the DEW line to be completed in the shortest possible time.

ment for the ex-Wien pilot we hired without realizing the extent of his drinking problem. Hiring that man, who was well qualified to fly the DC-3, was a terrible mistake, of course, and he very quickly proved it. On taking off from Point Barrow one day, he managed to drag both wing tips on one of the few times I wasn't flying with him as co-pilot. His drinking and this accident convinced me he couldn't possibly work out for us. This accident, at a time when every hour with that DC-3 was precious, was a serious blow and a bad omen if we ignored it. A personnel change had to be made quickly, and I lost no time in making it.

Getting that workhorse DC-3 back in the air as fast as possible took priority, however. We had to get it fixed without a moment's delay and lost no time in flying it down to Bob Reeve's Anchorage hangar, where his mechanics went to work on it. They worked all night installing new wing tips, making it possible for us to be back in Barrow the next morning with the DC-3. The kind of service the Reeve organization gave us and the speed and efficiency with which Reeve mechanics put the DC-3 back in shape speaks volumes for Reeve's maintenance crews and for the entire organization.

With the DC-3 earning revenue again, it was time to seek out a permanent replacement for the unfortunate pilot who was saddled with a drinking handicap. The "wonderful" aftermath of the DC-3 accident occurred when I contacted Rice, a very well known, highly experienced Alaska pilot admired and respected by all who knew him.

I don't want to leave the impression he could walk on water, and I knew that, by reputation, he could be highly independent and unorthodox at times. But anyone familiar with the remarkable cast of characters in Alaska aviation at the time would consider Rice a star and would confirm that he was a crackerjack pilot and a real go-getter who really knew how to do a flying job efficiently and well.

Best of all, Rice had a rock-solid, exemplary experience record, having worked for Wien and then having operated his own business with a small airplane. And Rice knew the bleak arctic terrain like the back of his hand. So hiring him in the wake of the DC-3 accident proved a real stroke of luck for us.

Rice's phenomenal skill as a pilot and his unrelenting dedication and determination never ceased to amaze me. And I wasn't the only one impressed by his performance.

Jim Dalton, construction boss for Puget Sound & Drake, with jurisdiction over the entire Alaskan DEW line sector, never stopped singing Rice's praises.

"I know the guy's healthy as a horse," Dalton told me once, "but every day I pray he won't get sick." Caught up in the feverish, nerve-straining demands for air service during the heyday of construction activity, Dalton told me solemnly, "Without Rice, my operation would almost come to a halt."

Unstoppable, tireless, Rice was truly indispensable, and having him share the heavy load we carried was a real godsend. He thought nothing of flying day and night for seven days a week, though regulations required that he fly no more than six. He was fully aware of the need for such involvement if the radar warning system was to be built in the shortest possible time.

On my first flight as Rice's co-pilot, he showed little concern when a red light flashed on indicating a fire in the right engine. He casually asked me to look out my window and see if there was any smoke coming out of the engine cowling. I reported that there was none, whereupon Rice reached up and removed the bulb from the socket and placed it in the ash tray. In maintenance that night, our mechanics found a frayed wire that had caused the problem.

Impulsive actions by inexperienced pilots have caused many mishaps when there was actually nothing wrong with the aircraft.

Rice's on-the-job performance needed no exaggeration, but the press, as it so often does, needlessly gilded his record on at least one occasion. An article about him claimed he had flown more than 350 hours in one month for our firm on DEW line work. This wasn't true, even though he occasionally flew more than double the allowable flight time.

Rice's overall safety record was outstanding and impressive. As far as I could determine, in all his career, he had only one accident of any significance, but it definitely wasn't his fault and was something that could have happened to anybody under similar conditions.

The accident happened in the early '50s when Rice was flying a Cessna for Wien. It was around 70 degrees below zero when he was making a landing at Fort Yukon. The plane's spring steel landing gear, weakened by the extreme cold, snapped in two as he touched down.

Rice was an uncannily innovative guy, gifted with the ability to improve and improvise in ways that would never occur to the average pilot. Getting big airplanes into small fields was his specialty. He could easily "grease-in" the Dewliner, our DC-3, into postage stamp sites we felt had to be serviced with much smaller planes.

One of his soft-field landing tricks was simply letting about half the air out of the plane's tires. Now, on landing, the tire surface would spread over a wider area and keep the plane from sinking into soft sand. Another of his short-field practices was shifting the plane's load to the back of the airplane as far as possible without putting the plane dangerously out of balance. Thus, when he landed, the tail wheel would dig deeper into the sand, stopping the plane in a much shorter distance than would otherwise be possible. Short fields previously "forbidden" to the DC-3 now became a piece of cake, and this helped immensely in moving large volumes of cargo.

On one occasion, I landed a Cessna 180 at a station limited by a 700-foot runway. I prided myself on making a short landing until Rice came along and landed on the same gravel strip in our DC-3, stopping six feet short of where I was able to halt the 180.

Some of the strips we flew into and out of were too narrow to allow a DC-3 to turn around for takeoff, so a vehicle had to be used to haul the plane back to the end of the runway for takeoff.

Rice never lost his cool even when something unexpected happened that would shake up or spook a lesser pilot. On one unforgettable flight, Rice was taking a group of Western Electric and Air Force VIPs out of Point Barrow on an extensive tour of Alaska and Canada DEW line sites. While letting down through thick fog on the approach to Barter Island's airfield, everybody came to attention when a terrible crashing sound resonated loudly through the DC-3 cockpit and cabin. A duck had collided with the right windshield and had shattered it and disintegrated inside the cockpit. Co-pilot Frank Gregory, wearing a crisp, spotless white shirt and neat trousers, was instantly transformed into a gory mess. Startled VIP passengers, still not sure what was going on, stared in disbelief as they saw him stagger from the cockpit and make his way back to the lavatory to clean himself up. One can only surmise what was going through their minds as they watched Gregory lurch by with blood streaming all over him and thick splotches of duck innards festooning him from head to foot.

There was no perceptible change in Rice's flying tempo. Coolly, as if absolutely nothing had happened, he continued his approach to Barter Island, landing there in his studied, unhurried way.

The inspection party assumed the trip was over. After all, the right windshield was shattered, something that could take days to replace there in the arctic. Here Rice's innovative skill came into play. He saw the shattered windshield as something that could be fixed in short order if one puts his mind to it and he did.

Hustling around, he located a heavy sheet of plexiglass. With the help of a Barter Island carpenter, he shaved the dimensions of the plexiglass down to fit the windshield opening. This improvised windshield fit exactly when they installed it and the briefly interrupted inspection trip continued.

Rice took great pride in grooming his co-pilots for better jobs. He watched with satisfaction as several of them went on to become airline captains themselves. Gregory, his co-pilot on the above-described trip, serves as a good example. A natural flight instructor, Rice very early spotted Gregory's potential. Gregory, a 1950 student at our Alaska Flying School in Fairbanks, came under Rice's tutelage not too long afterward. With Rice's help, Gregory progressed steadily to become a DC-3 captain, then a C-46 captain. He flew for our company for several years.

So considering everything that happened afterward, there's no question that the Point Barrow DC-3 accident was unique in terms of its ultimate significance. I've never liked accidents, of course, but looking back at this one and realizing the tremendous contribution Rice made to our firm, I can truly say that this particular accident remains dear to my heart. ✝

CHAPTER 28

Still More Planes
And More Pilots

Interior's planes in the early '60s. A C-46 and C-82 are in the background. A Twin Beech 18 is in front of hangar, a single engine Bonanza is in the foreground, and a Twin-Bonanza is at gas pump.

By the mid-'50s, we were caught up in the frantic pace of DEW line construction and pressured by Air Force officials impatient to get the critical job done. We were able to acquire two more DC-3s and began operating them out of Barrow, Barter Island and Fairbanks.

At this time, we were obligated to fly a growing number of workers and heavier cargo from the Fairbanks supply hub to main bases at Barrow and Barter Island, so we had to get our hands on one or more C-46s.

Previously, we had a policy of paying cash for our airplanes and maintaining a debt-free status.

In that regard, I am reminded of the time when we set up a three-day fishing and hunting trip for Roy Gaasland, president of the Gaasland Construction Co. of Bellingham, Washington.

The party on this trip consisted of Roy and his son, as well as Emil Kluckhohn,

Old "Sixty Volts" — the cargo C-46 used by the Flying Tigers and sold to Interior Airways — a trouble-free dependable workhorse.

president of the Bellingham branch of the Seattle First National Bank, and two other business associates.

We had set up a tent camp on Swede Lake, one of the Tangle Lakes chain just west of Paxson Lake in the Alaska Mountain Range. Fishing was fantastic. Our favorite contest was seeing who could cast out a spoon hook and retrieve it *without* getting a lake trout. To add to the success of that trip, Gaasland's son shot a fine trophy bull caribou.

On the return flight, Kluckhohn was riding up front with me, and as we approached Fairbanks, he asked, "Jim, who carries your paper?"

"What do you mean?" I asked.

"Who finances you? With what bank do you have your loans?"

I replied, "No bank. We have no loans. We don't owe a dime to anyone."

Kluckhohn said he simply couldn't believe it.

Now we had no recourse but to borrow money to buy larger planes.

Initially, when I approached the banks in Fairbanks, I was informed that the amount of money I required to buy the planes was beyond their lending limits. I was referred to the Seattle First National Bank, which backed them on most of their transactions. That bank gave us the money we needed, and we repaid the loan in full within a year.

From Doc Curtis I learned that the Flying Tigers in Los Angeles had a C-46 for sale. Curtis managed the Transocean Airlines hangar in Seattle when we licensed our

This Norseman, one of four flown by Interior Airways, was donated to the Pioneer Air Museum in Fairbanks.

first Grumman Widgeon there in the summer of 1952.

Fred Benninger, who ran the Flying Tiger operation, and Doug Duly, one of his key officials, discussed the matter with us and came up with a suitable price for the C-46.

It startled Benninger when I wrote him a check for the entire amount. He nearly spit out his cigar.

"That's the first time that ever happened to us on an aircraft sale," he said.

That first C-46 was for cargo only. Now we had to have a C-46 capable of carrying passengers as well. I was glad to learn that Benninger could sell us the second C-46, which was surplus to their needs.

We had to transform the seatless cargo cabin into a respectable passenger-carrying interior that could be converted to cargo operation if required. We installed payloader seats that folded against the wall to make room for cargo. For passenger operation, we installed a public address system, a no smoking sign, and a small galley where a stewardess could prepare food and coffee. Also, engine and cowling modifications were required before the plane could be licensed for passenger operation.

Our customers kept pressing us for more aircraft. The Flying Tigers couldn't supply us with another C-46, but Doug Duly told me that aviation entrepreneur George Batchelor, also based in Burbank, claimed he could get one for us. I hurried to Los

Angeles and George met me. We proceeded to the office of Kirk Kerkorian, who owned Los Angeles Airways. Kirk had a C-46 rigged for passenger operation. N1663M was a bit plush for our operation, but it had a very convenient passenger door that had been installed in one of the normal cargo doors. We closed the deal with Kerkorian. I assume he paid a finder's fee to George Batchelor and George probably had to slip a few bucks to Doug Duly. The plane was perfect for our DEW line schedule.

The purchase of four single-engine Norsemans — bush planes commonly called "the one-ton trucks of the air" — helped fill our never-ending need to supply additional aircraft to fulfill growing commitments. We bought two of the Norsemans from the CAA and later got another from Northern Consolidated Airlines following a meeting with Ray Petersen and Lanky Rice after Petersen became president of that firm. The fourth Norseman came from Alaska Airlines in a friendly transaction arranged by Charlie Willis, Alaska's president, and Leroy Peterson, executive vice president.

Willis was always friendly and accommodating to us. He favored our people with airline passes, and we returned the favor the best way we could by taking him and his family fishing in the Brooks Range.

Getting qualified pilots to do the tough, demanding DEW line flying wasn't much easier than getting planes. Initially, we solved the pilot shortage by assigning four of the instructors from our Alaska Flying School in Fairbanks to Barter Island duty: Charlie Hubbs, Fred McGuire, Alex Pitts and Bud Compton. Experienced bush pilots also were recruited successfully at this critical time. We were glad to get Red Williams, who had been flying out of Central, and Don Stickman, who flew out of Ruby.

We obtained two excellent experienced pilots for Barter Island from Seattle — Al Mosley and Bill Lindgren. To start with, Mosley flew an Aeronca Sedan on floats and Lindgren checked out in the Howard, making numerous flights between Fairbanks and Barter Island until we got a twin-engine plane to do that job.

These guys were the hardest-working bunch of pilots I've ever seen. They chalked up a remarkable safety record while amassing many hundreds of flying hours under the worst conditions: terrible weather, deadly fog, soft runways, minimal navigation aids and incredibly tough schedules.

The versatility, drive and tirelessness of these pilots never ceased to amaze me. Bud Compton, for example, flew more hours each month than any of the other pilots. Whenever a spare plane became available, our loaders would have it fueled and loaded and Bud would lose no time in jumping out of one plane and into another.

Occasionally, they'd have the engine of the second plane running for Bud as he parked the plane he'd been flying. That's toughness, skill and dedication. And that kind of performance was invaluable to us as we operated under the rush-rush crash

Fred Benninger (left) and Al Benedict, MGM Grand Hotel executives from Las Vegas. The Widgeon took them to good fishing.

conditions of Barter Island.

H.O. "Red" Williams, a *good*, dependable pilot who flew hundreds of hours without problems, was a constant source of amazement at the breakfast table because of his ability to put away an enormous number of pancakes.

An enviable, accident-free flying record was chalked up by colorful Jack Wilson, a noted glacier pilot who was especially skilled in difficult operations. After working for us on the DEW line, Wilson wrote an interesting autobiography, "Glacier Wings and Tales," including his hair-raising mountain and glacier flights in the rugged Wrangell mountain range.

Phil Gray came to work for us as a Widgeon pilot. He had flown in southeastern Alaska and loved water flying. He had also flown out of Kotzebue for Alaska Airlines. Later, after leaving our company, he obtained a Consolidated PBY and began operating it on contract to the Arctic Research Laboratory at Point Barrow. Sadly, on returning to the Lower 48 in the fall, he lost his life in a botched instrument approach at Ketchikan and the ensuing crash.

The incredible tempo of air haulage was punishing to aircraft and never was efficient maintenance so important. Jess Bachner of Fairbanks Aircraft Service would fly up to Barter Island from time to time to perform required aircraft inspections. His presence saved us all the time we'd lose flying the planes back to Fairbanks and then getting them back to the DEW line.

Though we insisted on topnotch maintenance, we never employed a large number of maintenance people. For a long time, our maintenance crew consisted only of Jim Hutchison, Harry Fowler and Ralph Brumbaugh. Not only did these men maintain our aircraft, they kept improving them. For example, Brumbaugh designed and built new doors for our Twin Beeches that were far superior to the original Beech passenger doors, being lighter and presenting a larger opening for passenger and cargo access.

Our maintenance crew built loading ramps for our C-46s out of steel tubing. These were designed to hook into C-46 boarding ladder fittings and were built strong enough to support fuel barrels which we would unload by rolling them down the ramps, facilitating our fuel haulage on hundreds of trips when seismic crews became active on the North Slope.

Our very innovative maintenance men designed an excellent fuel barrel tie-down system for the C-46s by putting bars inside the fuselage on each side and anchoring them solidly to the fuselage. This made it easier and quicker to sling ropes through them, around the barrels, and back over the bar. This was better than having to tie the barrels to rings in the floor, although we did use rings to supplement the braces on the sides of the aircraft.

Our maintenance staff installed hard interiors in our Twin Beeches to keep them from getting beat up by the many loads of freight they carried. They designed and installed folding side seats constructed of steel tubing with canvas stretched over it and seat tops made of plywood with foam rubber and naugahide on top. Though the seats didn't look too bad, they weren't comfortable because passengers had to sit with their backs against the wall facing the aisle, but for short flights they were bearable. They also built folding side seats for our Grumman Widgeons and Brumbaugh designed and built a bracket that greatly reduced the radius of turn of our planes on floats.

The countless improvements that made our airplanes better than when we bought them can be attributed to our maintenance personnel. Thanks to them, we had an absolute minimum of mechanical troubles during the many years that we operated piston-engine airplanes. ✝

CHAPTER 29

Fishing And Hunting Unlimited

Among our friends who have joined us for fishing trips to Walker Lake in the Brooks Range are the Charlie Willis family. Charlie was the president of Alaska Airlines.

Nothing in the Lower 48 can compare with the unequaled hunting and fishing spots I was able to explore year after year as our area of operation expanded.

Many of these places, when I first came upon them, had been literally untouched since the Russian era. But in checking out all the good places, I ran into trouble a time or two.

One day in 1949, Ward Carroll, a Fairbanks big-game guide, and I were out flying in the Chugach mountain canyons in the Aeronca Sedan on floats looking for hunting spots.

We didn't find any place we liked, so we decided to go back to Fairbanks and take our sheep-hunting clients to the Brooks Range instead.

On the way back, we were enjoying a brisk tail wind at 2,000 feet over the Gulkana flats when the engine quit cold. Fortunately, we had just passed over a big lake. I made a 180-degree gliding turn, landed on the lake and we drifted to the beach. There I climbed a spruce tree and strung out the trailing antenna.

Gulkana radio answered my call and passed a message to Fairbanks Aircraft Service, letting them know I was down on that particular lake with an engine problem.

Fairbanks Aircraft Service, owned by Fred Seltenreich and Jess Bachner with several mechanics working for them, was always very sensitive to the needs of bush pilots. This service-minded firm went out of its way to help pilots, whether they were in trouble or not, and the kind of service they regularly delivered to us contributed appreciably to the success of our company.

On this occasion, Jess Bachner, himself, flew in to give us a hand with our problem. When we removed the accessory case, we found that the accessory drive gear was lying loose in the housing. It was fastened to the back of the crankshaft with four cap screws, each having a hole drilled in it for safety wire. There wasn't a sign of safety wire anywhere. When that engine had been assembled at the Continental factory, the workman had neglected to safety the cap screws. This allowed the screws to back out and the gear to fall off, precipitating an immediate, complete engine failure.

When we put the gear back on the shaft, we found that the steel key that aligned it was broken. We didn't have another one, so we filed down a nail and stuck it in the slot. That engine ran its time out without any further problems.

What Fairbanks Aircraft Service, particularly Jess Bachner, did for us on this occasion illustrates perfectly how dependent pilots are on the services of firms like this.

* * * * * *

One day at Fort Yukon I ran into a young trapper, Bill Grinnell, who wanted me to give him a lift back to his trapping camp on Beaver Creek.

I was flying the Taylorcraft on floats and asked him about landing in the river. He assured me there was a good, straight, deep-water stretch near his camp.

As we circled the hills just west of his cabin at the confluence of Beaver Creek and Victoria Creek, we spotted a band of mountain sheep in the high country.

We landed at Grinnell's camp, unloaded Bill's small amount of freight, and I met his remarkable wife.

Mrs. Grinnell was a big, husky girl named Evelyn. When we were introduced, she shook my hand just like a man, and I noted that her arms were twice as big around as mine. She was really a rugged character.

She had been deprived of the sight in one eye early in life. Raised in a trapping family, she had fallen while driving a dog team, and the stub of a cut willow pierced her eye. She was able to manage quite well, nevertheless, and in every respect was a pleasant, friendly lady.

Her husband, who was as much into hunting as I was, said, "I'd like to get one of those sheep we got a look at. Want to try?"

"Sure," I said. "We can fly up river about a mile and land, then go up the mountain."

"We'll probably get one," he said.

After we landed up the river and I tied the airplane, Bill said, "I'll go around to the east. You can go straight up to where we saw the sheep."

I had the easiest climb. Carrying my .30-.30, I got up past the timberline. Peeking over the edge of the ridge, I spotted a white sheep standing not far from me. It had horns, so I figured, "Oh, boy, a nice spike buck!"

What I wasn't aware of was that females had horns, too. I took careful aim and shot it, but received quite a shock when I walked up to dress it and discovered it was a female.

Not long after I packed the sheep back to the river, Bill showed up with his sheep. I flew him and his sheep back to his camp, then went back, picked up my sheep and flew to Fairbanks. That was my first experience at bagging a mountain sheep. I've had a good many more since then, but never have I shot another female.

* * * * * *

Waterfowl season opened Sept. 1, and I was kept busy flying hunters to and from our Minto camp. For their accommodations, we set up tents on an island on the Minto flats. Goose and duck hunting there went well and we made a few dollars. Generally, the hunting was fabulous, and we had a lot of satisfied customers.

It was so good that most of the Fairbanksans who went over with us became repeat customers. These included George Norton, the chief of police; Percy Hubbard, who owned the Chevrolet agency; Dan Lahmon, owner of the Ford agency; Charles Clasby, a Fairbanks attorney; Roy Ferguson, manager of the Fairbanks Lumber Co.; Emil Usibelli, owner of the Usibelli Coal Mines; and Sen. John Butrovich and his wife, Grace.

Many of these people hunted with us for a number of years. One place on the Minto flats was named Clasby Point because it was the place where Chuck Clasby loved to hunt.

Another spot was Hubbard Point, Percy Hubbard's preferred shooting spot. On Percy's demise,

Frank Murkowski, one of our directors, and his sons Brian (center) and Mike, at the Minto duck camp. Murkowski, a long-time friend and now a U.S. senator, included his children in the outdoor sports whenever possible.

Hubbard Point was taken over by Emil Usibelli.

Our "facilities" at the Minto camp included a two-place outhouse situated in the woods 50 yards behind the camp. Dan Lahmon gave some special thought to this isolated structure and scribbled a poem on the end of a wooden gas box mounted inside. It read:

> A trip to this secluded spot
> Is something to remember.
> Its usefulness can't be denied
> In May or in December.
> In summertime, we take our time
> We like to sit and ponder.
> But when it's 42 below
> We hustle out then back we go
> And is it any wonder?
> And though we dally at our task
> Or finish in a jiffy,
> The comfort that we seek is here
> Magoffin's two-hole biffy.
>
> Signed: "Eighth Grade Dan"

I especially liked flying the Minto operation because sometimes it gave me the chance to do a little duck and goose hunting myself. We also used the camp for moose hunting and for pike fishing.

The only drawback was that it was quite a tiresome chore to fly a party of hunters over with their dogs and all their gear, including the cook and all the groceries, then fly everybody and everything back again at a time when I could carry only one passenger at a time.

This small-scale operation in our early days kept Dot busy hauling hunters from Fairbanks out to Pike's Landing on the Chena River where we kept our Taylorcraft on floats.

Dot had to buy the groceries and get them out to the plane, then meet the plane after the hunting was over and bring the hunters, their gear, their dogs and their ducks and geese back to town.

All this was more than a little awkward since we had no radio in those days, and we had to pre-arrange it so the vehicle on the ground would arrive at the landing somewhere around the same time the aircraft did.

I refused to operate off the Chena River adjacent to Weeks Field because the river there, in my estimation, didn't afford enough straight stretches for safe landings and takeoffs.

Some pilots operated off the Chena right in downtown Fairbanks below the main Chena River bridge where there was a fairly good straight stretch, but I never considered this a safe operation. In fact, several accidents occurred there. In one really serious crash, the plane being flown by pilot George Gilbertson struck the bridge on takeoff. Both Gilbertson and his passenger were injured and the plane, a new Stinson, was demolished.

* * * * * *

The arrival of moose season always gave us some badly needed business. In the fall of '49, the partners in a Fairbanks garbage service, Red McCoy and Amos Breen, were eager to go moose hunting but couldn't afford to charter a plane. I agreed to fly them out to a small lake in the Shaw Creek flats, making it within their means because that location was on my way as I serviced other hunting parties in the Big Delta area.

I dropped McCoy and Breen off the evening before moose season opened and instructed them to signal me by spreading a white sheet over the willows when they were ready to be flown out. I was surprised to see the signal in place early the next morning as I was heading for another lake farther east. When I landed, I noted that there were four men on the shore instead of two, the additional pair being federal game wardens, Ray Woolford and Frank Chapados.

The two hunters got into trouble because they weren't able to resist shooting a bull moose that wandered in close to their camp late in the evening, even though the season didn't open until midnight.

The game wardens must have had an informer somewhere along the Alaska Highway, which was several miles to the south, who heard the rifle shot and alerted them.

The country between the highway and the camp was terrible terrain, mostly swampland, commonly called "moose pasture," that was hard to traverse on foot. Even so, the two dedicated game wardens sloshed across this mess for hours in the dark arriving at the "scene of the crime" just after daylight, worn out and soaked to their armpits.

By this time the hunters had skinned and quartered the moose and hung it up to cool.

Arrival of the wardens out of the swamp startled them and struck fear into their hearts because the appearance of the law was so unexpected.

"Got yourself a moose, I see," Woolford remarked as he studied the hanging carcass.

"Killed it early this morning," one of the hunters replied.

Woolford wasn't buying that. He marched over to the hanging moose, whipped out his knife and made a deep slash in one hind quarter. Then he pulled a thermometer out of his pocket and inserted it into the meat. After a short wait, he retrieved it and told the hunters bluntly, "This moose has been dead more than eight hours." The wardens ticketed the two hunters.

I flew the wardens to Big Delta, where they could get ground transportation, then took the crestfallen, disgruntled hunters back to Fairbanks.

I couldn't help feeling sorry for the two hunters. Neither of them could afford the hefty fine and the loss of their guns. And what made it all the worse was that they unquestionably could have killed a moose legally if only they had waited just a few hours.

Marksman Jimmy Magoffin, our older son, immensely enjoys moose hunting — evident by his prized trophy.

There was nothing I could do, however. In territorial days, the federal game wardens were tough as nails and unrelentingly strict as they enforced game laws to the letter. Violations like this case were publicized, and this alone made hunters think twice before violating the law, even when they were located in the middle of a vast swamp.

* * * * * *

Bagging a moose each year was a must for our family. Our normal moose-hunting procedure was for me to get up very early and scan the lake shore with field glasses

The Magoffin boys' love for hunting and fishing began when they were very young.

while Dot and our boys continued to enjoy their sleep. If I spotted a bull moose, I'd wake up the boy whose turn it was to shoot and paddle him to within range in the canoe.

One morning while scanning with the glasses, I spotted the figure of a man on a hillside across the lake. I couldn't believe it. We'd never seen another human in that area. There were no native camps nearby, and we were many miles from the nearest white settlement.

Puzzled, I paddled the canoe across the lake and on the far shore I met a young man, Fred Schikora of Fairbanks. Fred said he was moose hunting and had been dropped off on the lake several days before by a pilot friend.

That chance and totally unexpected meeting in the wilderness led to a lifelong friendship and Fred's association with our firm. An accountant, Fred came to work for our company only a short time after that meeting. He did a superb job for us, was always a loyal employee, and an enjoyable hunting and fishing companion. Fred later became the distributor for Shell Oil products in northern Alaska.

Now retired, he maintains homes in both Fairbanks and Baja, California.

My low-level flights in small planes between the arctic and Fairbanks gave me marvelous glimpses of wild game roaming the north side of the Brooks Range.

Bands of white Dahl sheep could be seen on most mountains. Bare arctic hillsides disclosed grizzlies, wolves and wolverines. Herds of caribou browsed throughout the area. Some moose had crossed the mountains and were thriving in the willow thickets carpeting the valleys. In August of 1953, I was surprised to see a bull moose knee deep in the Arctic Ocean near Demarcation Point.

With hunting in mind, I had my eye on a small lake near the head of the Hula Hula River. It was perfectly situated in the heart of superb hunting country.

Though small, the lake seemed adequate for the operation of the Piper Super Cub Dot had just acquired so we planned a hunting trip when season opened in August.

The Cub was too small to carry two grown-ups, two young boys, and all our gear, so we had Charlie Hubbs fly a Piper Pacer on floats to the nearest big lake, Schrader Lake, with the bulk of the load. Charlie maintained our base camp there and "baby-sat" our sons while Dot and I used the Cub to ferry our gear to a spike camp on the Hula Hula Lake from which we intended to hunt sheep in the surrounding mountains.

I was stuffing grub into my pack-sack prior to leaving camp when Dot inquired, "Why are you doing that? We'll be up there and back with our sheep in two hours."

She had never climbed a mountain before. Five hours later, we were finally up to the sheep. I let Dot have the first shot, and she downed a fine ram. After dressing the sheep, there was still ample daylight, so I suggested we climb a bit farther and get another. We climbed, but saw only lambs and ewes, so we had to be satisfied with one ram.

On our way back down, we were approaching Dot's dead sheep when she suddenly stopped and exclaimed, "My sheep's moving!"

Sure enough, the sheep *was* moving. A closer look disclosed that a large wolverine was practically inside the sheep's carcass, methodically cutting the carcass in two, probably intending to carry it off one half at a time.

When the wolverine spotted us, it stood up on its hind legs.

Dot, now in shooting position, delivered a bullet squarely through its middle. The animal rolled over and bounded down the mountain, spewing blood. I figured it would drop dead any second, but it kept going across a valley and up over the next mountain and was gone. If a cat has nine lives, a wolverine has 29 — toughest animal in the North.

Our family enjoyed many fine hunts at that little lake. For 17 years, we appeared to be the only hunters in the area. We thought no one else had ever hunted there until one day on the crest of a mountain ridge we picked up the oxidized casing of a .25-.20 rifle cartridge used in the small, light-weight rifles popular with the Eskimos. The Eskimos had hunted there, probably after making a 40-mile trip to the south by dog team from Barter Island on the Arctic Coast.

Several years later, we acquired a Cessna 180 on floats with unusually good performance. I used the plane to fly my friend, Sen. John Butrovich, directly to the Hula Hula pond.

Bub Hallett — the illustrious Minto Camp cook. He couldn't boil water, but he sure loved to hunt.

We had a good hunt and "Butro" made a fantastic shot with his .30-.06 from the top of a ridge to bring down a huge ram a hundred yards below us. My ram, bagged shortly afterward, was also quite large, so we decided to relay the animals back to our camp, one-half at a time. All would have been well had not John's wife, Grace, just presented him with a sturdy new pair of leather hunting boots that hadn't been broken in. He didn't complain, but I could see he was in growing agony. When he removed his boots back at camp, his big toes looked like eggplants.

More recently, the area has been invaded by multiple airplanes and even two pack trains of horses. The wonderful privacy we enjoyed for so many years is history.

* * * * * *

Occasionally, snags developed in the operation of our recreational camps. Our practice was to hire a camp cook and take him to the camp a couple of days early to be ready for the hunters who usually came over to Minto Lake on the afternoon of Aug. 31 to be ready for the Sept. 1 opening day of duck season.

On this particular occasion, however, Aug. 30 had arrived and we had failed to hire a cook for the camp. Our general manager, Roy Isackson, handled the problem by assembling all the young fellows on the loading crew and asking if any of them could cook.

This brought no response, but when he added, "We need the cook for our hunting camp," one of the young men, Bub Hallett, swiftly raised his hand.

Isackson had Bub scoot home to pick up his personal gear and rush back to the airport. Bub showed up with a small sack of clothing, along with a shotgun, and was driven immediately to a waiting Cessna 180 seaplane piloted by Billy Magoffin.

Billy and Bub were not acquainted and the initial part of the flight took place in awkward silence.

Finally, to break the ice, Billy turned to Bub and asked, "How long have you been a cook?"

Bub glanced at his watch and replied, "Exactly 20 minutes!"

It turned out that Bub knew very little about cooking, but was an avid hunter. He was the first to go out hunting in the morning and the last one to return at night and, in the process, shot up lots of our ammunition. As for the cooking, it turned out that Dot Magoffin had to do most of it.

Joe Usibelli (age 13) was one of the many lucky hunters we flew to the Endicott Mountains. A local newspaper ran this story about Joe:

13-YEAR-OLD BOY BAGS MOUNTAIN SHEEP ON HUNT — Chalk it up to beginner's luck if you will, but one young Fairbank sportsman can boast about his first sheep hunt for a long time. He's Joe Usibelli, 13-year-old son of Emil Usibelli, who bagged a ram in one shot on his first hunt. On the third day of the current season, the youngster shot a ram that had a 38" curl and measured 14" at the base. His father got one too, but it wasn't that big. The ram was bagged at Jim Magoffin's sheep camp in the Endicott Mountains. While there are no official records on the subject, the 13-year-old youth's feat in killing a mountain sheep may make him the youngest successful sheep hunter in Alaska.

However, Bub Hallett's personality amply atoned for such sins. He became — and remains — one of our favorite people. The young cargo handler is now a captain with the airline and has a teenaged son who is likewise an accomplished hunter. ✝

CHAPTER 30

Tell 'Em To Go To Hell!

One of the most intimidating and discouraging business experiences Dot and I have ever been subjected to took place on a bitterly cold winter day in a cheerless New Jersey executive suite.

We had been summoned there by the Federal Electric Co. That company had just taken over from Western Electric as the prime contractor on the DEW line.

It turned out to be a humiliating, unhappy experience, probably the worst of its kind we have ever been a part of, but it taught us a lot about how *not* to do business.

Let me sketch in just a brief history leading up to that riling, awful encounter. There had been a changing of the guard on the DEW line prime contract. Western Electric was bowing out, and Federal Electric Co. of Paramus, New Jersey, was coming on the scene for the first time. The latter firm had underbid Western Electric as prime contractor.

About a year earlier, Wien had underbid us on the flying contract, even though they lacked the aircraft required to do the job, something they remedied by leasing our planes.

Wien's DEW line performance was plagued by a series of mishaps. In one bad crash of a Twin Beechcraft near Barter Island, the pilot, Tommy Thompson, whom I had fired a year earlier, and several passengers were killed.

Without much business and with only a few airplanes left, Dot and I took advantage of the lull by closing down our flight operation, leaving only our manager, Roy Isackson, secretary Marge Perkins and our crack mechanic, Jim Hutchison, who was rebuilding a wrecked Norseman.

We flew our Beechcraft Bonanza to Fort Worth, Texas, where we enrolled our two sons in the public school and enrolled ourselves at American Flyers, one of the best flying schools in the country. Here, Dot got her commercial pilot's license, instrument and multi-engine ratings, and I obtained my Airline Transport Pilot's rating.

After the "changing of the guard" and after we returned to Alaska, Federal Electric sent out bid invitations on the flying contract. We responded and were notified by wire that we were the low bidder and would take over from Wien. We were asked to report to Federal Electric headquarters in Paramus to "negotiate."

This in itself was irking. We had bid the contract very tightly since it was "the only game in town." Because there was very little cushion, I saw nothing to negotiate about. The contract was routine, fairly well defined and not radically different from the earlier one, so the need to go to New Jersey to "negotiate" escaped me and annoyed me.

But of course, we had to go. When we got to New York City, it was bitterly cold and snowing heavily. Our room at the Waldorf Astoria was a miserable deep-freeze because the steam radiator had gone on the blink.

The management's response to our complaint was far from lightning swift, and we fled to the warmth of the restaurant below.

In our absence, workmen came to the room and removed the shroud off the radiator. The metal cover was carelessly tossed on the bed where Dot had spread one of her favorite dresses, the one she planned to wear to the Paramus business meeting. The sharp-edged cover ripped the lovely dress, making it impossible to wear. The management assured us it would be rewoven, and by the time we got back to the Waldorf from Paramus, the dress was as good as new. Even so, it was just another of several annoyances on that trip.

Traffic on New York City streets was snarled by four inches of snow and getting a taxi to take us over to Paramus was another frustrating process, but we finally got one.

At Federal Electric headquarters we were met by Admiral Sowell, the chief honcho on the DEW line contract. He led us to the conference area, a large, dimly lit room with a huge, oval table in its center. Eight silent, stern-faced people were seated around the table. All were solemn and glum, as if gathered there for some mournful occasion.

Sowell, who must have known better, didn't bother to introduce us to this group of negotiators. Instead, he abruptly left the room, leaving Dot and me standing there awkwardly, the target of eight pairs of unfriendly eyes.

Being a woman, Dot, of course, couldn't be allowed to sit at the table with the rest of us, but had to be placed in a far corner of the room. I was permitted to sit alongside the others.

The strategy seemed to be to keep us ill at ease and intimidated, because I began to be assaulted from all sides with regard to items in the contract they wanted changed. I refused to budge on any of the items or to adjust any of them downward.

Seeing I wasn't going to capitulate, one of the guys abruptly raised his hand and hollered, "Conference!"

At that, the whole bunch trooped mechanically out of the room like a bunch of tenpins. It was a remarkable, seemingly well-rehearsed performance and was disconcerting for both of us since we had never witnessed anything of the kind before.

After a short interval, they filed back in and began badgering me again.

"Look," one of them declared, referring to a clause in the contract, "you're asking for $15 a night per truck to keep it in warm storage in Fairbanks. Jeez, I can get storage here in New Joizy for t'ree dollars a night."

The temperature in my thermometer kept moving steadily toward the boiling point. "That may be so," I said, "but here in New Jersey, when you open the garage doors, it isn't 45 degrees below zero outside. Keeping a vehicle from freezing when it's that cold in Alaska is costly, and $15 is not unreasonable."

None of them seemed to like the fact that once again I was refusing to budge. I was getting glares and an icy, awkward silence had set in. They persisted in the annoying questions and attacks, and it wasn't long before I had it way up to here with that meeting.

Wanting no more of it, in the midst of a hostile lull, I called over to Dot and said, "Well, Honey, what would you say?"

She came through admirably. In a loud, clear voice she declared, "I'd tell 'em all to go to hell! Let's go back to Alaska!"

Her marvelously delivered bombshell seemed to leave them all thunderstruck and shocked. And then it seemed to bring them to their senses, because suddenly they warmed perceptibly and were conciliatory and apologetic. Where before nothing was right about the contract, suddenly nothing was wrong. Now, they saw no reason why it couldn't be approved with a handshake, and why we couldn't all get along like one big happy family.

Despite their belated efforts at mending fences, I still couldn't condone the unforgivable way we had been treated. The needless trip and the rudeness we had been subjected to continued to irk me for a long time.

This bunch of so-called "top executives" had to be about the sorriest collection of human beings I'd ever run into. As I looked at them, I couldn't see a red corpuscle in the bunch. And their behavior was in sharp contrast to that of the people I had been used to dealing with at Western Electric.

When we left New Jersey, I was dejected. I wondered, what kind of a mess are we in? If the job's going to be run by people like that, it will be hell. The whole affair left a bitter taste and was getting us off on the wrong foot, through no fault of our own.

Nevertheless, we buckled down to perform the contract, just as if nothing had happened.

At first, the job seemed to be going pretty well. Our smaller planes and the DC-3s on the DEW line were handling, with apparent efficiency, cargo distribution from the main supply hubs of Barter Island and Point Barrow.

Unsettling things, however, began to happen.

One day I got a call from Bill Towsley, Federal Electric's local manager at Ladd Field (now Fort Wainwright).

"I've got to see you right away about a serious problem up on the DEW line," he said.

When I got to his office, he told me he had information that liquor, forbidden anywhere on the DEW line, was making its way to personnel in the DEW line camps.

"That liquor, Jim, is coming off your airplanes," Towsley said. "This has to be stopped — and fast. We just can't let it go on. Do anything you have to, but put an end to it."

I promised immediate action and got on it right away. A thorough investigation revealed that one of our C-46 captains had a cozy little business going on the side. He was smuggling in booze and selling it at high prices to DEW line construction workers. The evidence I was able to obtain about his bootlegging was conclusive and unassailable.

In cahoots with cargo handlers in Fairbanks and at the sites, he had arranged to place, regularly, several cases of whiskey into the belly of the airplane when it was loaded in Fairbanks. Accomplices at Point Barrow and Barter Island would assist in the unloading and distribution. They were selling a fifth costing $15 in Fairbanks for $30 or more up in the arctic. On top of his flying pay, the pilot was raking in a lot of money.

What I found out about this pilot was jolting and distressing, and it hurt me. He was an excellent pilot and had a likeable personality. Now he was faced with immediate dismissal and possible criminal charges.

When he found out that his illicit operation had been discovered, he struck back in a way he figured might save his job. Having flown for a number of non-skeds, he had become familiar with union activity. Now, in deep trouble, he made a lightning pitch to the Teamsters union. He suggested that the Teamsters unionize our DEW line pilots, and the Teamsters eagerly accepted.

Not long afterward, Jess Carr, the Teamsters boss for Alaska, came to my office. Exuding friendliness, he placed a two-inch-thick contract on the desk in front of me.

"Jim," he said, smiling broadly, "when you sign this contract, Wien will be No. 2."

After looking it over, I responded, "If Wien signs, then they are going to be No. 1, because I'm not going to sign it."

Leafing through it, I had seen it was a United Airlines pilots' agreement that had been hastily rewritten. By no stretch of the imagination could this rehash possibly fit our operations. It called for pilots to bid and to be awarded their bases according to seniority. This would mean we would have to assign all our junior pilots to the toughest jobs. And the inevitable result would be a rash of accidents.

I tried to explain my objections to Carr, but he either wasn't listening or didn't want to listen. Apparently, he wasn't in the least concerned with air safety.

At my outright rejection of the contract, Carr's smiles and friendliness switched instantly to livid anger. Mad as hell, he began throwing out all kinds of threats. And he warned me that my refusal to sign was going to destroy our airline.

As Carr stormed out of the office, I was thinking, "You S.O.B. We're going to outlast you!"

And we have. ✝

Snapshot Memories

Wien Airlines pilots Billy English and KeithHarrington in front of Magoffin's Howard at Fishwheel, 1949.

Territorial and State Sen. John Butrovich Jr. with ducks at Healy Lake, Alaska. The airplane behind him is a Grumman Widgeon, covered to avoid frost.

"Yukon Ice" Airport at Fishwheel, Alaska, October 1949. A Wien Airlines Norseman is parked behind the Howard.

*This 1928 Beech Travel Air 6000 was used by Interior Airways on the DEW line and throughout Alaska —
on wheels, skis and floats.*

*Jim Magoffin with Jim Jr. in front of Interior Airways' first Grumman Widgeon at the Transocean Airlines
hangar, Boeing Field, Seattle, Washington, in 1952.*

*Interior Airways' planes at Point Barrow, winter 1954. From left: Beech Bonanza, Aeronca Sedan and
Norseman.*

Top left: Mike Bergt — always ready to go fishing — holding a lake trout.

Top right: Jess Bachner, Fairbanks Aircraft Service mechanic and owner, who rescued me on two occasions.

Mario Fontana (left) displays Kingsford, Michigan, briquets with trophies at Schrader Lake, Alaska.

Bush pilots — old and new: Archie Ferguson and Dot Magoffin at Kotzebue, Alaska, 1951.

Dottie Magoffin — cocky but careful bush pilot with her own Cessna-185, 1969.

Interior Airways accountant Fred Schikora (left) and attorney Dick Cole with ducks bagged on an early October hunt at Minto.

Top left: Western Electric Co.'s senior vice president at Schrader Lake, August 1953. Vern Banall was often referred to as the "Father of the DEW line."

Top right: Butchering a moose is a big job, especially if he drops on swampy ground. This one yielded 800 pounds of delicious meat.

Our Grumman Widgeons transported geologists and supplies throughout the arctic. The pilot is Clint Schoenleber.

"The Dewliner," Interior Airways' first DC-3, N46496. This plane put in 16 years of hard work for Interior before being sold. Here it is shown on takeoff at Point Barrow.

Ralph Brumbaugh, Louie Metoyer and Jim Hutchison. Most of Interiors' employees participated in Alaska's clean, healthful outdoor sports.

In Alaska, the secret to eating well is shooting straight. Dot Magoffin downed this blacktail buck on Shuyak Island, Alaska.

Pilot Pete Cessnun of Ketchikan's Webber Air flew us to good steelhead fishing.

Alaska's premier aircraft mechanic, James T. Hutchison Sr. "Hutch," in his office at Interior Airways, Fairbanks, Alaska.

Summer or winter, bush pilots gotta eat. Dot Magoffin with a northern pike.

Peaches at Anaktuvuk Pass, Alaska. Most of these people had never seen a fresh peach. At right is Richfield Oil Co. Vice President Jim Wilson.

New name, same company, same people. A MarkAir Boeing 737 in maintenance at the Fairbanks hangar, 1992.

Top left: Mike Hamilton (right), construction manager for Puget Sound and Drake, with associate on the DEW line, Spring 1953. Top right: Dot Magoffin's shore lunches were always feasts.

Aviation gasoline in cases for a Texaco geology party being unloaded by pilot Bob Jacobs. Aircraft is a DeHavilland Beaver. Arctic Slope, Alaska, 1961.

Unloading from one of Interior's Fairchild C-82's at Sagwon, 1966.

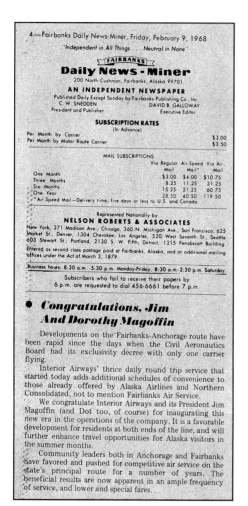

4—Fairbanks Daily News-Miner, Friday, February 9, 1968

"Independent in All Things . . . Neutral in None"

FAIRBANKS
Daily News - Miner
200 North Cushman, Fairbanks, Alaska 99701

AN INDEPENDENT NEWSPAPER

Published Daily Except Sunday by Fairbanks Publishing Co., Inc.

C. W. SNEDDEN   DAVID B. GALLOWAY
President and Publisher   Executive Editor

SUBSCRIPTION RATES
(In Advance)

Per Month by Carrier	$3.00
Per Month by Motor Route Carrier	$3.50

MAIL SUBSCRIPTIONS

	Via Regular Mail	Air-Speed Mail*	Via Air Mail
One Month	$3.00	$4.00	$10.75
Three Months	8.25	11.25	31.25
Six Months	15.25	21.25	60.75
One Year	28.50	40.50	119.50

* Air-Speed Mail—Delivery time, five days or less to U.S. and Canada.

Represented Nationally by
NELSON ROBERTS & ASSOCIATES

New York, 271 Madison Ave.; Chicago, 360 N. Michigan Ave.; San Francisco, 625 Market St.; Denver, 1304 Cherokee; Los Angeles, 520 West Seventh St.; Seattle 603 Stewart St.; Portland, 2130 S. W. Fifth; Detroit, 1215 Penobscott Building.

Entered as second class postage paid at Fairbanks, Alaska, and at additional mailing offices under the Act of March 3, 1879.

Business hours: 8:30 a.m. -5:30 p.m. Monday-Friday, 8:30 a.m.-2:30 p.m. Saturday.

Subscribers who fail to receive their papers by 6 p.m. are requested to dial 456-6661 before 7 p.m.

● *Congratulations, Jim And Dorothy Magoffin*

Developments on the Fairbanks-Anchorage route have been rapid since the days when the Civil Aeronautics Board had its exclusivity decree with only one carrier flying.

Interior Airways' thrice daily round trip service that started today adds additional schedules of convenience to those already offered by Alaska Airlines and Northern Consolidated, not to mention Fairbanks Air Service.

We congratulate Interior Airways and its President Jim Magoffin (and Dot too, of course) for inaugurating this new era in the operations of the company. It is a favorable development for residents at both ends of the line, and will further enhance travel opportunities for Alaska visitors in the summer months.

Community leaders both in Anchorage and Fairbanks have favored and pushed for competitive air service on the state's principal route for a number of years. The beneficial results are now apparent in an ample frequency of service, and lower and special fares.

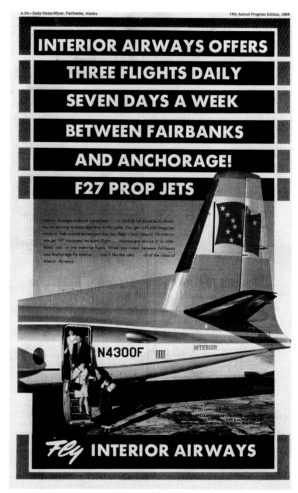

A-24—Daily News-Miner, Fairbanks, Alaska   18th Annual Progress Edition, 1968

INTERIOR AIRWAYS OFFERS
THREE FLIGHTS DAILY
SEVEN DAYS A WEEK
BETWEEN FAIRBANKS
AND ANCHORAGE!
F27 PROP JETS

N4300F   INTERIOR

Fly INTERIOR AIRWAYS

1968, when Interior Airways began offering daily flights between Fairbanks and Anchorage: (From top, left) Editorial from the Feb. 4, 1968, edition of the Fairbanks Daily News-Miner, advertisement from the same newspaper; and (at bottom) Laura Bergt and State Sen. John Sackett at the Anchorage Interior Airways' reservation and ticket desk.

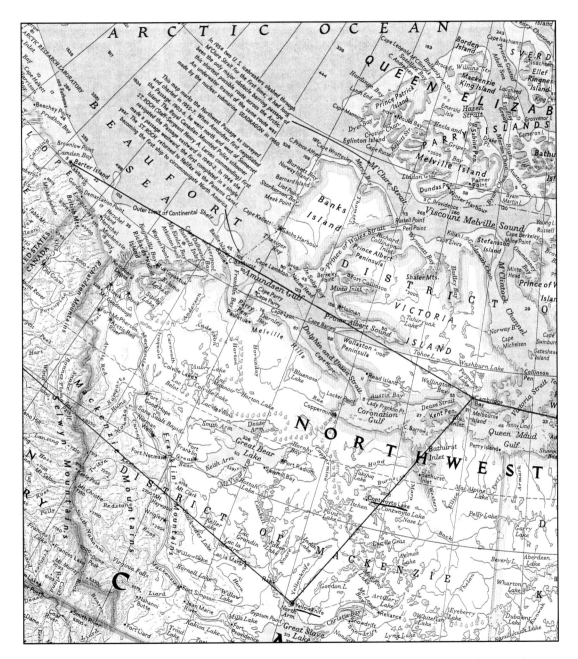

Flights carrying DEW line officials took Interior Airways far into the Canadian Arctic Islands and as far south as Yellowknife, Northwest Territories. Twenty years later, Interiors' Hercules planes carried on extensive cargo operations throughout the Canadian arctic.

*Right: Dick Roberts,
Interior's maintenance and
engineering vice president,
with a trophy buck at Tom
Culhane's camp at Stump
Lake, Montague Island,
Alaska.*

*Below: Jim Magoffin Jr. with
blacktail bucks taken at
Saltery Lake Lodge, Kodiak
Island, Alaska.*

Salesmen Dick Lankford (left) and Don Webster pitch their respective planes at the Magoffins' dinner table.

Old friends at Minto: Peter John and Elsie with Alaska's U.S. Sen. Frank Murkowski. Peter John, age 93, is the Traditional Chief of the Tanana Chiefs.

Jim Magoffin Jr., wife Elrita and sons David and Brent with their faithful retriever, Cessna, at the Minto Duck Camp.

Dot Magoffin and Alabama guest Voncile Jordan with a king salmon at Saltery Lake.

Alaskan "Dude" Brian Murkowski (left) bagged this gobbler on his first Alabama turkey hunt. Guide Noah Smith is at right.

Jim Magoffin says Alabama whitetailed deer are larger than Alaska blacktails — and much wilder.

240 years of Alaskan aviation: Jim Hutchison at 92; Dot Magoffin, age unknown; and Bill Munz at 81.

Jim Magoffin at his 75th birthday party along with his pal, Lulu.

Time together: the real blessing of retirement. Jim and Dot Magoffin can now make up for weeks and months in the bush or overseas. Their winters are spent in Alabama; summers in Alaska.

CHAPTER 31

Strike!

The unprovoked strike unleashed against us by the Teamsters had a tragic and terrible fallout. The deepest scars left after the dispute were those caused by the subsequent deaths of three of the striking pilots in three separate air tragedies.

We had never lost our regard for these fine young men, and I couldn't help but think that things might have been different for them had they stayed on the job.

Not only the three pilots who lost their lives after the strike was over, but all who went out on strike, suffered to some degree from the walkout. There were no winners and plenty of losers. The overall cost in terms of bitterness and turmoil was high. So there was no satisfaction on our part when the pickets gradually disappeared and the needless strike passed into history.

The pilots who had gone out on strike were eventually forced to go to work elsewhere. Some found themselves working for unfamiliar, uncontrolled operations where different standards of maintenance and safety prevailed. Under such circumstances, accidents could be expected. Yet we were unprepared for the news of the separate fatal accidents that later took the lives of the three fine young pilots.

When the end came for Buzz Sheldon, he was flying one of Wien's Cessnas. According to the official report, he was overcome while aloft by carbon monoxide escaping into the cockpit from a defective cabin heater. His death saddened us all.

Jack Hovland, a personable young man from the Midwest, was making fine progress with us when he decided to join the strike. Always meticulously dressed and well-groomed as if he'd stepped from the pages of *Esquire*, Jack was often referred to by his fellow pilots as "Dirty Jack."

After the strike deprived Jack of his job with Interior Airways, he was out of work until he started flying polar bear hunters out of Point Barrow, a very high-risk operation.

The circumstances surrounding Jack's final flight were especially shocking. He was trying to land on too-thin polar ice when it collapsed. His plane was swallowed up by the dark, icy ocean.

Jack's only passenger, a big, strong dude hunter, managed to get out of the plane and swim to safety, but Jack was trapped in the submerged aircraft and he drowned.

Bobby Fischer was a fine, well-liked young pilot. After the walkout ended, Bobby decided to remain at Point Barrow, where he had been stationed. He later took a job with the Arctic Research Laboratory there. Ultimately, he began flying the Aero Commander that took him to his death in a takeoff accident at Point Barrow.

If Buzz, Jack and Bobby can be considered casualties of the strike, then surely they paid far too high a price for their one serious error in judgment. While they were with us, they had been good, capable employees. And when they died, each in his turn, we mourned for them, along with their families and friends.

When it was all over, when the dust settled, it was time for lots of soul-searching and conscience-examining. I am as convinced now, as I was then, that short of outright capitulation to the union, there was absolutely nothing we could have done to avert the walkout. And capitulation, I was convinced, would have been disastrous for our business, an organization that was the product of years of uphill struggle. Had we caved in, it would have meant the end of Interior Airways.

Turning over crucial decision-making to the Teamsters would, I am convinced, have inevitably led to heavy financial losses and, unquestionably, more accidents.

Our only alternative was to resist, to fight every step of the way. We had to fight tooth and nail to keep our planes flying. In this, fortunately, we had the support of our more mature, experienced pilots who remained on the job and continued to be the backbone of our work force. It wasn't easy for them to tell the union to go to hell. That made them the target of all kinds of intimidation, name-calling, demonstrations and threats.

Having these fine, loyal men on our side gave us tremendous reassurance and bolstered our resistance to the union's unrelenting pressure. And we had to fight more when the Teamsters dragged the dispute into court.

In the years since the strike, I have thought about it a lot. Out of all this reflection has come one primary conclusion: Our firm simply didn't deserve it.

Right from the start, we tried to treat our employees as we would want to be treated. We considered our role in the employee-management picture as far more than just being responsible for providing a regular paycheck to our employees. We were genuinely concerned about them as individuals and did our best to help them solve personal, financial and other problems. Although the fact that several of them went out on strike seems to contradict this, I think we were successful in building a kind of family atmosphere that was marked by mutual respect and mutual regard.

We provided our employees with many valuable perks not enjoyed by employees of other companies. For example, we often advanced sizeable "no-interest" loans so employees could make down payments on new homes. Occasionally, when warranted, we forgave loans.

Further, I flew as much as time permitted and *always* took the trips that involved any hint of risk, such as questionable landing areas, and I "broke in" the younger pilots on how to safely make landings on frozen lakes, ocean beaches and river bars.

Interior employees were given free use of hunting and fishing camps, including use of airplanes, boats and motors. They and their families received free company transportation to and from the camps. We encouraged these clean, healthful activities.

Everything considered, at the time the strike broke out, our employees were enjoying a far superior job "package" than that offered by some other airlines. All this was callously ignored and discounted when the Teamsters launched their strike.

After picketing started, the Teamsters started giving our people a bad time. And it wasn't only the pilots who were subjected to constant intimidation. The drivers of our two big trucks were also right in the middle of it. They were subjected to demonstrations as they hauled cargo from Ladd Field to Fairbanks International Airport, where the cargo was warehoused before being flown to DEW line sites.

Fear was regularly used as a weapon against those who chose to stay on the job. In the first couple of days, demonstrations were so alarming that one of our captains wanted to carry a rifle in his car for self-protection as he drove to and from the airport.

Charlie Cole, Interior Airways, Inc.'s attorney and executive vice president. Here, in 1958, Charlie is hunting ducks at the Minto camp.

When he asked me about it, I told him I was dead set against it. "No matter what happens," I told him, "I don't want any gunplay. Leave your gun at home."

When the strike began, the North's blistering cold proved to be an ally. The 45- degree-below-zero weather was so miserable that few of the pickets the Teamsters had hired were enthusiastic about walking the picket line.

Being forced to fire striking employees was one of the hardest things I have ever had to do in my life. Yet I had to bite the bullet. The Teamsters reacted immediately by filing grievances with the National Labor Relations Board (NLRB).

With a serious court battle looming, we needed a good lawyer to run interference for us. Our attorney friend, Chuck Clasby, felt he could not represent us as he was Wien's attorney. He suggested we contact Charlie Cole, and Cole proved perfect for our needs. Though we had been in business for years, it was the first time we had found it necessary to put an attorney on retainer.

Cole proved to be a highly skilled, fearless, colorful and tough young lawyer. At the time he agreed to represent us, he was caught up in a far more spectacular case involving a hotheaded young homesteader who had been trying to get a squatter kicked off his property.

The essence of the story was as follows:

When the defiant squatter pitched a tent, the homesteader visited Cole's office to see what the attorney could do to eject the man.

At the time, Cole was preoccupied with a stack of papers on his desk.

"Now this guy just pitched his tent and says he'll stay 'til hell freezes over," the bewildered homesteader began telling Cole. "What am I gonna do?"

Without looking up, Cole mumbled, "You oughta *shoot* the S.O.B"

Before Cole could say anything else, the homesteader was gone. He reappeared a short time later to announce: "Well, Mr. Cole, I just did it!"

"Did what?" Cole asked.

"Did exactly what you told me to do. I shot the sonovabitch!"

Charlie Cole had to perform some real fancy footwork to extricate himself and his client from that terrible situation. Meanwhile, he agreed to take our case.

In the years to come, Cole became interested and absorbed in our entire operation. He obtained his pilot's license and frequently flew our small planes. He started spending more and more time at our office and was obviously far more interested in airline operations than in the tedious, mundane chores of his everyday legal practice.

Knowing this, I later made him executive vice president of our firm and moved him right into the office with me. This gave us the benefit of his excellent advice and guidance on a daily basis.

He fit into our operations like a glove. Whenever I was absent, he was right there to take charge of the extensive, complex activity that was swamping us during this period, and he did much of the needed travelling. His help was invaluable in representing our firm on numerous matters, including negotiating leases for the additional Hercules we required.

Right now, though, he began providing the legal clout in our crucial court dealings with the NLRB. That prolonged fight began consuming a lot of our time — and money. In addition to his help on NLRB matters, Cole pitched in on countless other complications that kept springing up. It was good having him around at a time, for example, when the CAA was all over us as they were known to be when labor strife threatened to cripple an airline.

Cole's leadership helped us through frustrating weeks in court defending ourselves against the NLRB action.

The usually boring hearings were occasionally enlivened by lighter moments.

We contended at one point that, since we were hauling the mail, we came under the Railway Labor Act, thus the NLRB had no jurisdiction over us.

A red-headed captain, the postal officer at Ladd Field, was testifying on this aspect and was answering questions when the judge interrupted the proceedings to clarify a point.

The captain turned sharply and stared at the judge, then asked, "Hey, whose side are you on anyway?"

The laughter that followed temporarily eased a situation that had been tense and serious.

After all kinds of legal maneuvering back and forth, the NLRB ruled against us and for the Teamsters. This was a heavy blow. I came away from the hearings with the impression that partiality had been shown. Moreover, I felt sufficient consideration hadn't been given to the fact that a criminal bootlegging operation had been at the heart of the labor dispute.

Circuit Court Rules For *1-4-62* Interior Airways on Dispute

The Ninth Circuit Court of Appeals last week ruled in favor of Interior Airways in a labor dispute case stretching back to 1957.

The case involved a strike against the airline by 15 pilots who claimed they were illegally terminated and charged Interior Airways with unfair labor practices.

The recent decision completely exonerates Interior Airways from the charges and is considered a major victory for local attorney, Charles Cole, who represented the company.

In the four years of continuous litigation, the case was first held in favor of Interior Airways, then reversed, and now it has been reversed back to the original finding.

The vicious Teamsters' strike finally comes to an end.

Losing the NLRB case dealt us a shattering psychological blow. I got to thinking about this serious setback, the strike, and other headaches we had to contend with and wondered whether we ought to close down the entire operation and go into some other less-troublesome kind of business.

Fortunately, Cole offered his typically wise counsel against throwing in the towel. He promised to act immediately to bring the case under the jurisdiction of San Francisco's 9th Circuit Court of Appeals. He pointed out that if we appealed, there was an excellent possibility that the Alaska decision might be reversed.

That is exactly what happened. In the new jurisdiction, the Teamsters lost and we won. That victory gave us new resolve to dig in and get on with our business.

It helped, also, that Federal Electric, from the outset, was understanding about our predicament. When the strike began, I was afraid we might lose our contract but this, fortunately, didn't happen. I hustled out to Ladd Field to discuss it with Federal Electric's Bill Towsley. To my surprise, he wasn't a bit shook up since, apparently, he had seen labor conflicts erupt before. "Just do the best you can, Jim," he told me.

It also was fortunate that we were able to obtain replacement pilots from Alaska and the lower states after word got around that we were hiring.

Our first new hire was a young kid from Anchorage, Neil Bergt, who was just 21 years old and had barely obtained the 200 flying hours needed for his commercial pilot's license.

Though Bergt was far short of the 2,000 flying hours that we normally required, he appeared bright and enthusiastic, and I felt we could start him flying our smallest and simplest airplane, a Piper Cub, and gradually advance him to larger planes, which we did.

The next pilot who showed up was Paul Palmer, a highly experienced, very capable man who later became our chief pilot. It helped a lot that Palmer was already checked out in DC-3s and C-46s, because this enabled him to start flying for us immediately.

Pilots like Palmer, Rice, Charlie Hubbs, Fred McGuire and Bob Jacobs along with other seasoned, dedicated employees, helped keep our operation functioning smoothly at a highly critical time. We were fortunate to have every one of them.

Neil Bergt — Interior Airways pilot since 1957 — fishing silver salmon at "Hell's Hole," Prince William Sound, Alaska.

It was the younger, less-experienced pilots who had been the most susceptible to Teamster propaganda. They were brainwashed, and the rug was pulled out from under them. And, as I have related, it was these fine young men who suffered the most.

All the tragedy, suffering and trouble experienced by strikers and loyal employees alike can be traced directly back to the deeds of one irresponsible man, our former C-46 captain. His greed, bootlegging and union agitation generated an incredible furor. His actions were the underlying cause of the triple tragedies I've described.

What happened to him? After the strike was over, we got word he was alive and well in Los Angeles, though reduced to pumping gas at a service station.

At no time, apparently, did he suffer any pangs of conscience for what he had done to his flying comrades and to our firm. It was clear he was totally blind to the whirlwind of trouble he had caused, because we had it on good authority that he was harboring a vision of maybe getting his job back.

When I heard that, I remember thinking, "Over my dead body." ✛

CHAPTER 32

Down On The Arctic Ice

A moment's inattention can lead to months of salvage, repair expense and lost productivity. Most airplane accidents are avoidable.

Neil Bergt's first assignment with us was flying a Piper Cub to service lateral DEW line sites along the coast east and west of Barrow.

Though he handled this without serious problems, he was involved in several mishaps in larger planes later on, and his record with us did not remain unblemished.

One of Bergt's off-duty exploits was a real hair-raiser and it caused us a sleepless night. Based at Barter Island, Bergt had been checked out in a Cessna 180 on skis. The emergency developed one day in early spring after he had taken off in the Cessna with Bert Stearns, our Barter Island mechanic, to hunt polar bear.

Over the frozen ocean, the pair spotted a polar bear and they landed near it. Bergt took off on foot after the bear and Stearns, who wasn't a qualified company pilot and not an accomplished a pilot to begin with, took off in the 180 to keep the polar bear spotted and Bergt in sight.

Stearns made several mistakes. He failed to keep in mind that there was a strong wind aloft just a couple of hundred feet above the ice. By the time Stearns was airborne and leveled out, the wind had drifted the plane and he lost all trace of both Bergt and the bear.

There was only one thing to do: get back to Barter and get a search organized. Fortunately for Stearns, the radios had been left on and he had sense enough to follow his Automatic Directional Finder (ADF) needle back to Barter.

In Fairbanks late that evening, we got the alarming news that Bergt was lost on the arctic ice. We were shocked. I knew the peril of being out on that polar ice. Visualizing this young pilot at the mercy of the arctic's terrible cold and fierce weather was a horrible sensation.

I had flown in the arctic for a good number of years, and I was well aware how quickly a ground blow could materialize to cut visibility to just a few feet. Such conditions could sock in the ice pack for days. Getting lost in that vast expanse of ice is always life-threatening, and when the weather closes in, chances of finding anybody out there are almost nil. All of us were terribly worried, and few of us slept that night.

Good fortune was with us, however. The night had been quiet and clear, and the weather remained good. Paul Palmer, our chief pilot, was off before daylight in a C-46 with several observers aboard. He flew to Barter, then out over the trackless ice. Visibility was good, and he soon spotted Neil walking around, seemingly none the worse for the incident except for being cold and tired.

Palmer was irate. He was all for firing Bergt immediately. Palmer felt Bergt had shown extremely poor judgment in allowing an unqualified pilot to fly a company airplane. Palmer wanted to discharge Bergt and consulted me.

I decided against it. For one thing, Palmer didn't like Bergt and the feeling was mutual. Their political views were completely opposite, Bergt being a staunch Republican and Palmer a confirmed, outspoken Democrat. Besides, Palmer was known to have a somewhat abrasive personality that made him unpopular with most of the pilots. This unfortunate personality trait led to his ultimate dismissal.

Bergt's own skill as a pilot occasionally left much to be desired. How he was able to wreck the new Twin Beechcraft we had bought from the Navy at Farmingdale, Long Island, remains a puzzle to me. The immaculate plane had just emerged from a Navy IRAN (complete overhaul). It had new engines and props and was so clean I couldn't see a speck of dirt or a drop of oil anywhere on the gleaming aircraft, even under the cowling.

Dot and I flew the airplane to Fairbanks and sent it up to Point Barrow where Bergt started flying it. One day he neglected to lower the landing gear as he was making his approach to one of the airports west of Barrow. The aircraft was equipped with a perfectly functioning landing gear warning horn. For the life of me, I've never been able to understand how any pilot would forget the landing gear with the warning horn sounding off.

That costly crash was a heartbreaker for us and a stunning blow to our then-shaky finances. +

CHAPTER 33

Surrounded By The 'Fuz'

On that bitterly cold winter day in 1961, we had no way of knowing, of course, that our charter flight from Fairbanks to Minneapolis with a planeload of school-teachers was a "target."

Our competitors hoped it would be our last flight. They alerted the "fuz," as we called federal inspectors, and they hoped we would be caught red-handed as far as regulations were concerned. If all went as they hoped, we'd be put out of business once and for all.

Fortunately, we didn't know about our planned demise, otherwise that C-46 charter to give a group of Alaska schoolteachers a head start on their 1961 Christmas vacation would have been a nerve-wracking trip. Thankfully, we were oblivious to the scheme. A festive spirit reigned among the passengers going "home for the holidays." Just about everybody was enjoying the flight.

Meanwhile, the fuz was keeping close track of us from the time we left Fairbanks. They kept monitoring our flight progress as we moved across Canada and into the Midwest. And they were waiting for us at our destination, all primed to throw the book at us.

Some of it was like comedy, some was adventure and some offered suspense.

We had been delighted to get the charter. It was one of the few bright spots in a terribly slow winter businesswise. We badly needed the chunk of revenue this flight would bring.

At first there was nothing particularly unusual about this flight on which I was the captain, Horace Black was the co-pilot and Dot was the stewardess. We were concerned, however, about the strong weather front moving across the western United States. Now we were positioned behind it. Minneapolis airport had been socked in — zero-zero — for hours, so we landed at the airport in Regina, Saskatchewan, to await further weather developments.

When we got word that the front was slowly moving out of the Minneapolis area, we took off and soon were moving across the Dakotas.

Black was as busy as a one-armed paper-hanger, spending a lot of time on the radio monitoring the weather ahead, fine-tuning the navigation and operating the de-icers. For a long time, the possibility of landing at Minneapolis remained a big question mark.

Then Minneapolis radio, at a time when we were just 20 minutes out, reported a 200-foot ceiling and half-mile visibility. That made it legal for us to shoot an approach and land, which we did.

We taxied up to the terminal which, at the time, was just a small building on the west side of the field, and parked. It was 11:30 p.m. The curtain on the drama to follow was about to rise.

Suddenly, the door from the passenger compartment burst open and an alarmed Dot rushed in. "We're surrounded by the fuz!" she exclaimed.

Startled by this introduction to Minneapolis, I glanced out to see a half-dozen Dick Tracy types clustered outside waiting to board the airplane.

Black's face fell. He knew immediately we were in big trouble. There were a number of things the inspectors could nail us on, but we knew there was one principal violation they were after. Strict regulations governed flying an aircraft of our type in instrument weather. Among the things required for this flight was a detailed, running record of the flight's history, including progress, radio contacts and a lot of other stuff. Everything had to be carefully recorded on the proper forms which had to be made available for inspection, if asked for, at our destination.

It so happened that none of this bureaucratic paperwork had been accomplished. Black had been busy checking the weather, operating the de-icers and handling vital radio transmissions, and there was no way he could drop everything to fill in these forms. No question about it, he — and our airline — were backed into a corner. And, as Dot had proclaimed, we were "surrounded by the fuz."

Dot was opening the main entrance door and the inspectors were preparing to storm aboard.

Black looked at me and I looked at him. He seemed paralyzed for a moment. Then he got to his feet, grabbed the flight kit off the floor and rushed to the back of the airplane, where he locked himself in the lavatory.

Now the inspectors were aboard and making their way toward the cockpit. I remained glued to the pilot's seat, braced for what was sure to come.

The inspectors' faces were stern and expressionless. "We want to see your paperwork," one of them said.

I scrambled for an answer. "The co-pilot's got it," I said. "Must be here in his flight kit."

The inspector looked annoyed. "Well!" he said crisply. "Where's the flight kit?"

"I guess — I guess the co-pilot's got it," I stammered.

"And where's the co-pilot?" he demanded, getting irritated.

"He just left."

While the inspectors were busy up front, Black was able to scoot down the steps and vanish into the night.

We didn't see Black again until we met several days later to go back to Alaska.

After his whirlwind escape from the plane, he had taken the flight kit and checked into a motel. There, for the next couple of days, he busied himself with drawing up an immaculate set of flight records, including all the countless details that were supposed to have been covered. It was a masterpiece of contrivance by a man who thought fast when cornered and devised a way to pull off a narrow escape.

Black knew a lot was at stake. He was fully aware that if the fuz had nailed us, we would have had one hell of a struggle to retain our certificate. This time, however, a calculated plan to shoot us down had failed by only a hair's breadth. It was a shame that he and the rest of us had to go through these heart-stopping maneuvers just to survive.

The odds against us had been merciless, and staying in business had always been a struggle for us. Each time we went in to renew our annual certificate, we were worried sick that we'd be turned down. Several times the authorities threatened to do just that.

Times kept getting tougher for non-skeds like us. To keep our certificate, we were required to provide annual proof of financial responsibility at a time when we were struggling to keep our finances in good shape.

The FAA kept looking with a jaundiced eye at the non-skeds because throughout the United States their safety record was far from satisfactory. Like us, most non-sked operators were flying war surplus aircraft. Some operators weren't up to snuff on maintenance and training. Accidents proliferated to such an extent that the FAA decided to send out "blue ribbon" inspection teams throughout the country to give non-sked operations a thorough going-over. Blue ribbon team members were tough. They looked for the slightest excuse to cancel a non-sked certificate, perhaps on the theory that this would be a contribution to flight safety. Certificated airline people kept feeding the federal teams tips on how to nail non-skeds. These small operators were being assaulted constantly from all sides.

Once a blue ribbon team nailed us on the wheels we were using on our C-46s. These wheels were the same size as those used on Boeing B-17s. The B-17 wheels, made of an aluminum alloy, were stronger and better and only a few pounds heavier than the original magnesium alloy C-46 wheels.

We put B-17 wheels on our C-46s, but didn't go to the trouble of plowing through the mountains of paperwork and doing the extensive testing required to get the B-17 wheels certificated. This meant we were illegal using them, though everybody admitted they were better.

As soon as the blue ribbon team left town, we took the magnesium wheels off and put the B-17 wheels back on. I'm sure our local FAA people knew what we had done, but didn't bother us about it.

The arrival of a blue ribbon team at your place of business could send a cold chill down your back. It was never pleasant. On one occasion, one of the teams spent several days snooping around our business when the time came for renewal of our certificate.

Team members rode with our pilots, checked our maintenance and record-keeping and delved into our administration and finances.

At the conclusion of their penetrating inspection, four blue ribbon inspectors converged on my office.

"How do things look?" I asked, on pins and needles.

"Not bad," one of them told me, "except for a few minor discrepancies. Not bad at all."

Yet, when they got back to Washington, they wrote a nasty report on us. Their recommendation was that our certificate not be renewed.

I immediately asked for a hearing with the FAA's regional director in Anchorage. Dot and I attended the hearing set up at FAA's regional headquarters in the Hill Building.

We were confronted with a whole passel of FAA officials all set to tell us how we had stumbled. We were told that inspectors found a propeller that was 300 hours over the allowable time between overhauls.

On the surface, it looked like we were guilty of a serious safety violation. I explained that Wien had needed a C-46 propeller, and we loaned them our spare. They ran it for several months, then returned it to us. They entered one figure in the log book for the flight time on that propeller. The propeller had actually been used more than the number of hours they had indicated. This was probably an unintentional mistake on Wien's part, something we had nothing to do with. But we were the owners of the propeller and had put it back on one of our C-46s and were still flying it when the FAA caught the discrepancy. We had a tough time getting out of that one despite the reasonable explanation.

We practically had to get down on our knees and beg those guys to renew our certificate, something that was humiliating as hell for us.

As I looked around the room, I could hardly keep from getting angry. The more I thought about it, the more incensed I became. We had been struggling for many years, knocking ourselves out seven days a week and investing a lot of money in Alaska's economy. After doing all that, I now found myself surrounded by a bunch of government employees, most of whom had never done a day's hard work of the kind we took for granted. They had never invested a dime in aviation nor provided a job for anybody. Now they were ganging up on us and trying to shut us down. It was a frustrating situation.

Weldon Bell (left), FAA maintenance inspector, in front of our third C-82. Bell was one of the "good guys" — strict, fair and practical.

They finally relented and renewed our certificate. I think the only reason they did it was because they knew if they didn't, I'd be heading for Washington again and the only thing most of them had much respect for was Washington power. This time, they probably wouldn't have had to worry because now my Washington contacts were gone and we weren't involved in a critical national defense contract.

My first two meetings in Washington, the first in 1954 with Administrator Fred Lee and the second in 1962 with Administrator Najeeb Halaby, had been successful. Halaby not only assisted us in solving regulatory problems, but displayed a genuine interest in Alaska and our airline. When he later became president of Pan Am, he sent me a lifetime first-class pass on any Pan Am route. This proved valuable when we started our international operation in the early '70s and I was required to travel extensively in Europe, Africa and Australia. I invited Halaby to Alaska to enjoy the superb fishing, but he hasn't made it yet.

Though generally our relations with the FAA during the '60s were not too good, we enjoyed some good years when some outstanding people were assigned to the Alaska regional office and the Fairbanks field office.

Some of the best FAA people we dealt with were fellows like Don Gretzer and Joe Miraldi in the beginning and then Bud Seltenreich. Seltenreich, a pilot himself, had been active in the industry and was genuinely interested in the business and genuinely concerned about aviation safety.

We appreciated guys like that who weren't merely paper shufflers and could be helpful with our problems. They could talk with us in a knowledgeable way about the condition of aircraft, the efficiency of pilots, and how best to promote common sense flying safety.

Typical of this exceptional FAA breed was Weldon Bell, a maintenance inspector who was one prince of a guy. Also, one hell of a fine fellow was Jay McCausland, who became chief of the Fairbanks Flight Standards office.

Jay had a distinctly non-bureaucratic way of dealing with the industry. Occasionally at meetings with him, he would politely give me hell. Then, when he realized I'd gotten the message, he would say something like, "Jim, I guess your communication with your people just isn't what it should be. See if you can improve it."

And this would let me off the hook.

Bill Reynolds, also first class, was among those who came along and took charge of the Fairbanks office. Though he was strict and kept us in line, we respected him. He got along well with Ralph Brumbaugh in our maintenance department, as well as with the rest of our people.

Anchorage regional office people were regularly troublesome. They were on the receiving end of constant complaints from scheduled airline officials who kept crying about the things they said we were doing wrong. They were constantly nit-picking and charging that in one way or another we were overstepping the bounds of our certificate.

We always tried to comply fully with regulations as long as they weren't injurious to our business. We had to walk a fine line between what the bureaucrats thought we should do and what we had to do to run a safe, efficient operation. This didn't endear us to a lot of people in government, but our business survived. ✛

CHAPTER 34

One Hell
Of A Struggle

The early '60s brought terribly tough times for us. DEW line flying had dwindled to next to nothing, leaving us practically jobless. Several times business got so bad we came close to shutting down but, like the saying "It's always darkest before the dawn," something always turned up to save the airline we had been struggling so hard to keep afloat.

Overall, the Alaska business situation was forlorn and grim. Except for scattered geology parties, there was virtually no oil activity either on the North Slope or elsewhere. Mining was almost at a standstill. Passenger travel was suffering. This, for example, was before the bountiful Native Land Claims settlement provided Alaska's natives with money for travel and for other things that for years had been out of their reach.

It was an incredibly tough situation. And it was also, in a way, a challenge for those, like us, who refused to quit.

Around us, businesses were biting the dust. We were hanging on as we had done so many times before. For us, it was a time to batten down the hatches. Interior Airways became a bare-bones operation. Expenses were given the closest scrutiny. Pay scales were adjusted, leveling out a little on the low side, yet we never had a check bounce. We never missed a payday.

The way we did business helped. Everything we owned was debt-free. Our bank balance was maintained at a healthy level. Our credit rating — both in Alaska and in the Lower 48 — was impeccable, something that helped a lot at a time when we were trying to do more with less.

During this period, Jim Dunlap, one of our pilots, summed up the kind of crunch we were in. After juggling figures in the pilots' ready room, he announced, "I've just figured out that with our 17 pilots, we're 23 pilots short in terms of normal airline standards."

We dug and scrambled and beat the brush for business. When Rudy Voigt, a Fairbanks sportsman, got the idea for ferrying a planeload of outdoorsmen to South Dakota to hunt pheasants, we pounced on this chance to make a few bucks. Rudy's newspaper advertising helped collect 48 hunters from Fairbanks, Anchorage and Nome. Just before Thanksgiving vacation, this happy throng, along with yelping dogs, showed up for an unforgettable trip.

Dot went along as stewardess and we treated our boys to this special hunting trip. Our general manager, Roy Isackson, came up with the idea that everybody on

Daily News - Miner

Fairbanks Daily News-Miner, Saturday, December 2, 1961 — 5

Edited By
JO ANNE WOLD

Social events, organizational news, personal items of interest are welcomed by your woman's page. To contact your new woman's editor,

Please Phone GLobe 2-1400

Or write the "who's, what's, where's and when's" to her at the following address: Jo Anne Wold, Woman's Editor, c/o Fairbanks Daily News-Miner, 514 Second Ave., Fairbanks.

Four Women Bag Pheasants

"Last Saturday, our last day of hunting, it was sixty above. Just perfect for hunting!" said Mrs. James Magoffin, one of the four women who went to South Dakota for the annual pheasant hunting trip during the Thanksgiving holidays.

Other women making the trip were Mrs. Art Hayr, Mrs. John Butrovich, and Mrs. George VanWyhe.

Dorothy, as she is known to her many hunting and flying friends (and to her non-hunting and flying friends) bagged the limit, twenty-five birds.

The trip this year was made in a C-46 and was filled to capacity.

The annual pheasant hunt began several years ago as a family affair. Jim and Dorothy Magoffin and their two sons are not only avid outdoorsmen (and woman), but they flit around in their own planes as if it was common to fly several hundred miles in one day to go fishing or hunting.

The first trip to hunt pheasant was strictly a Magoffin trip. The next year a good friend wanted to go along so a larger plane was used. The following year a couple more friends wanted to make the trip on a share the cost basis so a plane with a larger seating capacity was flown.

The passenger list grew and grew until this years' plane carried a total of forty-seven people and three dogs, all black laborador retrievers.

Eight of these passengers were hunters from Anchorage and two came from Palmer.

Mrs. VanWyhe and her husband came up from Glennallen to make the trip.

the trip should carry stacks of two-dollar bills which, when they began circulating in Huron, South Dakota, were soon all over town, putting Alaskans in the limelight.

The South Dakota pheasant hunt became an annual affair. It was thoroughly enjoyed by the hunters and helped bring in a few dollars to our business at a time when we needed the money most.

We were constantly on the lookout for new business. A small Alaska Road Commission contract for hauling fuel to the May Creek landing strip southeast of Gulkana was a shot in the arm. The first load went direct from Fairbanks to May Creek. Subsequent flights were made from the Gulkana airport where the Road Commission stockpiled the fuel.

The job went well with Ralph Brumbaugh flying as my co-pilot. Ralph was so husky he could sling full barrels around almost as if they were empty.

Knowing the job would take several days, Dot drove our family car to Gulkana, taking along our two boys. After they got there, Jimmy, our older son, began running a high fever and complained of stomach pains. The local medic urged that he be rushed to the hospital immediately. Jack Wilson, a former Interior Airways pilot who was then operating his own air service out of Gulkana, flew Dot and the two boys to Fairbanks. It was just in time: Jimmy's appendix was about to rupture.

Brumbaugh drove our car back to Fairbanks when the job was finished and I flew the C-46 back solo — strictly against regulations, but convenient.

During these grim times, no job was too small to pursue. In the summertime, when forest fires broke out in the hot, dry interior, we scrambled for firefighting flights, hauling crews from the villages

Dot, an avid huntress and crack shot, always enjoyed the South Dakota pheasant charters.

and dropping smoke-jumpers and equipment into fire areas. One of the people we worked with on these missions, Gary White, a Bureau of Land Management dispatcher, later joined Interior Airways and set up our dispatch system.

We were thankful for a small Corps of Engineers contract flying fuel to the site of the proposed Rampart Dam. We used C-46s on this job, with miles of runway at our destination. We landed on the ice-covered Yukon right in Rampart Canyon, where fierce canyon winds kept the frozen surface swept clean of snow.

Construction of the Ballistic Missile Early Warning Station (BMEWS) at Clear proved a real shot in the arm. Clear was one of several stations designed to provide America with warning of a Soviet missile attack (the DEW line was designed to detect aircraft only). When BMEWS got under way in 1959, America was still in the throes of the Cold War and it was another frantic, hurry-up job requiring air support because the good road between Fairbanks and Anchorage hadn't yet been built.

We dove tooth and nail into the Clear job, throwing in everything we had — DC-3s, C-46s and our small aircraft. Morning, noon and night we shuttled passengers and supplies between Fairbanks and Clear in an operation that functioned smoothly.

Even so, as there always was, there was a hitch. Though we were moving a lot of passengers and generating steady revenue, we knew we were running a scheduled airline without that indispensable certificate authorizing that kind of operation. No question about it — we were in violation and in trouble. Our scheduled airline competitors were yelping at our heels and angrily siccing the government fuz on us.

Clear Air Transport, Inc. — the phony company we created to legalize our scheduled operation.

The way we sashayed around this potentially explosive problem was like a Harvard Business School case history. We had George Foster, a longtime employee resign (on paper) and form a new company at Clear, Clear Air Transport, Inc. George then entered into a contract with us to provide three scheduled flights a day, seven days a week between Fairbanks and Clear, as well as a weekend schedule from Clear to Anchorage. Now, miraculously, to the disgust and annoyance of those thirsting to shoot us down, we were no longer a common carrier, but a firm that was fulfilling a specific contract. This made the operation legal and within the limits of our operating authority.

George set up an office at Clear to book the passengers. We provided ground transportation from the bustling construction site to the Clear airport. Dot Magoffin flew many of the Clear schedules, achieving a remarkable record of safety and on-time operation even though, in that era when there were few women pilots, her presence in the pilot's seat was sometimes disconcerting to her (mostly male) passengers.

Another contract that helped us through those lean times was the one we bid very tightly with the Air Force to haul fuel oil from Eielson Air Force Base to Indian Mountain. This required installing fuel oil tanks in the cargo compartment of a C-46. Associated plumbing in the aircraft held another 200 gallons, giving us a load of 2,200 gallons per flight. That extra 200 gallons, I figured, would probably be our profit for the trip.

Before the Air Force gave us their approval, they sent over an inspection team to evaluate the capability of our airline to transport such a huge tonnage of fuel to the outlying site within the restricted time period of one year.

A skeptical group of Air Force officers strolled into our little Fairbanks hangar to look around. "We're here to inspect the airplanes you plan to use to fulfill this contract," the team leader said. "Can you show us the planes?"

"Sure," I said, pointing out the window to our tired old C-46 cargo plane, N4860V, parked in the grass alongside the hangar. "There it is, gentlemen — right there."

When the C-46 had been towed there, the butt of the wing near the fuselage was positioned right up against a big telephone pole, making it look like the old work horse was leaning on the pole just to keep from falling down. The group studied the plane in amazement.

"You mean you're going to haul all the oil using just that thing? You can't do it," said the group's leader.

"We sure can," I told him.

''How?" he wanted to know.

"Easy," I said. "We'll fly around the clock."

"Impossible!" he protested. "The Indian Mountain strip is a daylight-only field."

"No problem," I said. "We're going to install our own runway lights there."

"I just don't see how you're going to do that," he said, looking at me sternly. "That's a very tricky runway. It sets on the side of a hill. You have to contend with one heckova steep grade. And you mean to tell me you're going to operate around the clock there?"

"That's our plan."

Though they seemed far from fully convinced, they approved us. We lost no time in installing a portable runway lighting system at Indian Mountain. The job went well.

It turned out that the best time to fly to this location was at night. Winter nights in the interior are usually clear and cold, virtually eliminating turbulence. We assigned a crew to each eight-hour shift and usually managed to complete three flights per shift without incident. The Air Force, it turned out, was impressed

Flying as my co-pilot on a good many of these oil hauls was Ralph Brumbaugh, our superintendent of maintenance and a commercial pilot. It was about 48 degrees below zero one night when we landed at Eielson and taxied to our usual spot for picking up fuel.

The procedure was for the fuel oil hose to be plugged into the outlet in the plane's belly through which the internal tanks would be filled, with the gas truck pulling up to the front of the airplane and pumping in enough gas for another round trip.

On this occasion, we got the oil hose plugged in okay but there was no sign of the gas truck. After waiting a long time, we spotted a figure coming toward us through the ice fog. Brumbaugh didn't know it but it was Col. Steve Henry, the base commander. He strolled over along the right side of the aircraft.

Ol' Brumbaugh slid back the cockpit window and hollered: "Where in hell's the gas truck?"

Col. Henry replied, "Yeah, where in hell is it?" He then headed for the operations office. Within a matter of a few minutes the gas truck zipped over. It was never late again.

On one of our Indian Mountain flights we lost a magneto. We radioed ahead for Hutch to bring a spare magneto out to Eielson and he was there a few minutes after we landed.

Getting that spare magneto installed in miserable sub-zero cold required a cooperative effort that reflected the way we had to improvise in the North. The Herman Nelson heater the Air Force furnished us for the job wasn't ideal, but it was all we had. Brumbaugh climbed up the ladder with the spare mag and began to work in the sub-zero cold as I held the heater ducts up his pants legs and under his coat to keep him from freezing. Insulated just a bit from the bitter cold, Brumbaugh managed to get the new mag installed, and a few minutes later we were on our way. We finished our three trips in the allotted eight hours.

Any concern the Air Force had about our capability of doing the job with "that" aircraft gradually vanished. We delivered the specified amount of fuel well in advance of the July 1 contract date. All of it was where the Air Force wanted it by the first week in May.

Our bleak Alaska business situation forced us, at one point, to look outside the state for something to do. Starting a new helicopter service in Seattle was a real roller-coaster for us but we were leaving no stone unturned.

We got word from a Seattle group that they'd welcome the same kind of operation being provided in New York by New York Airways. There was a real need, we were assured, for chopper service between SeaTac airport and downtown Seattle. Suddenly we found ourselves in the helicopter business.

We leased a helicopter from Republic Aviation, the U. S. distributor for the French Alouette, a turbine-powered aircraft designed to carry a pilot and four passengers.

We picked up airline passengers at the SeaTac terminal and shuttled them to

'Copter Taxi Gets Tryout

Aircraft Approaches Department Store

ROOF HELIPORT in downtown Seattle is about to be used on air taxi demonstration flight from Northgate by Sea-Tac Airways craft. Aboard are Wells McCurdy, vice president, and Norman Murray, promotion manager, for the Northgate Co., two television movie cameramen and the pilot, Bob Rice, Sea-Tac Airways vice president and general manager. In the immediate background is the top of the Northwestern Mutual Insurance Bldg. —(Post-Intelligencer Photo by Harvey Davis.)

Our helicopter operation in Seattle was profitable while it lasted.

the heart of downtown Seattle, landing on top of a garage at Third and Pine. Initially, the response from both the public and the airlines was good and the operation flourished.

We soon purchased another chopper of the same type to give us a spare when one was down for maintenance.

Everything went smoothly for several months until the fly in the ointment developed as it usually does.

The Alouette was a fine aircraft but noisy as hell, broadcasting a terrible screech as it settled for a landing. Work in downtown skyscrapers likewise screeched to a halt as secretaries and office workers abandoned their desks to rush to the windows to watch. Employers quickly tired of this constant loss in productivity and raised such a beef that the city fathers demanded that we seek another landing site.

For a time we tried to operate from a less-central site, Pier One on the waterfront, but this left airline passengers with a taxi ride or an uphill walk into the downtown area. Traffic understandably slumped and continuing would have been unprofitable so we had to abandon our Seattle chopper enterprise. We disposed of our helicopters and returned to Alaska. I'm convinced that had we been operating with a more modern, much quieter machine, we probably would have survived.

In the mid-'60s, our future looked bleak and I was concerned for our employees when I got word that Wien Airlines was looking for a maintenance boss. I encouraged Ralph Brumbaugh to take the job as Wien (a federally certificated, subsidized airline) was here to stay, I thought, and our future looked shaky. When he got the job and prepared to leave, it was a sad time for us because he had been such a pillar in our business.

There had been countless times when Ralph had been indispensable to us. Just one of those instances I remembered when our ways parted was the time I had trouble with a C-46 as I was approaching Fairbanks. One of the plane's rugged, highly reliable 18-cylinder Pratt & Whitney engines was backfiring and I thought it best to radio ahead and tell Ralph I had a problem.

When I taxied in and parked, the left engine was popping. As I shut it down Ralph came out of the hangar carrying a stepladder. I slid open the side window and yelled, "Ralph, that engine's been banging a bit."

Ralph climbed the stepladder, reached into the cowling and picked out the head of an exhaust valve. Holding it up in his hand, he said, "You suppose this had anything to do with it?"

After the valve broke, it came right out through the cylinder head and was lying in the bottom of the cowling.

We threw a sendoff party for Ralph, and for that occasion, I worked up a bit of so-called poetry that expressed to some degree how tough it was for me to see this longtime friend and exceptional employee go.

> *RALPH BRUMBAUGH*
> *There was a man of many skills,*
> *Who cured airplanes of daily ills;*
> *He'd cuss and fume and beller loud,*
> *For action from his little crowd;*
> *Who'd hunt and search 'til they had found*
> *What kept the aircraft on the ground.*
>
> *He used to fly but had to quit,*
> *For the manual and the paper bit;*
> *He'd had his fill of those who'd bitch,*
> *When they forgot to throw the switch.*
>
> *He'd start each morn with a cheerful grin,*

That would gradually fade as the squawks came in;
He'd tinker and fix till the end of the day,
While cussing the pilots and the FAA.

He'd scream for help and heat and parts,
And send a chill thru the helpers' hearts;
But in spite of the act and the noisy show,
In the end the plane would always go.

He's slaved in cold and mud and dust,
For many years to gain our trust;
But now it seems he's got his wish,
To sit on his SUBSIDY and hunt and fish! ✝

CHAPTER 35

A Day Of Recognition

OUTSTANDING BUSINESSMAN — James Magoffin of Yankovich Road was honored as Alaska's Small Businessman of the Year for his work as president of Interior Airways, Inc. Mrs. Magoffin, here with her husband before one of Interior's Super Constellations, was also cited for her part in Interior's progress. She is a multi-engine pilot. (This photo and caption appeared in the Fairbanks Daily News-Miner, June 2, 1966.)

One is never looking for approval or praise when struggling to keep a business going in the face of all the turmoil and headaches that confront and often frustrate any businessman. The way I look at it, working as hard as you can and dedicating all your efforts to building a future is just part of the job. Yet when recognition came as it did to Dot and me in 1966, it was deeply appreciated.

The Small Business Administration saw fit to honor us jointly at a special ceremony held at the University of Alaska in Fairbanks during which I was named Alaska's Small Businessman of the Year.

The honor was presented at a gathering of distinguished and influential business leaders as a key part of the program of the Alaska Bankers Convention.

It was a tremendous honor at a time when Dot and I were still in the throes of struggle, and we still cherish the recognition we were given.

The award was presented on June 2, 1966, by Brideen Crawford, chairman of the Small Business Administration's State Advisory Council. Mrs. Crawford was introduced to the large crowd by Robert E. Butler, regional director of the Small Business Administration for Alaska.

The history of our business and details of the struggle Dot and I had to get our firm off the ground were part of the review given the audience and it was highly gratifying. That morning was one of the highlights of our lives and the honor conferred on us by the Small Business Administration is one of our most cherished memories.

The summary of our careers was remarkably complete and accurate, so I'll merely repeat what was presented to the audience on what was a day of recognition for us:

"From a shoestring, part-time beginning in 1947, Jim Magoffin parlayed his love for flying into a full-time job as president of the airline company he built from scratch in Fairbanks.

"This company, Interior Airways, grosses some million dollars each year and provides a $270,000 yearly payroll for the company's 34 native and non-native employees.

"There have been a number of stops and starts in the company's history, but Jim Magoffin adapted to changing Alaska conditions. Through resourcefulness, he kept the company moving ahead.

"He did not build the company alone, however, for his wife, Dorothy, has been a working partner from the beginning and a commercial pilot partner since 1959.

"Dorothy Riddle Magoffin comes from Ashland, Alabama. She graduated from Massey's Business College in Montgomery in 1943. As secretary to the special services officer at the Southeast Training Command at Maxwell Field, Alabama, she met Jim, then a captain in the Air Force.

"A licensed multi-engine pilot, Dorothy applied her business training to good advantage and has been an indispensable factor in the steady growth of Interior Airways from 1947 to 1966.

"Jim and Dorothy were married in April 1946, the day Jim was released from active duty as a lieutenant colonel in the Air Force. The newlyweds drove over the highway to Alaska on their honeymoon. Jim had been trained as a mining engineer at Virginia Military Institute and Michigan Tech and gravitated towards the mining industry in taking his first job in Alaska.

"He went to work for the U. S. Smelting, Refining and Mining Co. at its Cripple Creek office at Ester, Alaska. Through savings, he was able to buy an airplane which he used part-time for charter air service. Jim decided the next year, in 1947, to make charter flying a full-time business.

"From this one-plane operation in 1947, Jim expanded operations in 1950 by acquiring the planes, equipment and personnel of the Alaska Flying School in Fairbanks. At the school, classes of 150 students were taught flying, most of them under the GI Bill. At this time, there were 12 flight instructors and 12 mechanics working for the school. Dorothy Magoffin took advantage of the flight instruction available and learned to fly.

"In 1953, the great demand for flight instruction was largely over in the Fairbanks area, and Jim Magoffin began scouting around for more air freight business. He sold off many of his light aircraft and acquired a more diversified fleet. He bid on a number of Air Force and Army freight contracts and was successful.

"When building of the DEW line in the arctic started in 1954, Jim's fleet was in position and ready to serve. Interior Airways had many successful years through 1959 in supplying the DEW line.

"By this time, Jim and his company had built a solid reputation with operations in the interior and arctic and, after the DEW line, Interior Airways continued to get military contracts for freight hauling.

"Other lines were now added to the company's service. Interior Airways was selling aircraft and components and entered the passenger business through its scheduled intrastate run from Fairbanks to Clear. This service was, and still is, provided twice a day, seven days a week. Dorothy Magoffin flies the early evening flight. In this way, she cuts down on operating costs and still has time to take care of the Magoffin household.

"In 1961, Jim Magoffin received a blow when the Air Force changed its policy on awarding air freight contracts to non-CAB certificated airlines. Since Jim's air freight volume was largely dependent on military contracts, it was necessary to change the gears of the business once again.

"In the face of adversity, Jim and Dorothy Magoffin began planning the future of the business they had built without assistance from government loans or subsidies. They researched their problem and eventually decided that a great part of the future of their company might be in oil exploration and development on the Arctic Slope. Soon thereafter, they were contracting with oil companies to supply equipment and crews to remote spots in the arctic.

"Conditions were most difficult, and after many months, Jim reasoned there must be a better way to supply this area. He then decided to take the biggest gamble of his life. That was to establish a supply base in the arctic near the oil exploration activity at which equipment and supplies could be stored and oil crews could be quartered, if necessary, and transported according to need and as weather permitted.

"Building a base in the arctic would be an expensive undertaking, but it was essential if oil exploration and development were to proceed at anything more than a snail's pace.

"Sagwon, some 90 miles east of Umiat and 300 miles north of Fairbanks, was chosen as the site for the base. It is at the confluence of the Sagavanirktok and Ivishak rivers.

"Construction began in 1964 on an airstrip that was to be 6,500 feet long and 200 feet wide — wide enough to take Interior Airways' largest plane, a Lockheed Constellation.

"After many months of hard work and frustration in some of the world's toughest terrain, the airstrip was completed and a number of buildings finished to provide communications, living quarters and storage of supplies. With the equipment at Sagwon, a long-distance telephone call can now be made from a tent in the arctic to Los Angeles or elsewhere.

"Through Jim Magoffin's faith in Alaska, Sagwon has become the operational supply hub of Arctic Slope oil activity.

"Interior Airways has invested over $100,000 in the Sagwon project and Jim and Dorothy's gamble and foresight have started to pay off. In years to come, after the base at Sagwon has served its usefulness, Jim has plans to convert it into a hunting and fishing lodge.

"The Magoffins have extended their flying services to Anchorage where they operate from a hangar at Lake Hood. Charter service is offered and freight is hauled to the McGrath and Nome areas. Here again, the Magoffins are planning for the future and expect to share in the role Anchorage has as a supply center for western and northwestern Alaska.

"Jim and Dorothy Magoffin have two sons, Jim Jr., who is 19 and a sophomore at the University of Colorado, and Bill, 15, now in his second year at Lathrop High in Fairbanks. Both love to fly and are avid outdoor sportsmen, each having bagged a number of big game trophies.

"Home life for the Magoffins centers around a hillside home on 160 acres which is five miles from Fairbanks on Yankovich Road. The place is especially satisfying to the family for two reasons. First, they built the house themselves in the true Alaskan tradition. Second, the place is built on a site from which the family can clearly see and keep an eye on the business at the Fairbanks International Airport.

"Jim and Dorothy Magoffin are true, enterprising pioneers, contributing greatly to Alaska's economy. We are proud of the achievements they are making to the growth of Alaska."

Further recognition came in 1970 when I was awarded the silver medal by the Michigan Technological University for "distinguished personal achievement and outstanding service to his profession." ☩

CHAPTER 36

Hiding Out In Paradise

Though it never got so bad that bloodhounds were nipping at our heels, there was a time when both Dot and I were fugitives of a sort after having been told that we'd better get out of town for our own good.

There are things worse than being forced by your attorney to hide out in a beautiful hunting and fishing paradise that would make Thoreau's Walden Pond look like a mud puddle.

So we didn't argue when we were told to get lost. Both of us loved our hideaway which offered as wonderful fishing and hunting as you'll find anywhere in the world. We enjoyed to the fullest our brief exile.

Details about why we were ordered out of town must await a few details on the island. Montague Island in Prince William Sound is a frankfurter-shaped, 50-mile-long narrow chunk of land crowned by a rugged spine of mountains just a couple of thousand feet high.

What is unique about the island is its beauty and its abundance of fish and game. Deer in incredible numbers roamed the open meadows, wooded hills and ridges. Shimmering schools of cutthroats could be seen in the streams pouring into the Sound. Flocks of Canada geese swarmed into and out of the island's lakes where feed abounded. In fall, thick clusters of blueberries loaded down thousands of bushes.

This is where we were glad to go when we had to get out of town.

Ward Gay, who operated a flying service out of Anchorage, introduced us to this wild, fascinating island. In mid-November 1959, Ward invited me there on a deer-hunting trip. I took along my 12-year-old son, Jimmy, flying a Widgeon to Cordova, where we joined the rest of Gay's hunting party. Included were Dan Cuddy, president of a chain of Alaska banks, and Tom Culhane, owner of a major Anchorage fuel business.

A boat operated by the Bilderback family took us to Rocky Bay on the north end of Montague. All the way over to the island, seasoned hunters kept giving an excited Jimmy tips on the fine points of deer hunting. He was told, for example, that he should be careful to shoot the deer in the neck to avoid spoiling the meat.

Hunting was never better. I had Jimmy sit on a hump in an open meadow covered by three-foot-high grass, giving him my packsack to use as a rest aim. Then I made a wide circle, zig-zagging back toward him through a thick patch of woods. I heard a number of shots.

As I approached the hump where Jimmy was stationed, I stumbled onto a dead deer lying in the grass. Then, to my surprise, I spotted another one.

"You killed two of 'em, Jimmy!" I hollered to him.

"Yeah, Dad," he said, "and there's two more over here!"

And there were two more. He was as proud as he could be. All four deer had been shot through the neck.

On the return boat ride to Cordova, Culhane told us about the wilderness cabin he'd built on Stump

Tom Culhane and Boat Captain Martin Samuelson visiting enroute from Cordova to Montague Island.

Lake on the south end of Montague Island. Tom invited me to hunt with him there, and we had several good hunts at his Stump Lake camp over the next few years.

On these hunts, everything I saw at Montague Island appealed to me. Later, while flying around the south end of the island, usually quite low due to the predominantly bad weather, I became intrigued by a sizeable fresh water lake just inland from San Juan Bay, the southernmost bay on the island.

One day in early October, Ward Gay and I prospected the area with the idea of building a jointly owned camp. The meadows, ridges and hills surrounding the lake were full of deer, and we could see silver salmon running in the lake.

Never did I go into a building project with more enthusiasm. Col. Steve Henry, the Eielson Air Force Base commanding officer, took leave to help us. He flew our old Travelaire 6000 on floats to Anchorage and spent several days hauling building material, including lumber and aluminum sheets from Lake Hood to San Juan Lake.

I stayed at the campsite. Ward, who was tied up in a business deal, sent an experienced carpenter, Frank LaVallette, to take his place. We cut logs and Frank, a brute of a Frenchman, could easily pick up one end. He expected me to pick up the other. The timbers were water-logged, as most everything on Montague Island is. They seemed to weigh a ton as I struggled to uphold my end of the job, almost ruining my back in the process. I almost had to crawl to get to the plane. Though I could still fly, I was really hurting. My back has bothered me some ever since.

That was the fall of 1960. After that, we enjoyed many good outings there and continued to use the camp to entertain customers and provide vacations for company personnel.

In a subsequent hot and heavy legal clash in Fairbanks, we found our camp would

Intra-State Air Paths To Go to Panel

1960

A three-judge panel will be presented a thorny case here on Oct. 24 when the constitutionality of the Civil Aeronautics Board to regulate intrastate air transportation in Alaska will be challenged.

This is the result of a charge by Wien Alaska Airlines that Interior Airways is violating CAB regulations. Senior CAB examiner William J. Madden came here from Washington, D. C. to conduct a routine hearing on Sept. 20 and found that it was blocked by a temporary restraining order from Judge Walter H. Hodge of Anchorage.

At a subsequent hearing in Anchorage Sept. 26, U. S. Attorney George Yeager moved for dismissal and dissolving the temporary restraining order. Judge Hodge denied dismissal but amended the order to permit hearings to proceed, but prohibited CAB from enforcing the economic regulations.

In a surprise move at the continued hearings here yesterday, James Magoffin took the stand but refused to testify without a required U. S. court order to do so. This stymied the hearings. Charles Clasby is the attorney for Wien.

Charles Cole, attorney for Magoffin, contends that the proceedings are in violation of the constitution and that part of the statehood act which provides for state perogatives. CAB moved to postpone the h e a r i n g s indefinitely and Judge Hodge appointed Judge Stanley Barnes of the court

serve another vital purpose. We were glad we had it after the uproar that followed my placing a small ad in the yellow pages of the Fairbanks phone book. Our competitors pounced, hotly charging that this ad violated our authority and was grounds for yanking our certificate.

The Civil Aeronautics Board (CAB) scheduled a hearing in Fairbanks. Being under the gun, I didn't make a move without consulting our attorney, Charlie Cole. He gave me some unusual counsel. When the CAB asked me to bring flight records to the hearing room, Cole told me to bring the records, but to neglect bringing the key to the dispatch case in which I carried them.

Hostile representatives from most of Alaska's scheduled airlines jammed the hearing room — all eager to give us the shaft. Noticeably absent was a representative from Reeve Aleutian Airways. Reeve, who never gave us any trouble, had always been friendly and helpful to Interior Airways.

Cole mapped out my every move, and I was careful to follow his instructions to the letter. He advised me to refuse to testify. So when the CAB attorney asked me a question, all he got was silence. This sent the hearing officer into a conference with another attorney. After stalling for a while, they temporarily dismissed the meeting.

Cole, wearing a very serious face, called me over for a private discussion, "I want you to get out of town, Jim," he said.

"Why?" I asked.

"Because they're going to get a court order, and when they get that, they're going to *make* you testify."

"I'm going!" I said, not a bit upset and looking forward to the exile Cole ordered. I headed for home, grabbed my deer rifle, shotgun, packsack, sleeping bag and some grub. Then I drove to the airport, got into the Widgeon and flew to our camp at Montague Island, about

Fighting the state and federal governments at the same time. We won, but it wasn't easy.

the most remote and safest place I could think of.

I enjoyed, to the fullest, being a refugee. Deer hunting was good, and soon two nice bucks were hanging on the deer pole.

I was contemplating the beauty and the stillness of this matchless wilderness when I heard the sound of an airplane approaching. The thought came: 'They're coming after me! There'll be a U.S. marshal on board for sure!"

I decided I wasn't going to be easy to capture. I grabbed my rifle and a little grub and headed up the side of the mountain. Every once in a while I'd stop and check on the incoming plane. I could see the paint job that told me it was from Ward Gay's outfit in Anchorage, Sea Airmotive.

The float plane circled the lake then settled down for a nice landing. I watched the plane taxi up to the beach. I saw the pilot's door open. Warren Wright, chief pilot for Sea Airmotive, stepped out. I expected the next one out to be the U.S. marshal, but was very relieved and happy to see that the one passenger was my wife, Dot. I hustled right back down to the camp.

Dot told me that Charlie Cole had advised her, also, to get out of town, pointing out that since she was the vice president of our company, she might be forced to testify in my absence. Like me, Dot lost no time in making her happy getaway. The days that followed were wonderful and unforgettable. The two of us enjoyed superb deer hunting for about a week, getting up early in the morning and returning at noon. Then we'd go fishing for the silver salmon that were in the midst of a late run in the lake. In the evening, we'd go up to the head of the lake and get in on the evening flight of geese. We weren't suffering.

When we cautiously ventured back to Anchorage, I called Cole to determine which way the wind was blowing. He informed me it was now safe to return to civilization.

By the time we got to Fairbanks, the CAB examiner and his attorney and all the airline people had gone.

The thing that saved us was that Alaska had just become a state.

There was great uncertainty about whether intrastate air commerce was to be dictated by the federal government or by the state.

Cole made the most of that uncertainty.

We lost our lake during the disastrous 1964 Alaska earthquake.

Powerful tremors raised the end of Montague Island, on which our camp was situated, about 35 feet. The lake, in a matter of hours, drained away into the ocean, leaving behind an ugly expanse of mud, logs and weeds. Within a couple of years, most of the lake bed was covered with a new growth of thick willows.

There was no longer a lake to land a plane on, but the upheaval created a new

The Coast Guard's way of paying for booze consumed during their stay at our Montague Island cabin.

beach several hundred yards wide where previously there had been none. We easily made subsequent landings on wheels on this solid new ocean beach.

In the early '70s, the Bureau of Land Management notified us that our camp was in trespass since Montague Island was part of the Chugach National Forest. The BLM told us our building would have to be moved or burned. We managed to convince them that the building was a valuable refuge for pilots and others caught in bad weather who might need emergency shelter.

We cited, in support of this, the case of Anchorage pilot Bill Renfrew, who had been forced to land his seaplane on the lake. Renfrew stayed in our cabin for several days waiting for the weather to clear.

When a Coast Guard Grumman Albatross crashed a few miles from our camp during a night flight in low weather, killing all aboard, a rescue party was brought into San Juan Bay on the Coast Guard cutter Storis. When rescuers tried to make shore, their boat was upset in the surf and everyone aboard was pitched out into the icy water. They all made it to the beach and were overjoyed to discover our camp equipped with an oil stove, propane lights and, incidentally, a plentiful supply of spirits. Members of the Coast Guard's rescue party used our camp as headquarters while bodies of crash victims were retrieved from the wrecked aircraft.

Several weeks later, I received a nice letter from the Coast Guard Base at Kodiak thanking me for the use of our camp. Included was a voucher to pay us for the supplies their men had consumed. Though no mention was made of our diminished cache of beer, wine and whiskey, which was far from neglected by the party, the voucher included payment for the booze by giving us the generally equivalent value of other groceries supposedly consumed, most of which we didn't have in our camp in the first place. We got a chuckle out of that.

Eventually, the BLM agreed to designate our cabin as a public-use facility. This was okay with us. We have since used the camp as have many other Alaskans and visitors to our state.

I might add that, knock on wood, we never had another occasion to go to Montague Island as "fugitives." ✝

CHAPTER 37

The Oil Hunters

Umiat. Once it was just another chunk of emptiness on a trackless sea of tundra. In winter, it was a forbidding, frozen wasteland; in summer, there was little there but mosquitoes.

Yet, when the search for Alaska oil began in earnest, Umiat sprang into bustling life. The sound of arriving and departing aircraft ended the round-the-clock silence of this bleak place. Geologists, construction workers, field crews and surveyors fanned out from this point for hundreds of miles in search of oil.

Few know that the real discoverers of Alaska oil were the Eskimo nomads who stumbled upon meandering surface oil seeps back in the 19th century. They carved out blocks of oil-soaked tundra from the widespread seeps, using them regularly for cooking and heating.

The Navy knew about Umiat's oil potential long before the gigantic Prudhoe Bay discoveries. Back in 1944, the Navy launched an ambitious eight-year oil exploration program, known as Pet 4, in a vast area that included Umiat. Thirty-six wildcat wells were drilled. Three gas fields and two oil fields were located, the largest of which was in the Umiat area.

Some estimates indicated that Umiat was sitting on a geologic structure containing up to 100 million barrels of high-gravity oil. So oil companies like Richfield, Humble, BP and Sinclair weren't gambling wildly when they began sending out their geologists, surveyors and field crews into the Umiat environs.

With the arrival of the oil hunters, the airplane and organizations like our own suddenly took on tremendous significance. The only way these scatterings from down south could be supplied and shuttled from point to point was by air. And soon Umiat, a once unknown spot on Alaska's endless tundra, was transformed and became a vital, throbbing air gateway to the clusters of oil exploration camps that sprang up like mushrooms after a spring rain.

Playing even a modest role in this surging development was exciting and challenging for any Alaskan fortunate enough to be called on to play a part in it. That's the way I felt about it.

There was never any secret about what was happening in the arctic. At a very early date, it became clear to me that this was becoming one of the hottest oil exploration areas on the continent. Many had all kinds of doubts about the future of Alaska oil exploration, but in guiding our struggling firm, I had to take the gamble.

I was convinced that if we were to get our foot in the door so far as participating in this exciting new development was concerned, we were going to have to act fast. And initially that action would have to be the establishment of our own airport in the Umiat vicinity. But where?

I took off one day in a Super Cub to scout the site for our new airport. This might seem to some like seeking a needle in a haystack, but I knew generally what I was looking for.

Skimming over the Canning and Sagavanirktok rivers, I rejected one potential site after another. Then my eyes scanned a nondescript gravel bar not far from the banks of the Sagavanirktok River. I knew instantly it had a lot of things going for it. It was far enough inland to be insulated from most of the summertime coastal fogs that often complicated air travel. It was above the river's normal high-water mark and not far from a lake that would be suitable for float operations. This was the place.

Though in the beginning our new airport was just a forbidding expanse of undistinguished river gravel covered with large rocks and brush, I knew the search for our airport was over.

I landed and carefully looked over the place and its surroundings. As far as my eye could see were just thousands of more acres of untouched tundra. Though the site was bleak and rocky, everything about it matched the specifications I had worked out. Now, there was no time to lose. I had an airport to build and I might as well get started. On that first landing, I cleared out a lot of brush and moved away what seemed like a ton of the bigger rocks. Gradually, in the days and weeks that followed, the new airport began to take shape. After some work, we were able to bring in successively a Cessna 170, a Norseman, a DC-3 and a C-46. Every time we landed there, we made more improvements. Before long, that dismal place took on the look of an honest-to-God airport.

Soon, a small building was on the site and a generator and a radio homing beacon were installed. Because of its location on the Sagavanirktok River, we named our little pioneer airport, the first to be built on the river, Sag No. 1.

Pilots approaching Sag No. 1 would slur the "sag one" in their radio transmissions, making it sound like "Sagwon" so that's what we named our tundra enclave. The name Sagwon stuck. Now, the newborn airport had a name. In the months to come, it was to play a major role in bringing Alaska oil to the world.

Having our own Sagwon radio beacon reminded me of an unfortunate unpleasantness with Wien at the time we were engaged in early DEW line flying. On flights between Fairbanks and Point Barrow, we had to rely on the Bettles radio facilities as well as the Umiat homing beacon to keep us on our course. The trouble was that Wien owned the Umiat beacon. The CAA informed us that we couldn't conduct instrument flights over that route without using Wien's beacon. We were told that we had to file position reports with the Wien operator at Umiat.

When we applied to Wien to use their Umiat beacon, there was trouble. Wien's attorney, Chuck Clasby, promptly advised us that we could use the beacon all right but if we did, we were going to have to pay $287 per contact. A strange sentence in Clasby's letter informed us that we were not to question the reasonableness of this charge.

The amount they wanted was so exorbitant that we had to decline. Immediately, we ordered a new homing beacon from the factory at Fort Lauderdale, Florida. We built an operations building at Umiat and flew in a cot and cooking equipment. When our beacon arrived from Florida, we proudly installed it in our own radio facility.

We put a one-lung Witte generator in a shack outside. Our experience with Witte generators amazed us at first, then taught us an important lesson. We bolted the generator down to timbers, never thinking it would move. The Witte, we were to learn, had a horizontal cylinder that produced a terrible lurch every time it fired. On the generator's first day of operation, it proceeded to march itself right out of the shack. To keep it in place thereafter, we had to reinstall it on a good-sized concrete pad.

There were some discouraging moments as we were getting under way at Umiat. Texaco had a geology party out on the North Slope. The firm's Fairbanks expediter and manager, Wayne Felts, was among the nay-sayers who seemed to think our little company would soon be gone with the arctic wind.

It was at the time when we put up our first Umiat building that Felts "leveled" with me, suggesting that our operation was vulnerable and expendable and would soon be wiped out by our competition.

"Jim," Felts told me, "we admire your guts, but we honestly think you're wasting your money and your effort. You simply aren't going to be able to compete so long as Wien is in the North. Wien has the federal certificate, they have the mail contract and they have the big planes. They're just too well established."

The message, I suppose, was that if we had any sense, we'd just fold up our tents. Though Felts was a nice guy and undoubtedly meant well, it's pleasant to report even at this late date, that he was dead wrong. Interior Airways became extremely well established in the arctic. We constructed an excellent airport of our own at Sagwon. And despite some initial setbacks, we prospered and survived.

Sadly, Wien, as important as it was in Alaska's aviation history, is no longer among the firms listed in today's Alaska yellow pages.

Even so, Interior Airways' year-to-year certificate crises remained a constant worry to us. This nagging uncertainty stimulated our search for permanent certification. One avenue to this was purchasing an airline that was currently certified.

Unloading case gasoline for the helicopter supporting a Shell Oil geology party. Dick Cole (in aircraft), Charlie Cole near chute rollers, Jim Magoffin stacking cases, and Paul Palmer in rear. Deadman Lake, arctic Alaska, 1961.

Thus, our interest was aroused when we learned that Kodiak Airways, which possessed both a federal certificate and a mail contract, was for sale. To check the matter out, Charlie Cole and I flew to Kodiak after arranging a meeting with Bob Hall, the company's owner.

Though Hall's asking price was reasonable, I was troubled by his lack of enthusiasm for the operation and by the condition of his planes.

Hall's pilots and mechanics, I discovered, were unhappy and the condition of his aircraft was disturbing. His Grumman Gooses and Widgeons were dilapidated. Aircraft wings were badly dented from constant contact with boats and dock pilings. Propeller blades were seriously water-eroded, having been filed down to much less than their original width. All of Hall's stuff looked bad, and some of it might even have been dangerous.

Even the Kodiak weather seemed to be warning us to back off. It was cold and utterly miserable all three days we were there. Although I could sympathize sincerely with Hall's plight, it soon became clear to both of us that if we took over that particular certificate we'd be buying ourselves a terrible bundle of headaches. I just had to turn it down, a decision I've never regretted.

As oil exploration accelerated, our planes and pilots were kept busy hauling personnel and their cargo from one site to another. Our pilots got used to packing and unpacking boxes filled with heavy rock samples and also became accustomed to loading and unloading 65-pound cases of gasoline and other supplies.

Working long hours and putting up with primitive living accommodations was tough on our pilots, and it helped if they had a sense of humor. Fun-loving, personable Richard Finnell, a competent Widgeon pilot, enjoyed the lighter approach and once put up a sign outside his living quarters proclaiming: "RICARDO FINNELLI, THE GREAT SPANISH FLYER."

Finnell, whose only bad habit seemed to be too much vodka at times, and other pilots soon discovered that loading and unloading the Widgeon could be a torturous operation. It was impossible to stand up straight in the small airplane as one wrestled with heavy stuff in an awkward, bent-over position.

Finnell established a good record with us with the single exception of one incident when he and I were using two Widgeons to transfer an oil crew from a tundra lake to Umiat. As we were loading up, a strong southwest wind was blowing at the exploration camp on the south end of the narrow lake which was oriented northwest and southeast.

I flew four passengers and their gear to Umiat and expected Finnell would depart the lake right behind me. He didn't show up at Umiat, however. I flew back to the lake. From the air, I spotted Finnell's plane on the tundra, some 60 yards off the lake's west side. He informed me that he had been forced to scoot up off the lake and onto the tundra because of the combination of propeller torque and weather-cocking action precipitated by the strong wind. At the same time, water splashing on his windshield deprived him of visibility.

Fortunately, the plane was undamaged and after we worked it back into the lake, Finnell was able to fly it to Umiat without further incident.

When winter ended Finnell's water flying, he took a Lower 48 job with a nonsked. It was saddening to learn some time later that, while flying as co-pilot, he was killed in a cargo plane crash.

Pilots had to adjust to flying all kinds of cumbersome things out to the field camps. Bob Jacobs, one of our early resident pilots at Umiat, flew a Norseman as well as the Grumman Super Widgeon. I happened to be there when Jacobs was preoccupied with jockeying a large refrigerator into a Norseman.

The bulky, awkward load wouldn't fit into the plane in the normal way because it was too long to go in the door. Bob had to remove the cargo doors from both sides of the plane to provide enough room to shove the refrigerator through. This left the ends of the refrigerator sticking out of both sides of the plane.

Seeing him ready to take off with that oddball load made me shake my head. I told him, "Bob, I'm afraid that load's going to blank out your tail. The way it's loaded, it won't fly so good." I wasn't telling Bob anything he didn't know already.

"I'll give it a try anyway," he replied, as unsure as I was about what was going to happen after takeoff.

Nothing serious developed when he took off, however, and when he returned from delivering the refrigerator, I asked, "Well, how did it fly?"

"Couldn't tell the difference!" was his reply.

As before, the CAA kept scrutinizing our operations so there was never any

FAIRBANKS NEWS MINER, FRIDAY, APRIL 19, 1957

News-Miner Photo by Phil's Studio

RADIO PLANNING—Jim Magoffin, left, and Don Andon pour over the final plans for what will be a unique radio operation in Alaska. Magoffin, who operates Interior Airways, holds the contract for flying supplies to isolated DEW-line posts. Andon is manager of KFAR radio. The radio station will be serving as a ground-to-air homing beam for Magoffin's planes on a frequency level which will not interfere with normal broadcast operations.

Government authorities could always think of some way of stopping us — but they didn't.

chance we'd start getting complacent.

Federal inspectors, for example, raised a fuss over our instrument flying between Fairbanks and Barter Island. They contended we couldn't maintain our course within limits because of the lack of navigational aids over the route.

We proved we could by tuning our Automatic Direction Finders to radio station KFAR in Fairbanks.

At this, they pointed out that navigating in this way wouldn't be legal unless KFAR transmitted an identifier code. We solved this problem by getting KFAR's station manager, Don Andon, to add the code to their broadcasts.

In the course of our fast-developing Umiat operation, it soon became clear that I lacked one very important flying skill: choppers. Most geology parties employed chopper pilots and kept small helicopters based right at camp. Pilots, and sometimes mechanics, lived right with exploration crews.

I didn't want to run the risk of being found wanting in an emergency or other situation that required me to fly a helicopter in one of these remote areas. So, at my earliest opportunity, I enrolled in Rick's Helicopter School in Los Angeles.

After a few days of intensive training, I was granted my helicopter license. Later, I flew some of the small piston-powered Bell machines as well as the jet-powered French Alouette II. ✛

CHAPTER 38

New State,
New Air Service

In 1959, Alaska becomes the 49th state and Jim and Dot Magoffin celebrate Interior Airways' newly scheduled operation between Fairbanks and Anchorage.

Not long after Alaska became the 49th state, we were prodded by some of the new state's officials to start a scheduled operation between Fairbanks and Anchorage.

It was pointed out that the existing service being provided by Wien and by Alaska Airlines had deteriorated to the extent that competition was called for.

The state granted us a limited certificate and our new service was launched with high hopes. We started the flights between Alaska's two largest cities using an Aero-Commander 690, a small, twin-engine turbo-prop, making three daily round trips.

LOOKING AHEAD—Jim Magoffin plans for future expansion of Interior Airways include the Fairchild F-228, a drawing of which he displays. It is now on order and delivery is scheduled for January 1971. Magoffin, who started his commercial flying career with a one-passenger plane after World War II, now has a fleet of 24 aircraft, and his wife Dotty, at right, is a certified multi-engine pilot, qualified to pilot many types of aircraft, wheel-based and on floats. Dotty makes many flights into the bush and Arctic, and is particularly active during the tourist season with sight-seeing charters.

(News-Miner Staff Photo)

FAIRBANKS DAILY NEWS-MINER   FEB. 1968

Interior Airways Inaugurates New Era

Jim Magoffin Started With a One-Passenger Plane After the War, Now Has a Fleet of 24

By CHARLEY MAYSE
Staff Reporter

When Dotty Magoffin recently broke the christening magnum of champagne over the nose of Interior Airways new F27 plane, a new era in flight operations was inaugurated by the company.

Jim Magoffin, newly separated from the U.S. Air Force in 1946, began his commercial flying career in Alaska.

His plane was a brand-new one-passenger Taylor-craft. It had been flown up from the smaller states by a friend.

His first commercial flying was with the Fairbanks Exploration Co. making ditch surveys for their mining operations.

Magoffin's second plane was a five-place Howard, a Navy craft bought in Michigan and flown to Fairbanks by Magoffin. It was in use in his expanding operations for many years.

The Fleet Grew

Additional planes became necessary to take care of the increasing work load and by 1950 Interior's fleet had grown to five.

Interior now has 24 flight-ready planes, two more on order and almost the entire 49th State is its flying perimeter.

It has planes on wheels, planes on floats, planes on skis and amphibians which have both water and earth landing capability. Thus, practically speaking, it is able, willing and ready to transport by air anything, anywhere at anytime, regardless of the terrain.

The little 65-horse "T-craft" was sold long ago—it's passenger capacity and load limitation were too marginal for profitable commercialization.

Now Interior's plane categories include DC3s, a twin Bonanza, a Beechcraft King-Aire, a Cherokee Six, several Cesna 180s and Piper Super-Cubs.

On order is a Beechcraft 99 of 15-20 passenger capacity scheduled for a June delivery.

During DEW Line construction days when mass transportation was called for, Interior had three C-46s, a DC 3 and numerous single and two-engine craft constantly in the air.

Statewide Hauling

After the DEW Line was completed in 1957, Interior turned to state-wide general contract air hauling, flying fish, oil, gasoline and mining equipment to their clients' specifications.

When the Clear Ballistic Missile Early Warning site began construction in 1960, Interior instituted a regular traffic flow between Fairbanks and that down-river community, and from there to Anchorage.

With the beginning of oil exploration on the Arctic Slope, Interior was engaged by the major oil and geophysical companies to ferry personnel, supplies and equipment to their operational sites.

Jim Magoffin qualified as a civilian pilot at Wold-Chamberlain Field, Minn.

A member of the U.S. Air Force in the Flight Training Command, he was based at Maxwell Field, Ala. from 1942 to 1946.

Had Mining Degree

He had graduated with a mining degree from Michigan College of Mining and Technology at Houghton, Mich. in 1941. Previous to that he had a degree in civil engineering from Virginia Military Institute, of Lexington, Va.

But once flying got into his blood, Jim Magoffin in no long while forgot all abut a mining or surveying career.

"Mining engineers and surveyors were not much in demand in 1946," he recalls. "And the pay was not very good."

He replied to a leading question, "No, when I began with the little T-craft back in 1946 I had no inkling Interior would go as far as it has. . . Then we got the King-Aire, which cost a half million . . . And now we've just taken delivery of the F27 and have it flight-ready. . . "

Interior now has authorization from the State Department of Aviation for a new Fairbanks to Anchorage run and will be involved during the next several days in tests involving the new F27 under auspices of the Federal Aviation Agency before a passenger schedule is set up.

Payroll of 61

The craft has been brought especially for this run.

The newest addition to the Interior fleet required a minimum flight crew of three: pilot, co-pilot and stewardess.

It is equipped with all the latest navigating and electronic gear available on the market, including automatic pilot and radar.

Magoffin pointedly refused to admit that it would fly unerringly through pea-soup fog but did say that its sophisticated instrumentation would allow flights under near minimal weather conditions.

"There will still be some limitations," he admitted.

Queried as to its cost, Magoffin said that the new aircraft and it associated equipment would add close to $1 million to the state's tax base.

As of now, there are 61 names on Interior's personnel roster. The job break-down includes pilots, co-pilots, stewardesses, mechanics, ticket agents, ground personnel, dispatchers and cargo handlers.

Flights regularly established will mean additional jobs in nearly all categories mentioned. It will mean not only an additional traveling convenience but an economy flow between Alaska's two major cities.

The new Fairbanks-Anchorage schedules will mean that a businessman may catch the 7:30 a.m. departure flight from Fairbanks and have his feet on his desk in downtown Anchorage by nine or nine-thirty.

There will be three flights in each direction seven days a week. The evening flights, of course, will be called, not inappropriately, "champagne flights."

Food will be available on all flights.

The public's reception to the new service was good and it looked like our new operation would take hold. However, the Aero-Commander was too small for the traffic demands, so we started searching for a bigger, affordable aircraft.

Our choice was a pair of used Fairchild F-27s. We painted the planes in the state's colors and had payloader seats of the same colors installed. We hired attractive stewardesses, made it a point to serve good meals, and were gratified when there was a steady increase in passenger loads over a period of many months.

Incorporated in our streamlined, scheduled F-27 operation were features reflecting what we believed an airline should be. Our goal was to give the greatest possible amount of service to the public on the vital, well-travelled Fairbanks-Anchorage route. We believed, for example, that it was possible to handle baggage more efficiently and with greater speed as another way of catering to passengers.

We had a standing agreement that any passenger who got to the baggage area before his or her baggage did would have the cost of the ticket refunded. Nobody ever got this refund. Our secret? The baggage area in an F-27 is situated between the pilot and passenger compartments. Immediately on landing and while the plane was being taxied to the terminal, the copilot would unhook the baggage restraining net and swiftly move the bags to the baggage doorway. A truck would back up to the doorway as soon as the plane had parked.

Saturday, Feb. 10, 1968   JESSEN'S DAILY '   Page 3

Champagne Flight

Interior Airways rolled out the red carpet and uncorked the champagne yesterday on their inaugural flights from Fairbanks to Anchorage and return. Here Chief Stewardess Pat Shortell invites participation during the inflight celebration while Stewardess Wynola Possento looks on.

Friendly people and good food made Interior Airways' flights enjoyable.

Pilots and members of the ground crew lost no time in transferring all the baggage from the plane to the truck which would quickly travel the short distance to the baggage rack where everything was offloaded. Invariably, following this system, by the time passengers walked to the baggage section of the terminal, their bags would be waiting.

It still irks me to take a jet flight and be forced to wait an unreasonable length of time for my baggage to show up. I realize, however, that most jets carry the baggage load in the belly, and airline pilots don't normally pitch in to handle baggage as our flight crews did.

We hired Red Boucher, the mayor of Fairbanks, to promote our Anchorage-Fairbanks schedule. He did such an outstanding job in presenting our service to the public that the news media which, for the past 20 years hardly knew we existed, suddenly discovered us.

Glowing articles began appearing about how far we had come and about what a remarkable job we were doing. Red's skill in public relations notwithstanding, this sudden glare of publicity didn't please me at all. At least half of the stuff being presented to the public as fact was inaccurate, exaggerated or just plain fabricated.

I was keenly aware that hoopla and publicity could boomerang and do serious damage to an aviation enterprise.

When I was honored as Alaska's Small Businessman of the Year, Herb Hilscher of the Anchorage Chamber of Commerce phoned me and invited me to speak to the Chamber. I had to decline, being fully aware of some of the negative aspects of being in the limelight. I had been following the sorry plight of Eastern Airlines which had been highly touted in the national media. A year later, the very same national publications were predicting the early demise of Eastern.

I was aware, also, that if I allowed Interior to be singled out and exposed to the merciless glare of publicity, our operating certificate could be yanked at any time and we would be history.

Wien had just suffered a major F-27 accident involving many casualties. If we experienced a similar misfortune, I was sure our certificate would be cancelled. To my mind, free publicity can often cost a lot, and it rarely thrilled me to see us featured on the front page.

Our new Fairbanks-Anchorage service had a very positive effect: Other airlines immediately improved their service to the public. Wien moved swiftly to add a Boeing 737 to their fleet. As soon as it started operating, our passenger loads diminished rapidly because our turbo-prop simply couldn't compete with the faster, larger jet. This brought our scheduled operation to a halt as we concentrated our efforts on the oil search on the North Slope.

Interior Airways' advance to turbo-props (Turbo Commander 690, F-27s, a King Air, Turbo Beavers and Twin Otters) relegated our older bush planes to the back lot. At the time, plans for a Pioneer Air Museum for Fairbanks were moving forward and our contribution was a Norseman and a Stinson SRJR— vintage aircraft that are now of real interest to a generation accustomed to sleek jets.

We later secured a 1936 Fairchild F-24 that had originally been delivered to the Pollack Flying Service of Fairbanks. That plane is also currently on display at the fast-growing Pioneer Air Museum at Alaskaland in Fairbanks. ✛

CHAPTER 39

The Cargo Haulers

As the tempo of oil exploration in the arctic increased, pressure on our flying capacity kept building up almost unbearably.

Cargo volume for tundra sites kept growing, threatening to swamp our ability to handle it. Waiting to be hauled out on a rush basis were such things as entire prefab buildings and vehicles of various types and sites. Our hard-working C-46s simply couldn't, by themselves, put a dent in the stacks of cargo that confronted us. And a lot of oil people were nipping at our heels demanding that their cargo had to go out right now.

We had to get a bigger aircraft, and fast. I kept sending urgent feelers all over the place in a near-frantic campaign to find a new aircraft. To my immense relief, I learned that the Ohio Oil Co. of Guatemala had two surplus C-82s for sale — just the kind of aircraft we needed to work our way out of the crunch.

It was arranged that Mike Murphy, the firm's aviation manager in Findlay, Ohio, would join me in San Jose, Costa Rica, where the two surplus planes were stored. I promptly made a deal to buy them, and soon they were flying north where no time was lost in putting them to work.

We found that the C-82s, though they required considerable maintenance, were pretty good airplanes. They were a good choice to fill in until we could realize our long-held goal to acquire one of the giant Lockheed Hercules.

After making arrangements to purchase the planes, I leafed through their logbooks and came upon a fascinating notation in one of them. That flight entry stated simply: "Cargo and herder lost." I was curious about that logbook item and asked about it. I was told that the ill-fated cargo referred to was 12 head of cattle accompanied by a herder. The clamshell doors from the back of the C-82 had been removed. On the flight, everything went all right as long as the pilot kept the plane flying level. However, when the pilot encountered a thunderstorm, he pulled the plane's nose up sharply to diminish its speed.

By this time, the cattle had glazed the floor and it had become slippery as glass. When the plane's nose zoomed upward, everything began sliding swiftly down the steep, slick slope of the climbing plane's floor. Cattle herder, cattle and virtually everything else in the plane slid down to the tail and tumbled out into the jungle below, never to be heard from again.

After loading up on arctic leases, oil companies lost no time in hiring seismic teams to help them determine the value of what they had bought. In the oil leasing frenzy, oil firms shelled out vast sums of money to snap up leases all over the North. There was especially brisk leasing activity in the vicinity of the Sag River, the Canning River, the Kuparuk River and some sections to the west. Seismic work was the next step.

As seismic camps began to sprout on the tundra, we found out very soon we had our work cut out for us. There was a somewhat disconcerting visit from a representative of one the first seismic companies to show up in Alaska, United Geophysical. The field manager visited my office and displayed a large spreadsheet showing exactly where the company's seismic crews would be situated and the exact times and dates they were scheduled to be there.

Also set forth in great detail was the precise schedule for delivering United Geophysical air cargo to the far-flung sites. We were, for example, to deliver so many drums of gasoline and diesel fuel to an array of lakes scattered over their leased area. Without any input from us, everything had been figured out to a gnat's eyebrow in terms of how their camps would be supplied.

This guy had been dealing with trucking people down in Texas. He was able to order them around and specify that deliveries had to be made to a certain spot on a certain day and at a certain time. Such wheeling and dealing worked in Texas transportation but was simply nonsense when applied to the arctic. There were thousands of things that could happen here to tear such a tightly worked-out schedule to shreds.

Weather conditions on any given day could run the gamut from fair to horrible where we operated. There were days when arctic blasts swept the tundra with devastating intensity. Widespread and much-dreaded whiteouts erased visibility over areas larger than most states and made it impossible for airplanes to pinpoint anything anywhere in a country where there were so few landmarks. There were many times when pilots, if they had good sense, weren't doing any flying at all. You don't precisely schedule air deliveries under such conditions.

Even so, I did my best to be polite to the fellow, but I wasn't sure I was getting through to him. I assured him that, conditions permitting, we'd do our best to make at least the first delivery as programmed. It turned out that first delivery was to the specified frozen lake at the specified time but the seismic party was still struggling along miles away. The seismic people got a better understanding of the North.

Our Sagwon homing beacon proved a godsend. We'd pinpoint our position over Sagwon, then take a compass heading to the lake on which we were supposed to deliver our load. By means of such precise guidance, we managed to successfully complete hundreds of trips into Alaska's outback. Tons of food, fuel, seismic equipment and other supplies were distributed to scores of camps where our arrival was always eagerly awaited. We also carried mail and packages to lonely crews.

Interior pilots Neil Bergt and John Robert talk to Jim Magoffin before boarding the Connie for a cargo haul to the Arctic Slope.

A good share of the nation's seismic firms was represented during the peak of testing activity. Besides United Geophysical, there were seismic crews from Geophysical Services, Inc.; Western Geophysical; Globe Geophysical; National Geophysical and Ray Geophysical.

All of these firms regularly made cargo demands that were either urgent or rush. I never heard anyone say, "Get the stuff out there when you have time." Typical of the difficulties we were accustomed to dealing with on a routine day was the urgent need of National Geophysical to get a recording unit—that had been trucked from Edmonton — delivered to their crew on the North Slope .

It was emphasized to us that nobody at the remote tundra camp could turn a wheel until the recording unit arrived. Personnel there were marking time while company brass kept fuming.

Frank Ganoe, the seismic firm's expediter in Alaska, seemed about to blow a gasket. A spell of bad weather had clamped down all the way to the Arctic Ocean and flying conditions were marginal at best.

To make things worse, the C-82 (flying boxcar) in which we had planned to haul the unit, had been giving us nothing but trouble. Though running okay in most respects, we couldn't control one of the propellers properly. One engine's rpm kept fluctuating all the way between 1,700 and 2,300. We'd be flying along normally when suddenly, for no apparent reason, the engine would change speed.

We kept wracking our brains for a clue to the cause of the trouble. We changed prop governors a couple of times. We changed props. Nothing seemed to help.

On the day when National Geophysical's man was badgering us to get going, the only plane available for the job was that cantankerous C-82. Our pilots knew all about its perversity and none of them were enthusiastic about flying it — especially in bad weather.

Though I had never flown a C-82, I decided that I'd fly the trip. I felt confident I could handle the plane despite its rpm problem. I wasn't totally unfamiliar with the C-82 since I had observed the operation closely while riding in the jump seat.

We loaded the recording unit — a rectangular building that entirely filled the cargo compartment.

Roger Burns, our radio man, kindly volunteered to fly co-pilot on the trip. The fluctuating rpm notwithstanding, we made the flight to the camp and back without incident.

After our return, we were determined to get to the bottom of the nagging trouble. We took the C-82's engine off and dismantled it. The gremlin showed up instantly. While being overhauled in Seattle, a workman had left a paper parts tag in the engine. Every once in a while that floating trouble-maker would cover up the oil inlet to the prop governor. This caused the puzzling rpm fluctuation that had been bedeviling us for so long. Otherwise, the engine was in perfect condition.

The environmental battle, usually confined to newspaper offices and the halls of Congress, occasionally made itself felt right out in the oil camps. One day, a party of dedicated naturalists, known locally as "moss-grabbers," showed up unexpectedly at one of the remote camps. One of the environmentalists lectured geologists about the correct way of carrying supplies from the lake shore, where planes delivered them, to the camp.

"It's important," camp members were told, "that you take a different path every time you travel from the lake to the camp. That way, you'll avoid damaging the delicate tundra."

Damage inflicted by geologists carrying supplies up the same path from the lake to the camp was certainly infinitesimal compared to what happened the following night.

A thundering herd of several thousand caribou swept by the camp. As the animals passed continuously through the camp area, their pounding hooves left foot-deep ruts that stretched for miles across the tundra.

Nature itself rarely spares the "delicate" tundra. In a matter of minutes, a summer rainstorm can touch off a flash flood that can chew up acres of tundra as the water surges downstream. My own view is that oil operations in the North have done little to disturb the environment.

Our major challenge, as seismic activity intensified, was the matter of adequately serving the scattered and frequently moving crews. At times, our logistics problems seemed almost insoluble. Thousands of barrels of fuel and other supplies destined for the camps kept piling up steadily. Seismic crews, prodded by the oil companies who hired them, kept demanding extra-fast service.

Faced with a mountain of supplies that just had to go, we were experiencing, at the same time, a shortage of qualified pilots. We couldn't hire just anybody to pilot these critical trips. That would surely result in accidents. Though we were able to hire a few good pilots, there never seemed to be enough to do the job that faced us. And flying in the arctic was far different from routine airline flying and even much of bush flying.

Well-honed flying skills and a real familiarity with natural hazards had to come from experience. Landing safely on nameless frozen arctic lakes requires special aptitude.

In the beginning, we had to land on lakes where no landing area had been cleared. Usually, we sent a small, ski-equipped plane ahead to test the ice. If landing a heavy aircraft was determined to be safe, the pilot would stake out the smoothest "runway" area with a series of black flags.

There were times, however, when we found it necessary to make landings on unmarked lakes without any such preliminaries. I tried to fly such trips myself, having gained a knack for recognizing the best landing spots and sizing up the feasibility of a safe landing. I was able to instruct younger, less experienced pilots on just how this was done. I pointed out to them, for example, how important it was to abort the flight if the landing area appeared to be too rough or was not feasible for any reason. In such cases, the pilot was instructed to deliver the load, instead, to the nearest safe landing spot or leave it at Sagwon to be delivered later.

The continuing pilot squeeze put heavy pressure on every available man. Out of necessity, our pilots flew almost continuously. Each month, as we approached the maximum flying hours permitted by regulations, we began to shave our trip times.

Had the fuz ever bothered to compare our flight times with mileage flown, they would have been puzzled to learn that Interior Airways planes travelled much faster than similar aircraft operated by other airlines.

On weekends when we figured no CAA agents were lurking around, many of our trips weren't logged at all. Had the inspectors simply checked our logbooks against control tower tapes, we'd have been caught red-handed, and it would have been tough to avoid cancellation of our certificate.

On one very productive Sunday, we successfully completed delivery of 180 barrels of fuel to the North Slope. This amounted to six loads. The operation required the use of two C-46s with Neil Bergt and Wayne Baily flying one plane and Chuck Evans and I flying the other, while Dot Magoffin drove the forklift used in the loading process.

To avoid serious fatigue during the course of an excessive amount of flying, co-pilots caught their sleep on northbound flights and captains slept on the return trip with the co-pilot flying the empty plane back to Fairbanks.

Air transportation is a seven-day-a-week business. We became accustomed to working every day, including Christmas and other holidays. There was, of course, grumbling and griping. Pilots would never complain to me but they would tell Dot, "Jim's okay, but it would sure be nice if he'd give us a day off sometime."

I was accused, only half-jokingly, of wanting, if I had my own way, to have all the pilots confined to a barracks-type building situated at the airport where I could control them and keep them flying. I lived by a strict, self-imposed discipline. My aim was not to play the role of some kind of a Simon Legree but to get a tough job done even under the worst kind of pressure. Working every day (and night) and bending regulations was not our desired mode of operation. It was a necessity since fully half the loads were destined for our own airport at Sagwon, the staging area for most of the seismic crews. Further, failure to deliver promptly would have resulted in unhappy customers who surely would have hired other flying outfits.

Having to work on Sundays made for infrequent church attendance. However, Dot eased our concerns about a certain road to hell by referring to the scripture in the Bible that says if one's ox gets in the ditch on the Sabbath, it is permissible to pull it out. It seemed that my ox was always in the ditch, and the federal government was intent on keeping it there. ✝

CHAPTER 40

Flood

The Magoffin home — where employees and friends took refuge during the 1967 flood. The garden helped feed our many guests.

In August, normally the wettest month in interior Alaska, the deluge began and it seemed as if it would never end.

It was as if the whole sky had opened up above us and some huge, unseen reservoir had ripped apart and begun dumping an endless surge of water on Fairbanks and the surrounding vicinity.

It rained around the clock for 14 days straight. The rivers just couldn't handle the drainage. On Aug. 15, 1967, the Chena River that flows through the heart of Fairbanks went absolutely wild. It surged over its banks bringing devastating flooding to downtown Fairbanks and all the surrounding vicinity.

The whole area was caught up in one of the worst disasters in Alaska history.

Never, since the town had been a raw gold camp, had it been inundated so badly.

People in aviation suffered like everybody else. Airports in the vicinity weren't spared. Taxiways and parking areas were flooded, but our airport runway, fortunately, remained about an inch above high water.

Our home, situated on a hill northwest of the city, became a welcome refuge for employees and their families, as well as many others driven from their homes by the flood.

The first to reach our "island" were a drenched Al and Millie Seeliger. They were forced out of their home in the Westgate suburb of the city, a location close to the Chena River and among the areas hardest hit by the flood.

Then, in the middle of one miserable night, in the midst of the continuing downpour, Neil Bergt showed up at our door with his four small children. After turning the kids over to us, he returned to his home to give a hand to his wife, Laura, who was

Roger Burns manning a pump during the flood that inundated most of Fairbanks in August 1967.

frantically trying to move their possessions above the steadily rising water level.

The next day, with rain still pouring down relentlessly, we were joined by Charlie Hubbs and his family, as well as several other friends.

Our available accommodations rapidly filled to overflowing as more people kept coming. Nobody was turned away. All the available beds and couches in our house had occupants. Clusters of children were sleeping on the floors. Cots we had set up in the garages were quickly filled. And still it rained and still the people came.

Our next major concern was making sure everybody got fed. Bob Fawcett, our Anchorage manager, would fly a DC-3 crammed with provisions to Fairbanks every few days. We'd use a Piper Cub to ferry the food from the airport to a small, grass field not far from our home. It helped, also, that our freezer was well stocked with wild game and fish. Flood victims also added many things to our larder and it seemed certain that there would be enough to go around.

Some of the ladies pitched in to help with the cooking and other work. A few of them went blueberry picking near Ester, and Laura Bergt baked a delicious blueberry cobbler, large enough to feed the whole crowd. Laura, an appreciative young lady, never missed an opportunity to thank us for giving them a start in the aviation industry.

Among our 25 guests were Roy and Frances Isackson. Frances had been employed as secretary to Woody Johansen, the boss of the Alaska Road Commission in Fairbanks, for many years.

Johansen provided one of the unforgettable lighter moments in the flood.

About the second day of the flood, Johansen stopped by briefly to check on the Isacksons. He was met at the door by Dot, who was caught up in the excitement of the tense situation and who had just been told that two dogs belonging to the flood victims were in heat. "Come in, come in!" she told Woody excitedly. "We have six dogs here and two females in heat!"

Woody grinned, then drew on his quick wit to respond, "In that case, I'd better not come in!"

This incident provided a much-needed laugh to a lot of people who were tense and anxious about the damage to their inundated homes.

In a few days, the flood began to subside, and gradually those being sheltered began going back to their homes to start the long, arduous task of cleaning up.

It's difficult to find something good to say about a disaster like the 1967 Fairbanks flood but looking back at it now, Alaskans can take real pride in the way Fairbanks citizens reacted. The flood brought out the very best in everybody. Everybody shared, everybody helped his neighbor, and those who could shelter others did it willingly and happily.

As for Dot and me, it gave us tremendous satisfaction to be able to be of real assistance at a time when a lot of people in Fairbanks were in such desperate straits. ✝

CHAPTER 41

Incredible Sagwon

An Interior Airways Hercules departing Sagwon.

In the mid-'60s, at the peak of the arctic oil exploration rush, our Sagwon airport was a restless beehive of activity, a far cry from the desolate acres of brush and rocks we started with.

Air traffic became so heavy, we were obliged to build and operate an aircraft control tower on top of our operations building at the airport. Where only birds flew before, now the field served a never-ending stream of aircraft. On any given day, one could see Beavers, Widgeons, Twin Otters, DC-3s, C-46s, C-82s, the Constellation and later on the huge Lockheed Hercules. The incredible tempo of air activity that developed at Sagwon included a flock of light planes as well — planes like the Super Cub, the Cessna 180 and the Norseman.

Float planes utilized Sag Lake, situated about a quarter of a mile east of the Sagwon runway. On this good-sized fresh water lake, we operated a Beaver on floats to serve seismic crews over a tremendous area.

It was not unusual for pilots of transient float planes to come into Sag Lake to refuel at the gas facility we installed there. Visiting pilots often took advantage of the opportunity to partake of our modern Sagwon camp facilities including showers, sleeping quarters and a warm mess hall serving good food.

In the early construction phase at Sagwon, buildings went up all over the place. These included a larger operations building, a fine mess hall and barracks for workmen. Communications improvement had a high priority. We installed a whole array of new equipment including single side-band radios at both Sagwon and Umiat. Now, we had round-the-clock access to instant weather data, so vital to our far-flung operations as well as three-way communications with a highly useful voice link to Fairbanks.

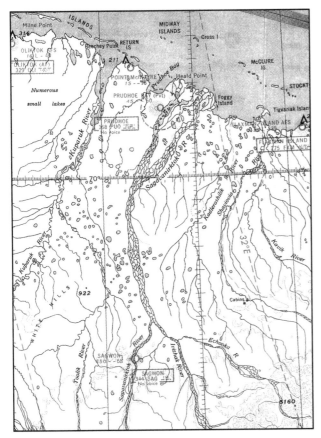

Sagwon, the site picked by Magoffin for Interior's own airport, was inland far enough to escape the coastal fog but close to the area of most interest to the oil companies. Sagwon paid for itself many hundreds of times.

A brand new, much larger generator went in; I'll have more to say about that later.

While work proceeded hucklety-buck on buildings and facilities along the airport's periphery, we urgently pushed expansion of the airport itself.

We flew in heavy equipment, including a rock crusher, to enable our contractor, Rivers Construction of Anchorage, to increase the runway length to 5,200 feet. They did a good job on our new mile-long runway, overlaying it with crushed rock and crowning it.

A permanent modern runway lighting system was installed. When work was completed, we had a solid, up-to-the-minute airport, so good that the FAA okayed it for use by some types of jet aircraft, although I never knew of a jet to land there.

Much of the feverish building activity came under the eagle eye of Roy Isackson, our vice president and general manager. He spent a lot of time at Sagwon during early phases, keeping constant track of logistics and riding herd on construction activity. Roy was an incredibly versatile fellow and actually designed the buildings we put up at the airport.

Roy liked to kid and, on one occasion, decided to pull the leg of a fresh-faced New York lad, a rank greenhorn on our loading crew at Sagwon.

To the amusement of others on the crew, though it was the dead of winter, the young fellow had brought along his fishing rod, some spinners and other tackle. And he meant to use them.

"I'd like to go down to the river and do some fishing," he told Roy one blistering cold day in mid-January.

Glancing at the almost solidly frozen Sag River, Roy grinned and nodded. "Sure, son," he said, "you can go right down there, cut a hole in the ice and catch all the fish you want."

The others stood around snickering, convinced that the river was nothing but ice all the way down to gravel.

Undaunted, the boy gathered together an ice chisel to carve out the fishing hole, an ax and his gear and loaded it all in a gas box that he put on a sled and pulled to the river.

After he had been gone about three hours, we began getting a little concerned. Finally, he came trudging back to camp just at dark wearing an ear-to-ear smile and dragging along a gas box brimming with beautiful arctic char.

The boy had cut a hole through the ice at the bend of the river. Here a good pool existed and a current of water flowed all winter long. The pool was teeming with fish.

"Every time I'd put my spinner down there, I'd yank out one of these beauties," he said proudly.

Those wonderful, fresh fish he caught fed the whole camp. They were delicious.

✻ ✻ ✻ ✻ ✻ ✻

Roy's light-hearted, spur-of-the-moment, usually harmless antics backfired on one occasion at Sagwon and scared the dickens out of a lot of people.

He came up with what he thought was a fool-proof, instant solution to the problem of eliminating a huge cache of blasting powder believed to be tainted and unusable.

United Geophysical had flown in the stuff for use in their seismic activity and stored it right across the Sagwon runway about 100 yards from camp.

Subsequently, word came through that much of the blasting powder had been condemned and was not to be used under any circumstances. We were told to get rid of the stuff as soon as possible.

The seismic firm's crew manager began griping to Roy about all the extra work involved in disposing of the explosives and having to fly in a fresh batch.

Roy was not found wanting in reaching an instant solution to the explosives problem as he characteristically did with so many other problems.

"Look," he announced, "it really isn't necessary to haul all that stuff away. I'll take care of it quick and easy and nobody's going to have to do any work at all."

At that, Isackson picked up his .30-.06, leaned up against the mess hall door and touched off a single shot into the cases of primers stacked on top of the powder.

The deafening blast that followed must have reverberated all the way to Russia. It startled everybody at Sagwon and scared the hell out of some people. Several windows in the camp were shattered. Roy, himself, was shook up. It took a long time for the debris to settle. It was a good thing that no planes were parked at Sagwon when Roy decided to get rid of all those surplus explosives by firing just one shot. They surely would have been damaged.

* * * * * *

The Grinch who stole Christmas was no more of a meanie than our little Witte generator that blew up at a time when 25 seismic workers were waiting at Sagwon to catch a special flight that would allow them to get home for the holidays.

A seismic exploration firm had chartered an Alaska Airlines Convair 240 to pick up their crew at Sagwon at 9:30 p.m. on a 45-degree-below-zero night less than a week before Christmas.

Now, the eager-to-get-going workers were crammed into a 16- by 20-foot shack alongside the runway, all of them listening intently for the sound of the aircraft that would make possible getting back to family and friends at Christmas.

At 8 p.m., just an hour and a half before the plane was due in, the lights in the waiting room went off, leaving only the flickering from the little oil stove everybody was clustered around. At the same time, our runway lights went off and our homing beacon and communication radios went off the air as well.

The Grinch, our Witte generator, well-mounted in concrete, had thrown a rod, completely disintegrating the generator into useless pieces of junk. Before that, it hadn't given us any trouble, and since the Wittes had a long-standing reputation for reliability, we hadn't bothered to keep a backup on hand.

Without the runway lights and without the radio communications, nobody was going to be flying anywhere. We had a serious problem on our hands, including what we were going to tell all those workers anxiously milling around in the waiting room.

But the Grinch had a guy named Roger Burns to contend with. Burns was a radio wizard who had been Shell Oil's radio man in Fairbanks until we hired him and put him in charge of our communications.

Burns had established a crackerjack communications setup that allowed Shell's Fairbanks officials to keep in constant touch with their geology crews on the North Slope. From on-the-air indications, I figured Shell must have an elaborate setup, so I visited their headquarters one day to have a look.

Their intricate communications system turned out to be not much more than an antenna wire stretched between two bushes. Though sloppy-looking, the system had been nurtured and peaked up to such a point by Roger that it was providing Shell with excellent communications at a time when equipment operated by the rest of us was squeaking and squawking, only occasionally emitting a clear word here and there. We hired Roger at the earliest opportunity and he remained with us for many years.

Sagwon, Alaska, on a foggy morning, 1966.

Much later, we were to find Roger's brilliance highlighted when he tackled another problem we had after acquiring our first Hercules. We were faced with making an overseas flight for the International Red Cross but were stymied because regulations required us to have a navigator if we were to fly over the North Pole from Fairbanks to London. We didn't have a navigator.

A couple of our Airline Transport-rated pilots did some in-depth studying and took the navigator's exam, but it proved so tough both of them flunked. Roger, who hadn't studied a bit as far as we knew, took the examination at the FAA office and came through with answers that were almost 100 percent correct. From then on, and until we began hiring professionals for the job, Burns was our one and only navigator.

Now, with the clock ticking away toward the time when the men were scheduled to be picked up to begin their Christmas holiday, it was Burns who came forward with an unexpected solution to our problem.

I was conferring with him after the generator conked out when he stopped in mid-sentence and declared, "Just remembered! Couple of weeks ago, United Geophysical's crew dumped a generator in a snowbank not far from here. Guess it wasn't running good enough to suit them. I wonder if we couldn't drag it out of the snow and get it going?"

Who but Roger Burns would come up with a possibility like that at a time like that? I was desperate and ready to try anything. "Let's go," I told him.

We hurried out into the terrible cold and headed toward the snowbank. Roger quickly found the place where the generator had been ditched and, as I held a lantern, Roger went to work. I placed the duct of a Herman Nelson heater next to Roger's hands so they wouldn't freeze.

Roger took the carburetor off, cleaned it and checked the magneto. We applied heat to the generator, gave it a crank and prayed. By golly, it ran.

We hooked the generator on to the line just 20 minutes before the Convair flight arrived, on schedule. Instantly, the runway lights were back on and our beacon and radios were operating.

It was real good, just a few days before Christmas, to see all those people filing aboard that plane which was their only ticket to a merry Christmas. Roger and I weren't going anywhere that Christmas, but as we watched that plane take off for Fairbanks and saw its lights gradually disappear in the arctic darkness, I think we both were feeling good about getting them all back to civilization at a special time like that.

Within a few days we had replaced our defective generator with a new 15-kilo-watt unit, much larger and able to easily handle the power requirements of a growing Sagwon.

Now, having said all those nice things about Roger, I've got to balance things a bit by revealing one outrageous incident that certainly didn't endear him either to me or to the company. People have been fired for far less.

On one occasion, Roger and his friend Bill Chadwick, a Western Geophysical employee, spent an evening making the rounds of Fairbanks bars, and there were plenty of them. By midnight, both were four sheets to the wind and Roger was boisterously bragging that he knew how to start every airplane in Interior's fleet — 30-some air-craft.

Naturally, Chadwick challenged him to prove it, so there was nothing to do but get a cab out to the airport. Roger was successfully upholding his claim until they climbed into one of our C-82s.

In their impaired condition, neither of the revelers noticed that the C-82's pro-peller on the right engine had been removed.

Roger engaged the starter and it turned over very nicely. Then he snapped on the ignition switch and the engine really began roaring. As engine speed quickly exceeded the red line, Roger fortunately sobered up enough to cut the switch.

To his credit, he was honest enough to tell us about the whole caper the next morning. We were afraid we might be faced with an engine change, but a thorough test revealed that no damage had been done.

* * * * * *

Among my favorite employees was a huge, black guy, Louis Metoyer, whom we hired for our loading crew during the Sagwon expansion period. Louie quickly became a star on the crew because of his incredible strength and his personality.

His strength was amply demonstrated to me one day while the two of us were loading barrels of fuel on a C-46. The barrels, after having been deposited on the flat landing opposite the cargo doors, had to be rolled up a steep incline, then heaved into an upright position.

Normally, it took two men exerting all their strength to tip the barrels on end. I was about to give Louie some help with the first barrel when he grabbed the lip of the barrel using one hand, swiftly setting it upright. After that, I decided I'd just keep out of Louie's way.

He stayed with us until his retirement. He loved to fish and it was a pleasure for me to take him along on several summertime fishing outings in northern Alaska.

* * * * * *

When the first oil well was drilled by Richfield in the Sagwon area, Interior's cook at Sagwon was Jim Eaves. Jim and his wife, Suzie, had a pretty little baby girl, also named Suzie, so the Richfield boys named their first oil well "Suzie." The parents were delighted even though that particular well wasn't successful.

* * * * * *

I am proud to say that our younger son, Billy, had a role to play, and played it well, during early activity on the North Slope.

Billy became a temporary ARCO employee about the time Richfield and Atlantic Refining Co. merged to become ARCO. It was shortly after Richfield drilled their first well in the Sagwon area. Bill had the job of watchman for the drilling rig during the summertime when there could be no drilling at the remote site. Crews had to wait for winter when the tundra became solid and heavy aircraft could get in. Meanwhile, Billy was out there all by himself, keeping his eye on the rig and making sure nobody pilfered it in any way.

Billy occupied deserted living quarters near the rig and kept in regular touch with Sagwon by radio. Though he usually did his own cooking, Bob Jacobs, our Sagwon resident pilot, would pick him up once in a while and fly him to Sagwon so he could enjoy a decent meal.

Mostly, Billy spent all that spare time getting acquainted with the foxes, ptarmigan and caribou, as well as other wildlife in the area.

* * * * * *

We had our share of incidents and accidents, of course, as can be expected in an

Longtime Interior Airways arctic pilot Bob Jacobs with a DC-3 at Arctic Village, Alaska. "Jake" was originally based at Umiat, but moved to Sagwon as oil company interest increased in that area.

operation of this scope.

The first of two serious setbacks took place in the spring of 1968 when a United Geophysical seismic party asked us to deliver a load of barreled fuel to Noluck Lake, aptly named, I might say.

Charlie Cole and I flew a Cessna 180 to the lake situated on the north slope of the mountains in the western arctic. We tested the thickness of the ice and found it safe for a C-46 landing. Then we flagged off a suitable landing strip in the middle of the lake where the ice was free of snow. We also marked out a spot for the plane to taxi to the beach to unload.

Getting the fuel oil cargo to Noluck Lake should have been an easy, safe operation. It ended up horribly. The captain on that flight, who shall remain unnamed, got the C-46 down on the lake all right and got the cargo unloaded. But when the time came to go, instead of using the safe, carefully flagged-out runway, the captain decided to taxi into a nearby snow-covered bay to begin his takeoff.

This was a serious, terribly expensive mistake. The bay he selected to begin his takeoff had a heavy snow cover that hid an overflow and weak ice beneath. When the plane taxied into this area, the main wheels plunged through the rotten ice and came to

Costly reflection. This valuable C-46 was left as a monument to poor pilot judgment. In less-hectic times, it would have been salvaged.

rest with most of the fuselage still above the ice while the wheels sank into the mud below. That plane wasn't going anywhere for several reasons: the remoteness of the lake, the arrival of warm weather and the fact that I was tied up in Chicago negotiating the acquisition of our first Hercules. That valuable C-46, now anchored in the lake, remains a monument to one pilot's poor judgment.

Our other notable mishap during that era resulted from allowing two airline captains to fly together.

In our industry, there's a well-respected belief, or a superstition, that nothing can be more dangerous than assigning two airline captains to the same flight.

To our later regret, we chose to ignore this unwritten rule because we wanted to perform a vital operation at a time when the only pilots available to do the job were Capt. Ed Brenner and Capt. Buzz Dyer.

On their late night arrival, at what they thought was their destination, they saw a runway marked out by lighted fire pots on a frozen lake. Without further ado, they proceeded to land on the runway that wasn't suitable for anything larger than a single-engine Beaver.

Of course, the C-46 swiftly gobbled up the entire length of that little runway and then some. It kept right on going past the lake and into the tundra. That terrible noise the pilots heard was the landing gear being ripped out. Fortunately, neither pilot was hurt.

We had one heck of a time getting that jinxed airplane out of there. We probably couldn't have done it without the dedicated help of Jiri Sorm of Boeing Field, an expert in metal work, and the hard-working technician who was his assistant.

We had a lot of confidence in Jiri because he had done considerable work for us earlier. Jiri and his young helper set up housekeeping right inside the stranded plane. It was terribly cold and miserable out there but these two guys were tough and determined, camping in that marooned plane for several weeks and knocking themselves out every day to get the plane set to go again.

We kept in constant touch with Sorm and his assistant. Our resident pilot at Sagwon, Bob "Jake" Jacobs, made a point of visiting the two men every day, flying out to the lake with the Beaver to make sure they had enough food and fuel and were okay in every other respect. Jake would shuttle in whatever items the craftsmen needed such as tools, screws and rivets.

The pair did a fine job of completing a temporary fix. This included bolting metal plates on the bottom of the aircraft, reattaching the landing gear and bolting it securely in the down position. Though the gear couldn't be retracted, it was in good enough shape to ferry to Fairbanks.

When we got word that the airplane was ready to go, Roger Burns again volunteered to accompany me. Jake flew us out to the crash site aboard the Beaver. He picked up Sorm and his helper and flew them back to Sagwon, where they couldn't wait to get showers, some decent food and a well-earned rest.

Roger and I brought the repaired C-46 to Fairbanks without incident, flying it with the landing gear down. We parked the plane near our hangar at the Fairbanks airport. Sorm arrived in Fairbanks a short time later to finish the job.

He got the C-46 back in shape and, by the time he was finished with it, there was no doubt that it was just as airworthy and stronger than when it was new.

Both these young men deserved kudos for the outstanding job they did in the face of terrible arctic conditions. ✝

CHAPTER 42

Oil!
And Hercules!

The Feb. 1968 oil discovery changed Alaska forever. For Interior Airways, 1968 and 1969 were wild years of non-stop flying and expansion.

News of the discovery of large quantities of oil at Prudhoe Bay in the spring of 1968 electrified the world.

ARCO's triumph at Prudhoe came after a series of failures and part-failures including the $4.5 million dry hole named Suzie, near Sagwon back in 1966.

The 1968 discovery was *big!* DeGolyer and McNaughton, an internationally recognized petroleum consulting firm, reported after the discovery that "Prudhoe Bay could develop into a field with recoverable reserves of some 5 to 10 billion barrels of oil." This, according to the firm, would make it "one of the largest petroleum accumulations known to the world today."

Oil authorities termed it the largest oil field ever to be found in the United States. The field was twice the size of the next largest field in North America, the giant East Texas field. It contained around one-third of the nation's known oil reserves.

To jump ahead a bit, on June 20, 1977, the first oil began to flow through the Trans-Alaska Pipeline, costing about $8 billion, to Valdez 800 miles away. Tankers there began loading as about 1.6 million barrels a day poured into terminal facilities.

What did all this mean to our business back in 1968?

Years of legal, political and engineering activity were ahead before Valdez got a drop of oil. Building of the pipeline was almost a decade away. Yet, the incredible ocean of oil that was about to be tapped had revolutionary significance for air transportation in general and for us.

After two weeks filled with hectic meetings, an agreement more crucial to our company's fate than any we had ever signed was consummated. We were getting the Hercules! It was delivered to us Oct. 18, 1968.

One thing I was sure of long before the Prudhoe Bay discovery became global news: We had to expand, and do so rapidly, to keep pace with events.

Exploration activity continued, even accelerated, after the big discovery. The strain on our facilities continued to grow. No question about it: We had reached a crossroads. Decisions we made at this crucial time would decide the fate of our firm.

With the highly intensified pace of oil activity in the North, our C-82s and C-46s simply couldn't do the job. Unless we began expanding, we wouldn't be in the picture very long. Our earlier aircraft acquisitions simply were inadequate to cope with the huge surge of cargo activity we faced.

Flying Tigers made us a deal we found hard to turn down for a Lockheed Super Constellation. Fred Benninger, who was then running the company, put it this way: "If, within the first year, you decide you don't like the plane, you can return it to us and all we'll charge you is a monthly rate for the rental."

We were glad, later, to have a way out of the agreement we signed because early on we had trouble with the aircraft. Our crew had flown it to Richfield's Suzie well site. While it was taking off on a bitterly cold day, one of the engines disintegrated internally.

Oil development progressed until Interior Secretary Walter J. Hickel failed to issue the pipeline permit.

Never before had we had an engine go completely to pieces. The Constellation had Wright 3350 engines. We had been operating Pratt & Whitney engines in our DC-3s, C-46s, C-82s, Beavers, Norsemans and Twin Beeches.

The Tigers contended that our pilots had been using excessive power under the extremely low temperatures prevailing in the arctic. Nevertheless, we just weren't going to take a chance on such touchy engines. The plane had to go back where it came from.

It was then that I began to think that the huge, multi-million-dollar Hercules might not be such an impossible dream in light of the startling new developments in the North. More and more, I became convinced the Hercules was a plane worth fighting like hell for. Boeing and Lockheed representatives were giving me sales talks without knowing that my mind was pretty well made up.

Dick Lankford, the Boeing salesman, and Don Webster, who had been sent to Alaska by Lockheed, were both guests at our home.

It was amusing to see them sitting at our table enjoying the dinner, each with a model of the airplane he wanted to sell us placed prominently in front of him.

Though Lankford did his best, when the dust settled we remained determined to get our hands on a Hercules and lost no time in pursuing that desire.

Webster accompanied me to the Lower 48 to help run interference on financing the huge aircraft, something way beyond the lending limits of Alaska banks.

We talked to money men in Seattle but didn't meet with much interest there.

Then we talked to the president of World Airways, who was enthusiastic about buying us a Hercules, but only provided we gave him 40 percent of our stock, a deal we politely declined, of course.

In Chicago, we began to hit pay dirt. We talked to Richard Oldacre, a young investment banker associated with a small investment banking firm, Douglas Securities. He had been to Alaska and knew about the economic potential there.

Through Oldacre and his firm, we were put in touch with Marvin D. Juliar at the powerful Chicago First National Bank. Juliar lost no time in setting up meetings for us with key bank people. They began to express guarded interest.

Don Webster, Lockheed Hercules salesman, is assisted by pretty Interior Airways stewardesses when he visits Prudhoe Bay, March 1968.

The board of the Chicago First National Bank sent Juliar out to confer with top officials at the home offices of oil companies involved in Alaska to get more information on the feasibility of what was to us a gigantic loan.

Discussed were such things as cargo tonnages and sea and air competition. Other possible investors, including Baxter Laboratories, were consulted.

One of Lockheed's top officials rushed to Chicago from Burbank to be present in the discussions and, hopefully, the ultimate deal.

Not everybody on the Chicago bank board was enthusiastic about the deal. These conservative bankers were particularly troubled that there might not be enough cargo to haul to justify such a large aircraft.

Knowing that Alaska's governor, Walter Hickel, was thoroughly familiar with the North Slope situation, I phoned him and told him of the problems I was having with the reluctant bankers.

He reacted immediately with a long telegram to the bank giving his appraisal of the oil situation and emphasizing that a sizable airlift would be required.

July 1975. The Grumman Widgeon coming ashore at Saltery Lake on Kodiak Island, Alaska. The left wing float is retracted to avoid hitting high ground.

With the active support of the oil companies, the governor of Alaska and Bob Reeve, we got very close to signing the agreement. I advised Charlie Cole about the status of negotiations, and he flew in from Alaska to assist me in finalizing the purchase details. At one point in the discussions, we were just $100,000 apart in reaching full agreement. I volunteered to fill that gap, but bank officials quickly took the step themselves.

After two weeks filled with hectic meetings, an agreement more crucial to our company's fate than any we had ever signed was consummated. We were getting the Hercules! It was delivered to us on Oct. 18, 1968.

Along with those already mentioned, Bob Reeve deserves a great deal of credit. I'm convinced that his all-out support was of great importance in weighing the decision in our favor at a critical time.

When Reeve heard that I was negotiating with the Chicago First National Bank to acquire a Hercules, he took it upon himself to direct a letter to a longtime friend, James Douglas, a former assistant secretary of the Air Force, who happened to be one of the Chicago bank's directors.

I knew nothing about Reeve's letter until several months after it was written when I was furnished a copy by Al Johnson, who was a senior vice president of the bank. He sent it to me with a handwritten note saying, "Jim, you have a real friend in Bob Reeve."

The letter, which remains among my prized possessions, is worth citing in full. It follows:

REEVE ALEUTIAN AIRWAYS, INC.
P.O. BOX 6027
Anchorage, Alaska 99502
Sunday, 9/1/68

Dear Jim:

Excuse the handwriting, but my secretary's piled-up desk dictates this won't get out for several days, and I deem it of sufficient importance to get out to you ASAP.

First, see attached news-sheet. Maybe you Middle-Westerners don't realize it, but this is just about the biggest thing that ever happened to Alaska, and its transportation requirements are going to be tremendous.

First, let me tell you about Jim Magoffin, founder of Interior Airways. I have known him for 20 years and he has an impeccable reputation for honesty and integrity and paying his bills. His present operations, principally above the Arctic Circle, have been profitable, and he has the confidence of the oil operators in that area for good service, and in view of this, I predict he will have first priority on any bulk freight hauls to the North Slope. Magoffin is not a cheap operator or a cut-throat. He has built up a good business by good service, and he has gained the loyalty of his customers — in this case, people like Atlantic Richfield Co. who made the big strike. I called the Atlantic Richfield people and asked them would they use Magoffin. They said, "We highly respect Jim M,. and while I can't obligate any haulage as an individual, there are going to be thousands of tons of cargo to be hauled there exclusively by air, and only a plane of the Lockheed Hercules type will fill the bill."

Now as to other Hercules craft available, one is owned by Alaska Airlines and being used, but it in no way fills the bill for all to be hauled. Atlantic alone is flying in (going to) two complete drilling rigs, and there are others like Standard Oil, Phillips and British Petroleum who are going into the area. I can foresee at least two Hercules flying night and day to get the job done. I would be in the act myself, but I already have almost more than I can handle, with serving the Aleutians and one MAC contract to service the DEW line.

The present CAB-certificated carrier now serving the North Slope is a combination of two Alaskan air carriers merged into Wien-Consolidated, Inc.

They also contemplate a Hercules, but they are so absorbed in financing three Boeing 737s that I personally know any more money for a Herc is out of the question. They do business with the First National Bank of Seattle which dominates the financing in Alaska and the Pacific Northwest. I believe they are also Magoffin's bankers, and the reason they won't finance Magoffin is because they are protecting the business for Wien-Consolidated, who have to raise $10-15 million in the 737s. The old protective society which is right, depending of course on what side of the fence you are on. I am positive in my own secret heart that this is the reason Jim M. hasn't had money luck on the West Coast.

I am friendly with Jim M. but not intimate. In all truth and frankness, I tell you that this situation has all the positive facts to merit favorable consideration of this loan — but it should be at least a five-year term loan and should include enough for training and plenty of spares, and some leniency in the first year's payments until he gets the plane integrated. Personally, that's about a thousand-dollar-a-day interest charge. That would scare the hell out of me — but, of course, my grandmother was a Campbell, and a few drops of that blood sure make a man aware that the intake has to exceed the exhaust.

Jim M. gets along very well with his help, and his pilots and mechanics are non-union. However, in a recent conversation, I warned him to do his best to keep his shop clean and root out any potential trouble-makers (I named one or two for him!)

Well, Jim, I guess I have covered the matter. If you want any other info let me know. Incidentally, I saw Jim's premises the other day. He has very clean shops and offices and is getting a new freight dock area.

He was recently involved in a scheduled operation between Fairbanks & Anchorage. He would have made a good success of it except for all the government and state agencies that got in the act — and, of course, when the big strike came, he smartly withdrew to devote his major efforts to the North Slope. Also, he can get a good price for his Hercules. The oil operators are all working on free money from oil depletion funds and price is no object, for they have at stake the biggest oil development of modern times.

All the facts are on the plus side, and I see no obstacles to a lender. In fact, this deal in my opinion, is much less speculative than most big airplane deals.

I am most pleased about Dick Nixon. I have conducted my own poll over the last 15 months — over 1,000 people from all states in the union and all walks of life — only 14 were not against the present administration and six of them didn't know what it was all about! I predicted a landslide last spring and present developments only strengthen my position.

We are all fine. I got in the jet business last spring (Lockheed Electra Turbo-Prop), but I paid cash for it. I don't have that interest keeping me awake nights.

I have much to talk with you about. I hope to see you in Chicago one of these days. Warmest regards and every good wish, Jim.

Most sincerely,
(signed) BOB ✝

CHAPTER 43

BP: The Only Game In Town

A positive development in the pre-pipeline years was leasing out our first Hercules to British Petroleum for one year.

Though the lease was on an exclusive-use basis, BP did not refuse the use of the aircraft for others at critical times. On several occasions when an emergency situation arose and we couldn't get piston airplanes into the air because of the cold, we asked BP to "loan" us our Hercules for other customers.

BP was most gracious in letting us use "their" plane to take care of our critical situations although I'm sure they were somewhat reluctant to assist persons who were actually working for their competitors.

Before the pipeline permit fiasco, it seemed obvious that there would be plenty of room for additional Hercules aircraft on the Alaskan scene.

Red Dodge, an enterprising young Western Airlines captain in Anchorage, got financial backing from a trucking operation on the East Coast and came up with two stretched Hercules. Unfortunately for Dodge, these two huge aircraft were delivered to him just at the time when the four-year delay in issuance of the pipeline permit was beginning.

All kinds of problems grew out of the temporary collapse of the pipeline plan. The oil companies, realizing that they were not, at least in the near future, going to be able to transport their oil to market, sharply decreased the scope of their Alaska activities. Most of them discontinued drilling and seismic efforts. Sadly, activity on the North Slope came to a near-screeching halt.

Our flying business diminished drastically. Now, we found ourselves stuck with some terribly expensive aircraft and very little for them to do.

Our British Petroleum contract was about the only thing that kept us going. BP was among the very few firms maintaining a fairly active tempo of North Slope operations. Being well financed, they probably figured they could take a chance on going ahead with some of their development plans and thus be in a good position if and when the pipeline permit was granted.

So our BP contract was about the only game in town. When our year expired, the contract came up for bid. Red Dodge, with two new Hercules to feed cargo to, severely underbid us, drastically cutting contract cargo rates about in half. His bid was incredible because there was no way Dodge could survive flying for such outrageously low rates.

Worse, to be considered for the few other charters that became available, we had to match Dodge's ridiculous rates. We found ourselves flying for cost and sometimes below cost just to maintain a little cash flow. The inevitable result was that both Dodge and our firm were forced into bankruptcy.

Apparently, Dodge lacked the valuable financial backing we enjoyed. Now an established corporation, we were able to weather the storm. Dodge, however, had his Hercules aircraft yanked away from him, and they were never to appear in Alaska again, even after the pipeline permit was finally granted.

Our operation had been going well until it was stalled by the failure to obtain the pipeline permit. Although getting our first Hercules financed in Chicago had been like pulling teeth, strangely enough the situation changed drastically later.

Our agreement with the Chicago bank required us to submit financial statements every two weeks. One day, I got a call from Al Johnson, one of the bank's senior officers, who told me, "We've been studying your financial statements and your progress, Jim. We're concerned that you're going to be faced with a horrendous tax liability. We believe you should purchase another Hercules. That will allow you to take advantage of the investment tax credit and the depreciation. We'll handle all the details."

The bank's foisting on us another Hercules after we had struggled like the devil to acquire the first one came as a shock to me. Nevertheless, within a short time a brand new stretched Hercules had been ordered from Lockheed. I didn't even have to leave our Fairbanks office to work out the details of the loan.

Dot and I flew to Marietta, Georgia, to accept the new aircraft when we were notified it was ready for delivery. Because this delivery coincided with the time that Secretary of the Interior Walter J. Hickel failed to issue the pipeline permit, we notified Lockheed that it looked like we might be getting into a bad situation. We wanted to delay taking the airplane to Fairbanks until we found out that the permit had actually been issued.

The outcome was that we never did pick up the airplane and Lockheed subsequently sold it to another customer.

The hectic rush during the winter of 1968-69 prompted a study of our cargo problem, revealing that we were using too much Hercules time to haul cargo that could be carried in other aircraft. For instance, we were hauling lumber and powder, cement and barreled and bulk fuel products in the Hercules that could just as well have gone into an airplane that didn't have the large cargo door and the rough field capability of the Hercules.

We contacted Boeing and concluded arrangements to purchase a Boeing 727 configured for cargo only. Boeing got the airplane ready for us, painted it in Interior's colors and notified us it was ready for delivery. Once again, delivery of a key aircraft coincided with the permit delay preventing us from taking delivery of that aircraft as well. Boeing later sold the plane to a South American customer.

Aircraft additions to Interior's fleet included a new Beechcraft C-90 King-Air, which we leased with pilot to ARCO. ARCO eventually wanted to upgrade, so we ordered two British DH-125 executive jets, one to be leased to ARCO and one for our company use and as a charter aircraft.

When the pipeline permit was delayed, ARCO informed us it no longer wanted the jet. We sold our position on one plane to Beech Aircraft Corp. and cancelled the order for the other.

When oil activity increased, ARCO purchased their own DH-125 and we bought an Israeli Aircraft jet, the Westwind, for company use. ✝

CHAPTER 44

The Hellish Winter Of 1968-69

The winter of 1968-69 was a terrible nightmare.

For weeks, we got hardly any sleep at all. It was just plain miserable. Interior Alaska was caught in the grip of bitterly cold weather — 55 degrees below zero or worse for weeks on end. It was the worst winter in 22 years. Thick ice fog frequently closed our airport and wiped out all flying. Ground equipment operated sluggishly, if at all.

Heating piston-engine aircraft to get them into some semblance of flying condition was often frustrating and extremely hard work.

Because we had our operating base at Sagwon, the eager oil companies directed the seismic crews they had hired to contact us for their transportation needs. Fresh from Texas, Oklahoma, California and other warm areas, these people were ill-prepared to challenge winter in the arctic, and most of them had no idea of what hazards lay ahead.

We did our best to guide them and assist them, but even so, there were plenty of emergencies that arose.

We were shook up when Bob Jacobs at Sagwon notified us that he had flown the last of the fuel oil over to a seismic crew of about a dozen men. They were situated out on the frozen tundra, some 20 miles west of Sagwon.

"They're down to their last barrel of oil!" Jacobs said. "If something isn't done soon, those guys could freeze to death!"

The stranded crew had used almost all their available fuel back-blading a runway on the tundra with a tractor. It was a very poor runway, rough and unsuitable for a large aircraft, but we realized that we had to get oil to those people or we'd have a tragedy on our hands.

The weather was terrible, with blowing snow and lousy visibility, but the mission had to be flown. One of our senior captains, Jerry Church, volunteered to take a DC-3 in on the makeshift runway, a terribly risky operation.

It was so marginal we loaded only half of the allowable load in the plane. After Church took off, the crew shifted the barrels so the plane would be quite tail heavy.

Jerry was able to bring the DC-3 down in a full stall, managing to get the airplane stopped without wiping out the landing gear. The possible tragedy was averted, but until the plane was safely back in the air and inbound for Sagwon, we experienced some very uneasy moments.

To further complicate things that winter, one of our C-82s developed a serious problem. Apparently, while the crew was on the ground at Umiat during the worst of the cold, one oil cooler congealed. While enroute to Fairbanks, the cooler split and the engine lost its oil. They were obliged to shut it down and were unable to maintain altitude on one engine.

The C-82 was forced down in the Yukon flats, 100 miles north of Fairbanks.

There were no injuries and the crew was airlifted out by one of our Beavers on skis the next morning. The C-82 was severely damaged and left in the thick spruce as a home for rabbits, squirrels and birds.

It was tough to lose a freighter we needed so badly at the time.

Cargo kept piling up much faster than we could handle it. We kept in constant touch with the oil companies to get estimates on their needs and what they told us was alarming. We estimated the tonnages scheduled to be moved would require about 20 or more Hercules operating right around the clock.

Of course, there was no way we could supply that many airplanes. We were able to lease a couple of airplanes from the National Equipment Rental, Ltd. in New York through their aircraft subsidiary, International Aerodyne of Miami, a company run by aviation entrepreneur George Batchelor.

I made a trip to see if I could line up some help from three other operators of Hercules aircraft. In Miami, I met with Bill Boyd, who was running Airlift International. He agreed to furnish us a Hercules at a time when we desperately needed it. In Oakland, Howard Korth, who ran Saturn, informed me that his planes were tied up on military airlift contracts and were not readily available. In Vancouver, British Columbia, I met with Rusty Harris and Jack Moul of Pacific Western Airlines with good results.

Intermountain Aviation of Tucson gave us some help by bringing in two C-46s and a DC-6. Intermountain, a well-organized company, brought in good mechanics who operated their own ground heaters. Despite the most miserable conditions, the firm did a good job of helping us get a lot of cargo up to the slope. Their Fairbanks manager, Bill Demmons, conducted an exceptionally efficient operation.

The Hercules we leased from Airlift International came up with several crews and they did a good job of helping us move freight. Unfortunately, on one trip, they undershot the runway going into Deadhorse and wrecked the airplane. They quickly replaced it and went right on operating.

Our operating area at the Fairbanks Airport became too crowded with the constant addition of more planes. I arranged with the airport manager to lease 19.7 acres of undeveloped swampland on the west side of the airport toward the southern end of the runway. We engaged a local trucking firm to clear the tract and bring it up to ramp level using gravel fill.

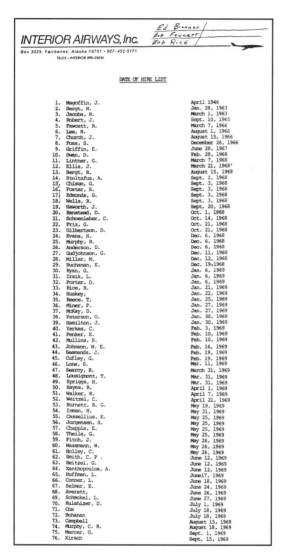

The pilot's list tells the story of unbelievably rapid
expansion — necessary to keep hundreds of people
from freezing or starving during the Alaska oil
rush of the late '60s.

The GHEMM Co. of Fairbanks took a contract to build us a new headquarters on the site. Later, Modern Construction of Anchorage built the hangar that the company uses today.

Our own subsidiary, Alaska International Construction, efficiently guided by its president, Lon McDermot, eventually paved the ramp providing a level surface to facilitate loading the Hercules aircraft in a hurry. Our smaller aircraft remained at our operation situated at the north end of the airport.

In normal circumstances, the terrible winter of 1968-69 would have been taken in stride by our people because we were prepared for it. We had the right equipment and we had our base at Sagwon. Many others suffered during that bitterly cold winter, but thanks to luck and vigilance, there were no fatalities associated with our operation.

Our Fairbanks headquarters office was burdened as much as the flight operation. Executive Vice President Charlie Cole and I shared the same office.

Dot packed enough lunch each day for both of us, and we ate without leaving the building as there was a steady stream of frantic customers demanding that they be given priority. Further, longtime oil company friends stopped in our offices daily and we had to devote time to them.

There were hundreds of things to be done, people to employ, planes to acquire, contracts to be written and dozens of deals to be made.

The almost unimaginable strain that the oil discovery and subsequent frantic efforts of the oil companies put us under, is amply illustrated by the pilot's date of hire list.

INTERIOR AIRWAYS, INC.	EXHIBIT B
STATEMENT OF INCOME AND RETAINED EARNINGS	
SIX MONTHS ENDED JUNE 30, 1969	
Operating revenues	$16,440,545
Operating expenses (including depreciation of $214,877)	12,335,919
Operating income	4,104,626
Other income	4,120
	4,108,746
Other deductions	57,291
Income before corporate income taxes	4,051,455
Estimated federal and state income taxes (Note 2)	2,041,889
Net income	2,009,566
Retained earnings, December 31, 1968	23,132
Retained earnings, June 30, 1969 (Exhibit A)	$ 2,032,698

In spite of the unusually severe winter, Interior Airways had a two million dollar profit in the first six months of 1969.

From nine overworked pilots in 1967, the list ballooned to 76 during 1968 and 1969 — and still we desperately needed more. When one considers that other company departments were proportionately enlarged, it becomes clear that administration, training and accounting were put under terrific pressure.

To complicate things, there were a large number of promoters and "wannabes" who took up our time when we couldn't avoid them. In the middle of one hectic day, a white-haired gentleman entered our office and proclaimed, "My associates and I are prepared to pay you $30 million cash for your operation and flying certificate!" We politely declined — too busy to even consider it — and we had multiple obligations and contracts that we couldn't have ignored if the offer had been twice that much.

Cole worked diligently, full time, with me and was invaluable in the office — negotiating, preparing contracts, acquiring aircraft and solving the multitude of daily problems. Though we had been in business for more than 20 years, we were ill-prepared for such a rush of business. We were short of help in all departments and short of space in which to put them. Accounting was a nightmare. We ceased all maintenance in our smallest hangar and divided the area into offices for the accounting department. Frank Leffler, our chief accountant, hired help as best he could but was grossly understaffed, requiring him to work day and night. Remarkably, the figures he presented were confirmed in audit by a national accounting firm to be unusually accurate. I will always be indebted to Frank Leffler for his loyalty and effort during the worst logjam with which an accountant could possibly be faced.

Cole and I kept a reasonably good handle on things and, until Secretary of the Interior Walter Hickel failed to issue the permit to build the pipeline, our operation was showing a handsome profit. However, the lack of a pipeline permit brought activity to a screeching halt, and our accumulated cash was quickly whisked away paying for leases on planes that were no longer earning. ✝

CHAPTER 45

"What In Hell's Wrong With Hickel?"

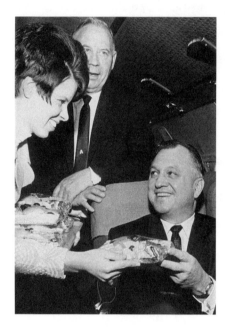

Governor Walter J. Hickel accepts lunch while riding on an Interior Airways DC-3 with other members of the "North Commission."

Walter J. "Wally" Hickel was — and is — Alaska's most spectacular "do-er," and he had a lot to do with the fate of our business during the early part of the oil boom in Alaska, beginning in 1968.

Hickel went to bat for me when he was Alaska's governor by helping me with the Chicago bankers at a time when the loan for the new Hercules was hanging in the balance.

Yet, it was during his 22 months in office as the country's interior secretary that he was our company's executioner, so to speak. His failure to act at a critical time precipitated the greatest crisis in our business life: *bankruptcy.*

Hickel, who is our governor as this is being written, also served as governor in the '60s when the crucial decisions concerning Alaska's oil pipeline were being made. Later he became President Nixon's interior secretary.

Hickel, who helped bring statehood to Alaska, came to the territory more than 50 years ago with only a few cents in his pocket. Along with the almost-legendary "Cap" Lathrop, Hickel rapidly became one of Alaska's dynamic moving forces.

But when the oil people were desperately trying to get a permit that would launch the pipeline from Prudhoe Bay to Valdez, many found Hickel, then in charge of the Interior Department, wanting.

Getting Alaska's oil out of the arctic to the world's markets initially seemed to be a challenge that was impossible to meet. All kinds of fantastic "solutions" to the oil transportation problem were cooked up. Ice-breaking oil tankers, under-ice submarines and under-ice barges were among the fanciful possibilities considered.

Finally, it was generally agreed that a 789-mile pipeline from the North Slope to the ice-free port of Valdez, tough as it would be with its anticipated price tag of $800 million, was the only feasible choice.

This project, the largest privately financed engineering and construction project ever undertaken, got under way in the fall of 1968 with the organization by three oil companies of the Trans-Alaska Pipeline System (TAPS).

The organizers were Atlantic-Richfield, Humble (a subsidiary of Standard Oil of New Jersey) and British Petroleum. Joining the consortium early in 1970 were Mobil Oil, Phillips Petroleum, Union Oil of California, Amerada Hess and Home Oil of Canada. The latter sold out its 2 percent interest to the others in the group before the year was up. (TAPS ultimately became the Alyeska Pipeline Service Co. or ALPS.)

A hectic and frustrating period, both for the oil companies and for us, was about to begin. TAPS directors were in a rush to put together firm contracts with the companies that would be involved in the engineering, construction and supply of the pipeline project.

We were among the companies invited by TAPS to attend a critical meeting at their Houston headquarters, where the contracts would be finalized. Representatives of construction companies, trucking firms and several other businesses converged on Houston at the appointed time.

We were invited to the TAPS offices to work out the agreement, in our case, to provide a substantial part of the air transportation and haulage for the pipeline project.

Fairbanks News Miner 2-10-1969

Three Firms Join On 800-Mile Line

Three major oil companies announced plans today to construct an 800-mile, 48-inch, $900 million pipeline from Prudhoe Bay on the Artic Ocean to the Gulf of Alaska, but did not disclose its terminus.

The huge pipeline, designed to carry oil from North Slope wells to a port on the Gulf, is scheduled to be completed in 1972 and will have a capacity initially of 500,000 barrels daily.

The announcement today by Atlantic Richfield, Co., BP Pipeline Corp., and Humble Pipeline Co., apparently settled the question of whether the pipeline would be built to an Alaskan port or through Canada, but left unanswered a major question of whether it would terminate at Valdez, Seward or some other deep water port in south central Alaska. Valdez has been mentioned prominently as *the possible terminus.*

The three companies said, "the precise routing may not be finally determined for as long as six months or more."

The announcement also said "planning studies on alternate routes are continuing to determine the best method to move the oil to the Midwest and Eastern sections of the United States." Oil carried through the Trans-Alaska Pipeline System, as it will be called, would supply oil to the West Coast of the United States.

The full text of the announcement from Anchorage follows:

"Atlantic Richfield Co., BP Pipeline Corp., and Humble Pipeline Co. announced today plans for the construction of an 800-mile, 48-inch pipeline to move crude oil south from Alaska's North Slope to a site on the Gulf of Alaska.

"The announcement said the total cost of the Trans-Alaska Pipeline System, as it will be known, would be about $900 million, with completion scheduled for 1972. Construction surveys will begin in the spring of this year. The pipeline system, the companies said, would have an initial capacity of about 500,000 barrels daily.

"At the outset, the announcement continued, ownership of the pipeline system would be on an undivided interest basis in the following anticipated percentages:

"Atlantic Pipeline (subsidiary of Atlantic Richfield) 37 1/2 per cent; BP Pipeline (subsidiary of BP Oil Corp.) 37½ per cent, and Humble Pipeline Co., (subsidiary of Humble Oil and Refining Co.), 25 per cent.

"The three companies said they intend to invite other firms anticipating a need for crude oil transportation from the North Slope to participate in ownership of the line. The agreement among the three also permits each party to reconsider up to April 1, 1969, whether it wishes to continue to participate in the project.

"Surveys are continuing to determine the exact route and to determine the location of the pipeline which would run generally in a southerly direction from the Prudhoe Bay area of the North Slope to the Gulf of Alaska, according to the announcement.

"'The announcement concluded: While the planned pipeline to the Gulf of Alaska would make North Slope oil available to the U.S. West Coast, planning studies on alternate routes are continuing to determine the best method to move the oil to the Midwest and Eastern sections of the United States.'"

Everything seemed in order and there was excitement in the air as the huge undertaking was about to be launched. Most of us arrived in Houston on a weekend, a time when we understood that the absolutely essential pipeline permit was on the desk of Interior Secretary Hickel. We understood also that this document, on which all of TAPS' endeavors rested, would be signed on Monday morning.

On Monday: bad news.

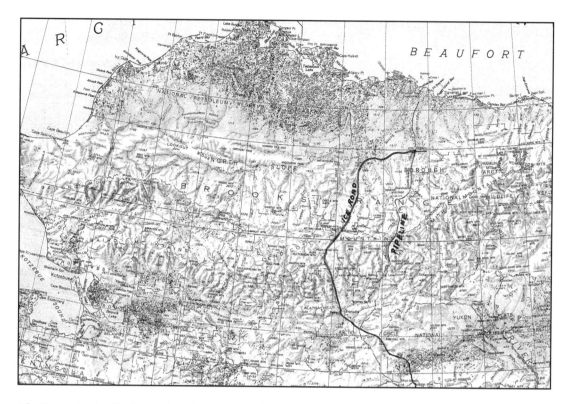

The Trans-Alaska Pipeline and, to the west of it, the temporary Ice Road, commonly called "The Hickel Highway."

TAPS people told us that no contract could be put into effect until the key pipeline permit was received — and so far there was no permit. In the meantime, individual meetings were being arranged at TAPS offices in anticipation of the prompt receipt of the pipeline permit.

There was agitation, annoyance and frustration among the Alaskans staying at our hotel. They felt their time was being wasted in Houston, where nothing was going forward. They expressed the feeling that they were needed in Alaska and that's where they ought to be, keeping their current work rolling while they prepared for the big pipeline push.

By Wednesday, a sense of desperation began to set in among the Alaskans. Several members of the group wanted to get Hickel on the phone to get his answer as to when the pipeline permit would be issued.

It was felt that someone who knew Hickel personally should make the call, but there were no volunteers. Finally, concerned about the inaction, I told the group that I'd known Hickel for several years but was not a close friend. Dot and I had been among his guests when he opened the Traveller's Inn in Fairbanks, and we had met casually on several other occasions. Hickel had flown to the North Slope aboard an Interior plane on which I was the pilot, and we had visited some enroute. And I pointed out that he had been of great assistance to us in getting our first Hercules. So I was elected to make the phone call.

"The permit will be signed either today or tomorrow," Hickel assured me when I got him on the line. I thanked him and passed on the information to a greatly relieved group of Alaskans.

And the frustrating waiting game began. The next day, the Alaskan contingent converged on my hotel room, all of us waiting for the phone to ring. TAPS had a man in Washington who was keeping them informed up-to-the-minute on developments there, and we were told we'd be notified as soon as TAPS got word.

When no word had been received by Friday afternoon, a tense anxiety began taking over. My hotel room became the Alaska group's crying headquarters.

As the hours dragged on, anger began to be expressed. Guy Rivers, representing his Anchorage construction firm, was among those chewing nails. "Jim," he demanded, "what in hell's wrong with Hickel?"

"I wish I knew," I said.

Bitterly disappointed Alaskans launched a heated discussion about what to do.

Some of our associates conjectured that Hickel was playing politics.

"He's in bed with the preservationists and environmentalists," one of the group insisted. "He doesn't want to do anything to alienate all the groups that have been opposing the pipeline!"

"Hickel has the support of most Alaskans, of the national business community, and most Republicans," another stated. "He must figure that if he can gain favor with the hippies, the long-hairs and the various other groups of street-screamers, he can be president."

We really weren't getting anywhere. I was pressured into phoning Hickel again. This time, however, I was informed that "Mr. Hickel isn't available." Minutes later, a TAPS official called to tell us that no permit had been issued in Washington so we might as well go back home.

On my return to Fairbanks, I wrote Hickel a polite letter. I wanted to know what went wrong. I pointed out the hardship being caused by the failure to issue the permit. Many Alaskan businesses, I reminded him, needed an answer — and soon.

Hickel never answered my letter. And, to the best of my knowledge, he has never, to this day, explained to Alaskans why he didn't issue the permit at that time. The fact that he had assured me that a permit would be issued made me wonder even more.

His failure to act dealt our firm a shattering blow. We had to declare bankruptcy

INTERIOR AIRWAYS, Inc.

Box 3029, Fairbanks, Alaska 99701 · 907-452-5171

Sept. 23, 1970

AIRCRAFT LISTING

MANUFACTURER	MODEL & NAME		IDENTIFICATION	SERIAL NO.	DESIGNATION
Lockheed	L-382E	Hercules	N-9265R	4300	8 - Cargo
Lockheed	L-382B	Hercules	N-921NA	4209	8 - Cargo
Lockheed	L-382F	Hercules	N-9266R ☆	4250	8 - Cargo
Curtiss-Wright	C-46T	Commando	N-1663M	22548	3 - 44 Pax/Cargo
Curtiss-Wright	C-46T	Commando	N-74689	32975	3 - 42 Pax/Cargo
Curtiss-Wright	C-46	Commando	N-4860V	30240	3 - Cargo
Curtiss-Wright	C-46F	Commando	N-7848B ☆	273	3 - Cargo
Curtiss-Wright	C-46F	Commando	N-74811	22451	3 - Cargo
Douglas	DC-3C	Dakota	N-46496	9499	3 - 28 Pax/Cargo
Douglas	DC-3C	Dakota	N-95460	20190	3 - 28 Pax/Cargo
de Havilland	DHC-6	Twin Otter Mod 300	N-6868	235	2 - 19 Pax/Cargo
de Havilland	DHC-6	Twin Otter Mod 200	N-6767	189	2 - 19 Pax/Cargo
de Havilland	DHC-6	Twin Otter Mod 200	N-4443	151	2 - 19 Pax/Cargo
de Havilland	DHC-2	Turbo Beaver MK III	N-4478 ☆	1653	1 - 8 Pax/Cargo
de Havilland	DHC-2	Turbo Beaver MK III	N-53011	1646	1 - 8 Pax/Cargo
de Havilland	DHC-2	Turbo Beaver MK III	N-4482	1629-TB17	1 - 8 Pax/Cargo
de Havilland	DHC-2	Piston Beaver MK I	N-2843D ☆☆	565	1 - 5 Pax/Cargo
de Havilland	DHC-2	Piston Beaver MK I	N-9762Z ☆☆	302	1 - 5 Pax/Cargo
Beech	A-90	King Air	N-870K ☆☆	LJ183	1 - 6 Pax
Beech	B-80	Queen Air	N-7835L ☆☆	LD348	1 - 10 Pax
Beech	D-50	Twin Bonanza	N-4353D	DH 117	1 - 7 Pax
Beech	C-45H	Twin Beech	N-9330Z ☆☆	51-11769	1 - 9 Pax/Cargo
Beech	TC-45H	Twin Beech	N-9499Z ☆☆	51-11534	1 - 6 Pax/Cargo
Beech	C-18C	Twin Beech	N-5338N ☆☆	7089	1 - 6 Pax/Cargo
Grumman	G-44	Super Widgeon	N-13122	1312	1 - 4 Pax/Cargo
Grumman	G-44	Super Widgeon	N-750M ☆☆	1341	1 - 4 Pax/Cargo
Grumman	G-44	Super Widgeon	N-708C ☆☆	1313	1 - 4 Pax/Cargo
Grumman	G-44	Super Widgeon	N-69067	1338	1 - 4 Pax/Cargo
Cessna	180A	180	N-7884A	32781	1 - 3 Pax/Cargo
Cessna	180	180	N-4643B	31541	1 - 3 Pax/Cargo
Fairchild Hiller	F-27	Friendship	N-4300F ☆	60	3 - 40 Pax/Cargo
Fairchild Hiller	F-27	Friendship	N-4302F ☆	58	3 - 40 Pax/Cargo
Fairchild Hiller	C-82A	Jet Packet	N-5102B ☆☆	45-57782	5 - Cargo
Fairchild Hiller	C-82A	Box-Car	N-209M ☆☆	10165	5 - Cargo

Interior Airways fleet as of Sept. 23, 1970.

under Chapter 11, as did the Hercules operator in Anchorage. While other companies had to shut down and never made a comeback, we were fortunate in being able to survive.

Alaskans haven't forgotten Hickel's failure to act. His subsequent tries for public office over a period of the next 20 years were failures, though his campaigns were well-organized and well-financed, and though he was probably the best-qualified candidate.

In the 1990 gubernatorial election in Alaska, Hickel did not enter the race until mid-September. He ran under the banner of the Alaskan Independence Party, a secessionist fringe group. *Time* magazine said Hickel used that party merely as "a flag of convenience." After spending more than $800,000, he became governor again.

How did our firm work its way out of bankruptcy after the permit debacle? Our successful struggle to get back on our feet is attributable to three things.

First: Our willingness to surrender corporate equity in favor of creditors. This was nowhere as painful as it might appear. Our maturing investments over a 24-year period had eliminated our dependency on our company for financial security.

Second: A substantial and continuous cash flow from our newly undertaken international operations, the most significant of them being our intensive flying activities in southern Africa.

Third: The loyal and unswerving support of our creditors. They had dealt with us for many years and recognized our impeccable reputation for integrity, both in Alaska and the Lower 48. These creditors recognized that our bankruptcy came as a result of political considerations which were completely beyond our control.

Our bankruptcy was one of the very few in Alaska, or elsewhere, in which all creditors were paid 100 percent of their claims with accrued interest and these payments were made considerably ahead of schedule. I'm proud of the way we were able to handle this distressing situation.

And how do I feel about Wally Hickel today? Despite my misgivings, I retain admiration for him. During his first term as governor of Alaska, he proved to be an able, conservative administrator. His was a businesslike approach to government and the development of Alaska's natural resources. It was Hickel who proposed extension of the Alaska Railroad to the arctic. It was Hickel who conceived and promoted the much-publicized "ice road" from the interior to Sagwon on the North Slope. This remarkable road was completed in the midst of frenzied North Slope cargo activity, boosting the movement of vital goods, though for truckers it was a long, rough trip.

Initially, critics charged that the ice road, also known as "The Hickel Highway," would ruin the environment. Exactly the opposite has been true. The scars have all but disappeared. The roadway has mothered new vegetation. Observation from the air has disclosed that the old roadway is now a favorite browsing ground for moose. Along the route vast growths of tender willows have proliferated — a favorite with moose.

Now that Hickel is once again our governor, he appears to be pursuing no-nonsense, progressive, conservative policies and attempting to inject sorely needed discipline into Alaska's government. Alaska should prosper if we can just keep Hickel out of Washington and isolated from the powerful "do-gooders."

It is true that Hickel disappointed us and many other Alaskans while he was interior secretary. However, we should never lose sight of the fact that even the most well-intentioned politicians become unpredictable when they become enveloped in the Washington fog.

Perhaps for the best, Hickel's term in Washington, where he served under President Nixon, was unusually brief. Confirmed as interior secretary on Jan. 23, 1969, he was dismissed on Nov. 25, 1970. His delay in granting the pipeline permit gave pipeline opponents the opportunity and time to organize stiff resistance. Prolonged hearings were required, causing endless delays and multiplying the cost of the project many times over.

The pipeline permit we had all waited for in vain wasn't signed until four years later, Jan. 23, 1974, by then Interior Secretary Rogers C.B. Morton.

Walter J. Hickel left his mark on Washington. Even now, some 23 years later, when some Washington bureaucrat or politician does an inexplicable about face, the remark is sometimes made that this person has been "Hickelized." ⊥

CHAPTER 46

Reorganization

The pipeline permit delay and the serious financial blow it dealt our company were particularly distressing for me as its founder and chief executive officer. For a business to seek Chapter 11 protection at that time was not as fashionable as it is today.

For more than 24 years, we had operated an independent, profitable and debt-free business with no government assistance but plenty of government interference. Somehow, we had survived gruelling spells of very poor business and tough competition. We had successfully fought off several government attempts to shut us down. We had weathered a vicious Teamsters strike that had tragic consequences. Each time we had bounced back and been able to move forward again.

Suddenly, through no fault of our own, we were faced with a virtual shutdown of our business and the grounding of our costly fleet of aircraft. Having one of Alaska's sharpest attorneys, Charlie Cole, as executive vice president and being in constant contact with our advisors at the Chicago bank, I had been comfortable with our rapid expansion to meet the airlift needs of the North Slope development.

Now with trouble assailing me from all directions and our aircraft lessors clamoring for their monthly lease payments (George Batchelor would phone me promptly at 6 a.m. each day that a payment was due to make certain his check had been mailed), there was a physical price to pay. Within weeks, without proper sleep, I developed high blood pressure, an irregular heartbeat and chronic headaches.

There seemed to be no way out for me, yet there was. The solution to these all-but-unbearable problems came from our two major creditors who supplied us with the Hercules: the Chicago First National Bank and National Equipment Rental, Ltd.

They wanted, understandably, to see our business remain afloat. Otherwise, they'd be stuck with aircraft not easily disposed of at a time when flying activity was at a low ebb both in Alaska and elsewhere.

These two creditors agreed to advance us funds to keep us going, though they demanded a healthy price in corporate stock. And they required a vital management change. As if by magic, Jim Magoffin and Charlie Cole, who had been dubbed "The Golden Boys" by Bill Douglas of Douglas Securities when the fat aircraft rental checks were rolling in, suddenly became country hicks who couldn't manage a pig farm and needed help — desperately.

Though I was to remain as chairman of the board, they wanted their own man,

Duncan McLaren, as company president. That was fine with me, and I executed an employment agreement that was generous to McLaren, and he accepted the job as temporary president. Activity at the airline was practically nil, allowing Charlie Cole to resurrect his long-neglected legal practice. We then promoted Neil Bergt to take his place.

I had never met McLaren. I knew of him only through Charlie Cole, who had traveled to Miami to negotiate our leases on the Hercules planes that we obtained from National Equipment Rental, Ltd. Charlie had meshed well with McLaren, and together they produced lease agreements considered fair to both parties.

McLaren set to work to ensure that our business carried on its long tradition of profitability — the one big reason that his friends in Miami and New York agreed to lease us planes in the first place. However, he quickly learned that there was virtually no business on which to demonstrate his management skills. It was gone, disappearing with one "non-stroke" of Interior Secretary Hickel's pen.

McLaren's stay with us must have been a nightmare for him. Here he was, supposedly an experienced aviation executive in whom our two major creditors had placed great faith to quickly solve a growing financial problem. I felt sorry for him, away from his family — a wife not in the best of health and a small boy — and facing a problem of enormous magnitude. To help him maintain sanity, Dot and I frequently invited him to our home for dinner, and after a few drinks he would relax somewhat. On the first such occasion McLaren stated, "I could never have done what you two have done. I'm just not that much of a gambler."

When McLaren came aboard with Interior, the expectations for early issuance of the pipeline permit were still high. He was well liked by me and by Dot and practically everyone else in the company.

However, it didn't take McLaren long to realize the problem was not one of deficient management. Neither he, nor anyone else, could quickly replace the rug that Hickel had jerked from under us and, other than a few minor office procedure changes, McLaren had no solution to our problem. When it became more and more evident that the pipeline permit was going to be delayed for an extended period of time, he threw in the towel and recommended a filing under Chapter 11 of the federal bankruptcy laws.

The following income summary, certified by a national accounting firm, illustrates the devastating blow caused by the pipeline permit delay:

1969 — $26,192,134		1973 — $12,763,395
1970 — 9,034,884		(Pipeline permit granted)
1971 — 4,566,400		1974 — 45,120,000
1972 — 9,522,040		1975 — 89,073,000

The Interior Airways, Inc. staff — 1970. From the left: Roy Isackson, vice president; Charlie Yerkes; Neil Bergt, vice president; Chuck Murphy; Dick Roberts, vice president; Jim Magoffin, chairman (standing); and Duncan McLaren, temporary president.

In spite of our admiration of McLaren, we were upset and angered by some of his later self-serving writings in which he came down hard on Interior Airways' previous management. His criticisms were especially hurtful since Interior had enjoyed the reputation for running a "tight ship" and having efficient management for many years. Such criticism, coming from someone who had reportedly been fired from a management position at Pacific Western Airlines and whose one attempt to run his own business (Somac Products, Ltd.) had been a total failure, was not appreciated. Interior Airways had been favored with several citations for efficient management and major contributions to our industry.

Our application for protection under Chapter 11 was quickly approved. McLaren returned to the lower United States, and we promoted Neil Bergt to company president. Neil had practically grown up with our company and was much more business-oriented than McLaren.

Now, with Neil in place in our Fairbanks headquarters, I was free to pursue flying opportunities in other parts of the world, and I lost no time in getting to it. Within a relatively short period of time I was in Canada, Singapore, Switzerland, France, Denmark, England, Australia, New Guinea and the African countries of Zambia, Botswana, Rhodesia (now Zimbabwe), South Africa, Swaziland, Kenya, Niger, Togo, Angola, Mozambique, Gabon and Zaire.

Most of my efforts produced flying contracts, although a potentially prosperous job in Niger was thwarted when our customers abandoned that country.

In the mid-'70s, we got word that National Equipment Rental, Ltd. was being forced to sell the stock they held in our company. NER held a strong position in the Flying Tigers, and regulations prohibited them from having a financial interest in multiple airlines.

Neil Bergt suggested that he and I try to acquire the stock ourselves. I declined since Dot and I had each retained a considerable block of stock, and personal investments over 30 years had matured to a point that I had no financial need that would impel me to take further risks. Further, years of investing had taught me that airline stocks were not always the best gamble.

Neil declared that he had nothing to lose and, if the deal went sour, he could declare personal bankruptcy. He was determined to make a try for it, so I executed a release that would permit him to own the stock. This was necessary since Dot and I were the original owners and we had given up some of our stock under duress to save the company when Hickel's inaction all but shut us down.

When Bergt wanted to take the company private in 1979, we agreed, with certain conditions. We felt it was time for us to let the younger generation continue the expansion we had struggled with and nurtured for 34 years.

Although Bergt didn't join us until 1957, he advanced rapidly and was now one of our senior officers.

Ironically, National Equipment Rental, Ltd. ultimately vanished from the scene, reportedly the victim of some unfavorable management decisions, while our company, now called MarkAir, continues to operate in Alaska and has expanded as far south as San Diego, California, and as far east as Newark, New Jersey. This should, once again, dispel the myth that all intelligence originates on the East Coast and terminates at the Mississippi River.

Now, our biggest crisis, like all those others over the years, was overcome.

A promising reconstruction period was beginning. For the first time in its history, our company would take on a global look. ✝

CHAPTER 47

To The North Pole By Dog Team

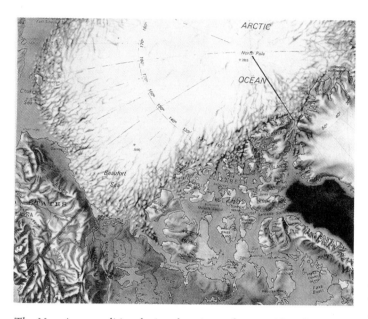

The Monzino expedition during the winter of 1971 widened our operation to Greenland, Denmark, Ellesmere Island in the Canadian arctic, and to the geographic North Pole.

Since the days of Peary, Amundsen and Byrd, the desolate, landless North Pole has been harrowing to human beings. This bitterly cold, boundless realm was the source of unimaginable suffering for early explorers and their crews. Men and dogs collapsed and died when caught in howling gales as they inched their way across the barren, trackless icepack seeking to reach an undistinguished and for centuries unknown point on the globe.

I had never imagined that the time would come when we, too, would become involved in not one but two missions to this miserable top-of-the-globe area. The first was an attempt to reach the exact North Pole; the second, a supply mission to Fletcher's Ice Island, a scientific research station that the U.S. Navy designated T-3.

Our first involvement was when we were called on to give aerial support to an expedition that would travel by dog team to the Pole. Those we worked with on this expedition were so unusual they might have stepped out of a book of fiction. We got our second bitter taste of the high arctic when one of our aircraft, a giant Hercules, crashed and was stranded there. Our struggle to get that plane back into the air is a story by itself.

The dog-team expedition was unforgettable. We got involved in it because we were clutching at all kinds of straws at a time when the oil companies had virtually shut down their operations on the North Slope. Any charter, even one to the North Pole, looked good to me at a time when we were frantically seeking any business at all to fill the enormous gap created by the seemingly endless delay in getting pipeline work under way.

My good friend Ward Gay, president of Sea Airmotive, Inc. at Anchorage's Lake Hood, got us headed in the direction of the North Pole.

In the winter of 1971, Ward called me. "Jim," he said, "I've got a woman from Denmark in my office right now. She's been offering to charter our Twin Otter to provide aerial support for a dog-team expedition going to the North Pole."

"Well, will you do it?" I asked.

"No, darn it," he replied. "At first we thought we might. But when we got to looking at it from all angles, we came to the conclusion that there were too many obstacles and problems for us. We just didn't want to get involved."

"So you're calling to find out whether we might be interested?"

"That's right."

"We're interested!" I told him.

"Great!" Ward said. "Hang on. I'll put the lady on the line."

In a few moments, a woman speaking in halting English began telling me about the unusual expedition. "I'm Mrs. Lillian Von Kaufmann from Copenhagen," she said. "I'm arranging an expedition to the North Pole with mushers and dog teams. We need a Twin Otter on skis to help supply the expedition and give other support."

"For how long would you need the airplane?" I asked. Several weeks," she said. "Months maybe."

"Well," I told her, "let's get together and talk about it."

She paused. "Oh, I'm very sorry," she said, "but I have to leave for Copenhagen today. Could you meet with us there to work out an agreement?"

"Sure," I said, "I'll wire you our date and time of arrival."

I related the unusual phone conversation to our temporary president, Duncan McLaren. He wasn't at all enthusiastic, being a meticulous planner and paper mechanic and not inclined to gamble on far-out business deals. He concluded that it was just an inquiry that wouldn't amount to anything. I, on the other hand, had a nose for business, had been a business gambler for many years and practically all of our gambles had been successful. Further, I felt that Ward Gay, my good friend and hunting partner, would not entice me into any deals that he did not have faith in.

Two days later Dot and I were on our way to Denmark. Waiting for us at the Copenhagen terminal was Mrs. Von Kaufmann's limousine and chauffeur. The uniformed driver took us to the elegant Palace Hotel, one of the many commercial properties in Copenhagen owned by the Von Kaufmann family. That evening, we joined Mr. and Mrs. Von Kaufmann and several of their 13 children for dinner in their ornate dining room. They were an unusual family. We got a laugh out of Mr. Von Kaufmann

Monzino Expedition support planes. The Turbo Beaver and Twin-Otter on the ice near Monzino's camp.

after he described his family of 13 children and eight dogs. "There's only one problem," he said. "I just don't like kids or dogs!"

Mrs. Von Kaufmann disclosed that her role in the whole affair was merely that of
an arranger and expediter. She told us she was acting for a wealthy Italian citizen,
Guido Monzino of Milan. Monzino's family owned all kinds of African property and
he was, as the saying goes, "loaded," so skimping really wouldn't be necessary. As it
turned out, there was no skimping.

We discussed, in general terms, the entire operation, at which time I learned the
charter had also been refused by a Swiss airline. It was agreed that we would meet on
the following morning with Mrs. Von Kaufmann and her attorney.

Though Dot and I were both tired from the long flight, we borrowed a typewriter from the hotel desk. I dictated a five-page contract to Dot, and she whipped it
out on the typewriter. We presented the neat, professional-looking document to Mrs.
Von Kaufmann and her attorney the next morning.

Knowing that additional aircraft might be required before the expedition was
concluded, I inserted rates in the contract not only for the Twin Otter but for the
Hercules and a single-engine Beaver as well, should they be required. As it turned out,
there were times when all three aircraft were simultaneously involved in the operation.

Since the North Pole operation called for long hours of flying over vast distances,
I had the contact specify that the customer would pay for both the cost of all fuel

consumed and its transportation to where it was needed. Needless to say, this operation contained an element of risk and we appeared to be the airline of last resort, so I was determined to make it lucrative — and it was.

The Danes had no major objections to the contract and we were able to finalize it before flying back to Fairbanks the next day — over the Pole.

I handed McLaren a copy of the contract that I had executed on behalf of Interior. He was shocked that our lightning-fast trip to Copenhagen had produced such an agreement. There had been no phone calls, telexes or any other communication and the terms of the contract were favorable to us beyond McLaren's wildest imagination.

There was absolutely no question about Mrs. Von Kaufmann's credit. Our billings were presented in the usual manner after each month's flying, and payment was prompt and in U.S. funds.

A few days after we returned, Mrs. Von Kaufmann notified us she would arrive in Fairbanks shortly and would be prepared to proceed to the arctic with the least possible delay.

Einar Pedersen, chief navigator for SAS and Monzino's guide to the exact location of the North Pole.

Mrs. Von Kaufmann had her youngest son, Eric (6 years old), with her. Dot invited them to our home for a delicious evening meal and a good visit. We liked the lady and admired her energy in undertaking such a project. Both Lillian and her son were decked out in the very best and warmest fur clothing, and they had an incredible amount of baggage. Lillian explained to us that one of Monzino's most fervent pastimes was participating in challenging, exotic expeditions. Conquering the North Pole would, of course, be another feather in his cap.

Monzino was, in a sense, going to lead the expedition. He would, of course, rely on the expertise of the mushers he had hired from Thule, Greenland, and the endurance of hardy dog teams.

Monzino's sled-dog trek to the Pole got under way from the northern tip of Ellesmere Island in the Canadian Archipelago on the very fringe of the polar region. They headed straight north, at times tracing the route that Peary took to the Pole way back in 1909 when it was "discovered." Peary's starting point had been from Etah, a settlement in northernmost Greenland.

Our Twin Otter was based at a place called Alert, which is a tiny outpost of civilization near the northernmost point of land in the Canadian arctic.

It was arranged that our flight crew keep in constant radio contact with the expedition. The Twin Otter delivered food, fuel and other supplies to the group at designated points along their polar route.

Monzino hired Einar Pedersen, chief navigator for Scandinavian Airlines, to be aboard the aircraft on the final flights. As soon as the sleds reached the immediate vicinity of the North Pole, Pedersen was to give the expedition radio guidance to the precise spot where the party, on the drifting ice pack, would be directly over the Pole. Then Monzino could chalk up another daring achievement.

I had an uneasy feeling about the expedition. Monzino was certainly no Peary or Amundsen. He had limited experience in conducting this kind of gruelling operation in the bitter cold and unpredictable weather he was bound to encounter. All kinds of unexpected hazards faced him.

Ice over the North Pole, where there's no land at all, moves constantly, impelled by ocean currents. Fixing a precise location, which could be so many hundreds of yards to the left or right, could be difficult, if not impossible. Nevertheless, Monzino was determined to reach the North Pole, even though when he got there it would look just as forbidding as all the thousands of square miles of shifting ice that surround it.

There was no turning back. Monzino had done considerable travelling throughout Canada in preparation for the expedition, we were told. Though I saw Mrs. Von Kaufmann in Fairbanks from time to time as she visited the expedition, Monzino, for some reason, never set foot in Alaska.

The pilots we selected for this unusual operation were all seasoned arctic veterans: Bob Jacobs, Clint Schoenleber, Dave McKay and Terry Reece.

The first flight took off from Fairbanks at night. This was done so the landing at Sachs Harbor on Banks Island would be in daylight. From there, after a few hours for rest and refueling, the plane would continue on to the main base at Alert.

This initial flight in the Twin Otter carried drums of extra fuel that would be needed to reach Alert on the northernmost tip of land in the Canadian Archipelago bordering the Arctic Ocean.

Though at first the Alert operation and the expedition seemed to be moving forward normally, we began to get a series of rather unusual requests from Mr. Monzino. Some of the orders seemed way out, but we did our best to fulfill them. For example, Monzino once ordered 30,000 pounds of T-bone steaks. Joe Franich who owned the Quality Meat Co. in Fairbanks, was thoroughly shaken up by this mammoth order for 15 tons of meat. Franich somehow managed to fill the order, but not all the meat flown out was T-bone because there simply wasn't that much T-bone in Alaska at the time.

Another time Monzino had one of our Hercules fly from Fairbanks to Copenhagen to pick up 45,000 pounds of pemmican. He pointed out that the dried concentrated lean meat was needed for dog food. We managed to fill this order successfully but it was at great cost to the expedition. Cost didn't seem to matter to Monzino.

We called a halt however, to Monzino's strange order for two .44-magnum pistols with ammunition. We refused to send the guns out. For one thing, it is against Canadian law to transport handguns into Canada, and we were not about to get crosswise with the Canadian authorities. And we were getting a bit concerned with the Peter Pan atmosphere surrounding the whole enterprise. People living for long periods of time under isolated circumstances were known to get a little snow happy at times. We didn't want any shootouts taking place at the North Pole.

Yet it turned out that all our fears had been groundless. Monzino and his party and our aircraft and crew got to the North Pole and back without anything sensational happening.

For us, this unusual contract was a godsend at a time when our income had been practically nil. Over a short period of time that "gamble" contributed well over half a million dollars to the Interior Airways coffers, with an almost unconscionable margin of profit. ✝

CHAPTER 48

Canada Beckons

During the disturbing lull in our Alaska air activities because plans for the Trans-Alaska Pipeline were moving with glacial slowness, our attention turned very naturally to Canada.

This vast land, rich in raw materials, has a population that is smaller than that of California. The more I looked at Canada, the more it seemed that the potential for air cargo there had hardly been scratched.

And now was the time to explore whatever potential Canada offered. I was convinced aviation possibilities in Canada rivalled and perhaps even surpassed those in Alaska.

The tremendous Prudhoe Bay oil discovery stimulated oil exploration in the Canadian arctic, increasing the demand for air support.

We possessed hard-won experience in this respect and worked hard at discovering any possibilities that would keep our planes and crews flying.

In the spring of 1972, a chance to participate in oil developments in Canada gave us a shot in the arm. We were contacted by Pacific Western Airlines (PWA) of Vancouver, British Columbia, the Canadian Hercules operator. They were familiar with our work in the arctic.

I flew to Vancouver and met with PWA's Rusty Harris and Jack Moul, who gave me the amazing information that between 600 and 700 Hercules loads of cargo were stacked up waiting to be flown into the Canadian arctic, and the recent gas and oil discoveries on Ellef Ringnes Island promised to intensify the air cargo demand even further. The emerging air potential here, I could see, was really mind-boggling.

Though PWA and our firm were competitors in bidding for overseas contracts, this meeting, and those held subsequently with them, were cordial and positive.

From our standpoint, we wanted to be able to call on PWA for help when the Alaska pipeline stalemate came to an end. Speaking for PWA, Rusty Harris emphasized that they were eager to do business with a reliable Alaskan operator during their own rush periods.

There were handshakes and smiles all around, and for us some lucrative over-the-border business developed. For a time, we had as many as three of our Hercules delivering cargo to points in the Canadian arctic islands. Our aircraft were serving Cambridge Bay, Resolute, Helicopter Bay, Rea Point, Dumbell, Drake Point, Romulus, Eureka and other seismic and drill sites. We also were making trips to Yellowknife and Edmonton.

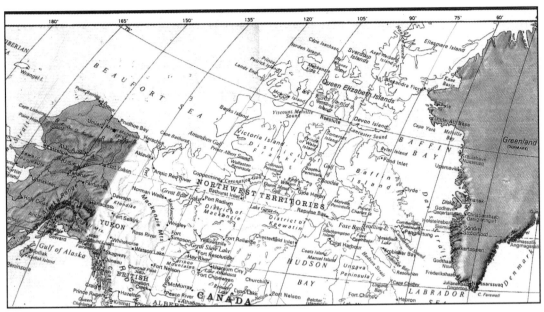

Our Canadian flight operations covered several provinces and the Northwest Territories and extended east to Labrador.

Throughout, PWA provided us with strong and efficient ground support. There were times when it was embarrassing the way we had to lean on them but they always responded very helpfully and with goodwill and friendliness. Since we were so far from our base in Alaska, we had to go hat in hand to them for such things as starting units, generators, bulk fuel tanks and rollers, to say nothing of a host of smaller items that we required from time to time.

In one instance, PWA even went so far as to let it be known that they would not object to a temporary Hercules operation by one of their competitors, Northwest Territorial Airways of Yellowknife, a firm owned by my friend Bob Engle. (We were classmates at American Flyers in Fort Worth, Texas, in 1958.) PWA was, however, against Engle obtaining a permanent license to operate the Hercules.

When Engle applied to Ottawa for a license to put one of Interior's Hercules on his certificate, a hearing on the matter was scheduled. He asked me to testify on his behalf at this very crucial hearing in the Canadian capital and I was glad to do it. The Canadian government finally gave him permission to operate a Hercules but not without the usual extended bureaucratic delays.

Acting on my conviction that Canada offered immense potential for our business, I suggested a merger to Engle. Being a fiercely independent individual, he was quite cool, at first, to my proposal. Subsequently, however, he warmed up enough to

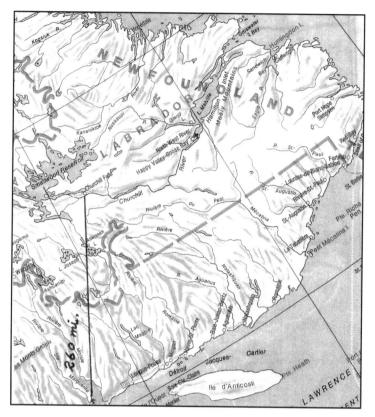

Flying for the huge hydroelectric project at Churchill Falls, Labrador, created welcome income during bad times in Alaska.

join with us in exploring the possibilities at some depth. Some of our executives flew to Yellowknife, and their people and ours looked at the matter from all angles.

It was not to be. A cross-border merger, when all the intricate international aspects and bureaucratic involvements on both sides were considered, was just too big a can of worms. Trying to marry a Canadian and an Alaskan firm, it was decided, would be far too complicated, so the merger wasn't pursued any further by either side.

Another Canadian operation we entered into during our slow period was associated with the construction of a massive hydroelectric project at Churchill Falls in Labrador.

Badly needed construction equipment and other materials for the project were to have been transported by railroad from the seaport at Sept-Iles, Quebec, to the construction site some 200 miles inland. The railroads, however, were paralyzed by a strike, so a substantial airlift became necessary.

Before we could turn a wheel flying cargo to Churchill Falls, however, we first had to get approval from the Canadian Department of Transport. That agency, in turn, had to get approval from the Canadian Hercules operator, Pacific Western Airlines. It so happened that at the time all of PWA's aircraft were busy and weren't available for the Churchill Falls job. They let the Department of Transport know that they had no objection to our taking a job in Canada that normally would go to them.

With this green light, I flew to Sept-Iles with a loadmaster and inspected their airport, finding it suitable.

When we got to Sept-Iles, my attention was caught by a Hercules parked off the runway. It was owned by Airlift International of Miami.

The construction contractor complained bitterly that the airplane flew infrequently at a time when he was desperately trying to get his "rush" cargo moved.

The loadmaster and I looked over the cargo stored there and the loadmaster stayed in Sept-Iles to line up the Herc loads as dictated by the needs of the contractor.

The crew of a cargo DC-4 operated by a Canadian airline invited me to go along with them on a flight to Churchill Falls. There I inspected the runway which was adequate for our Hercules.

The Canadian pilots were kind enough to warn me that the material the runway was composed of was primarily crushed chert, an extremely hard rock. When crushed, the rock chunks were angular with some edges as sharp as knife blades. These rocks cut aircraft tires to pieces after only a few landings, requiring tires to be changed frequently.

We flew back to Sept-Iles via Goose Bay where the DC-4 crew dropped off some cargo.

When we wrote up our contract, we specified that the customer would have to pick up the cost of the frequent tire changes.

With everything looking okay for the operation, I called for a Hercules from Fairbanks. When it arrived we completed six round trips within the first 24 hours, delighting the contractor who had been fuming until then. Without any hesitation, he sent the Airlift International Herc back to Miami. We had made another friend in Canada. ✝

CHAPTER 49

Crash Near The North Pole

Hercules wreck at T-3, Feb. 28, 1973.

Our second venture into the Polar region didn't go anywhere near as smoothly as Monzino's.

In the winter of 1973, we became involved in the airlift of supplies to Fletcher's Ice Island, an unusually thick chunk of ice floating with the polar ice pack. The Navy designated this site T-3 and maintained a group of Arctic Research scientists there. The contract was administered by the University of Alaska in Fairbanks.

This was not our first contract to supply T-3. Ten years earlier we were hired to air drop cargo to the scientists on T-3 during the summer, when landing on the ice would not be safe.

Our cargo C-46, N4860V, was fitted with an extra gas tank in the cargo compartment, thus giving us sufficient fuel for the lengthy round trip. Capt. Roger Edgerton and Ralph Brumbaugh, with Roger Burns navigating, made the first trip. Edgerton and I made the subsequent flights in which we would shove the cargo (securely boxed with parachutes attached) out the aft door as we passed near the tiny settlement. The entire operation was a complete success.

Our bid for the current Hercules job turned out to be identical with that submitted by Red Dodge. While the contract award was still being considered, I lost no time in setting up a meeting with Dr. William R. Wood, the president of the university. I explained to him the advantages of dealing with a firm located in Fairbanks. I pointed out that because we were near the university, and we had many more Hercs than Dodge, we'd be able to fulfill the contract far more efficiently than Dodge, who was located in Anchorage. The university could get together with us at a moment's notice to resolve any problem that might crop up.

I must have made a convincing pitch, because we were awarded the contract and proceeded to fly it. Although the bid was tight, the long flights developed a cash flow that proved to be substantial.

Our North Pole operation went well until the Hercules crash that resulted in a swarm of headaches. Like nearly all aircraft mishaps, it was an accident that shouldn't have happened.

On the night of the accident, uncleared snowdrifts, some up to three feet high, had frozen solid as rock, creating what amounted to a series of booby-traps on the runway. The tractor driver responsible for clearing away the drifts had been partying and neglected his job. He assured the camp manager the runway was clear when it wasn't. At that time our Hercules, piloted by an excellent young pilot, Jerry Chisum, was on its way. Poor Jerry had no inkling what was awaiting him: The field was totally unsuitable for landing.

As he neared touchdown, Jerry was unable to distinguish, in the glow of the landing lights on the snow, the solid snowdrift barriers ahead. He proceeded to bring the aircraft in and land it.

In the spectacular crash that followed, the big Hercules took a savage beating. One wing was ruptured so badly it practically fell off. And even though the crew escaped injury, the accident must have been an agonizing experience for them. Jerry certainly could not be blamed for the crash.

Having a severely damaged Hercules stranded near the North Pole in the dead of winter was a special kind of calamity. None of us knew at first what we ought to do. Some believed it would be impossible to salvage the big bird. Dick Roberts, our maintenance VP, hustled to T-3 and inspected the wreck. His conclusion was: "We can fix it!"

But how? The prospect of trying to repair a plane of this size in the bitter cold was absolutely staggering. To repair it, we would have to install numerous new panels, ribs and stiffeners. Thousands of rivets and associated pieces of hardware were required, and we'd be working under an ominous time limit. Spring would soon arrive. We would have to have all the necessary tools and parts in place before summer temperatures made the ice runway unusable or else they would have to be air-dropped — not feasible for large objects. With millions of dollars involved, we couldn't afford to fool around. We had to move fast.

I appealed to Lockheed for help, but their response was very discouraging. We were told it would take at least several months to get together the intricate package that would be required for the repair job. What they were telling me, actually, was that they weren't going to be able to help us out of the fix we were in near the Pole.

Swallowing my disappointment, I decided to pay a call on Hayes Aircraft in Birmingham, Alabama, the maintenance contractor for all Navy and some Air Force Hercs. They told me we could get most of what we wanted but that it would take a long time. Time we didn't have.

Another obstacle was that they would have to get military approval before they sold us any parts.

The Hayes people suggested I appeal directly to military officials on the Air Force side at the Pentagon. In Washington, however, I met with the expected frustration, bureaucracy and roadblocks.

The terrible urgency that surrounded my mission wasn't easing a bit, and the whole effort began taking on a sense of hopelessness.

Things began to change, however, on the day I was steered to a high-ranking civilian official who was familiar with getting things done at the "puzzle palace."

"Magoffin," he urged, "you're not going to accomplish anything here. You ought to go down and talk to a real sharp guy I know who's with the Navy at Falls Church, Virginia."

With that, he picked up the phone and arranged immediately to have me meet with his Navy friend. I walked into his office that afternoon.

He looked familiar. And the instant he saw me he stood up, saying, "We've met somewhere before!"

Then I remembered. "Weren't you the operations officer at Pensacola back in 1942 when I was taking aerial gunnery training there?" I asked.

He grinned as it all came back to him. "Yeah. I was on duty when you had a problem with jammed ailerons!"

I got a warm handshake from Capt. Mitchell, the man I'd met 30 years before, now a high-ranking officer in the Naval Supply Command.

After I outlined the problem, he mused a while then said, "Well, Jim, we have a lot of parts for the Hercules stored down at Cherry Point, North Carolina. If you want to go down there and see if there's anything you can use, I'll arrange to have someone steer you through our warehouses."

I caught the first plane I could get to Fayetteville, then got a car to take me over to the Cherry Point Air Station.

When I checked in at the guardhouse, a gentleman was on hand to drive me to the warehouse area and guide me through the compound. What a place! Not only did they have all kinds of parts, but there were complete Hercules wings still in the original crates. One of the wings looked like the one we needed. I copied the serial number and consulted Lockheed by phone. Within a half hour, Lockheed called back to say, "Yes, that's the wing you need to replace the one on the Hercules wrecked at the Pole."

Now things were beginning to move, but my ordeal wasn't over quite yet. When I got back to Washington and conferred with Capt. Mitchell, new doubts arose.

He maneuvered gingerly around the problem saying, "We've got to figure out how we can do this and still stay within our rules and regulations."

He called in his legal counsel. It quickly became clear to me that neither one of them wanted to risk getting into hot water over this irregular deal.

Then, after a discussion, I sensed a change in the attorney's attitude. "There's no way that we can sell you the wing," the attorney said. Then, after a pause, "But there's nothing to prevent us from *lending* you the wing."

"Great!" I said. The burden was starting to lift.

"However," the attorney said, "If we lend you the wing, you're going to have to insure it for the value shown on our books."

He called their accounting department to get the book value of the wing. Immediately, I signed an agreement binding us to insure the wing for about three quarters of a million dollars with the U. S. Navy as the beneficiary.

Right away, I got Bob Heath in our Fairbanks office on the phone and instructed him to dispatch a Hercules immediately to pick up the borrowed wing and deliver it to T-3 as fast as possible.

On my return to Cherry Point, Navy personnel fished out the crate I had just acquired. It included not only the wing, but complete engine mounts and a full set of flaps and ailerons — all extremely valuable items. On the following day, our Hercules arrived and we loaded the crate aboard. Then we were off and headed for T-3.

We arrived on May 22. This was cutting it awfully close. It was getting warmer and the ice runway already showed signs that the sun was taking its toll. Our lead mechanic, Art Walker, directed the repair project. Innovation was called for. For example, our mechanics discovered that they didn't have a level large enough to do one aspect of the job properly. Then they hit on the idea of filling a large, clear plastic tube with coffee and found it made a dandy level.

Jerry Chisum finally completed the return leg of his flight in N921NA on Thanksgiving 1974.

Art Walker received an FAA commendation for his outstanding leadership in performing this remarkably difficult recovery job. Dick Roberts' recommendation had saved a valuable aircraft.

It turned out, however, that this was not the last of our trouble with this particular Hercules. As fate would have it, during construction of the pipeline, the aircraft finally met its end. We were using it as a tanker. While bulk gasoline was being off-loaded from the plane at one of the construction sites, the cargo caught fire.

In the explosion that followed, a young loadmaster supervising the job was severely burned when flames engulfed the gas pump and surrounding area. The Hercules was destroyed.

The Navy received payment in cash for the borrowed wing. ✝

CHAPTER 50

A New Global Perspective

Our recurring ups and downs in Alaska compelled us, finally, to take a much closer look at other parts of the globe as a possible source of new aviation business.

Having a fleet of Hercules sitting out on the ramp with not much to do but add to expenses was hard to tolerate. At one time, a not-so-funny joke made its rounds in Fairbanks. According to the story, when anybody called us to charter a Hercules, we would say: "What color would you like?"

So we were forced to look elsewhere. As pointed out in the previous chapter, a developing Canada offered several lucrative opportunities. When times were good in Alaska, we never gave the slightest thought to other parts of the globe. Now we had to, if we were going to stay afloat.

Our conviction that there were other areas of the globe that needed us solidified after our Canadian projects and some jobs that came up in New Guinea and Australia.

We went to New Guinea at the request of British Petroleum. That company requested that we fly an oil drilling rig from Port Moresby, New Guinea, to their proposed well site high in the mountains about 100 miles to the north.

Dot accompanied me to New Guinea where Ken Trott, BP's resident manager, and his wife briefed us on the country while we were their dinner guests. Dot was quite shocked to learn that cannibalism still prevailed in some areas there. We learned also that more than 700 tribal dialects were spoken by New Guinea jungle dwellers. From time to time wars raged between the numerous tribes.

Northern New Guinea was captured by the Japanese during World War II, but Port Moresby withstood aerial assaults and became one of the most powerful allied military bases in the South Pacific. The island was recaptured by the United States and Australia in 1944.

Trott gave us a fascinating rundown on native customs, their culture and their dress. "The women wear only ausgraus," he remarked.

"What's that?" Dot asked.

"Well, Dottie," Trott answered, "I guess in America you'd just call it 'ass grass.'"

Our inspection of BP's proposed landing strip resulted in second thoughts about the project that sounded so good on paper. The proposed airfield was nothing more than a 3,200-foot cleared area that dropped off sharply into steep, awesome cliffs on both ends. The field was way too short to allow a safe operation in hot weather and at high altitude. Also making us back away was the fact that the surface of the field was too soft to support the heavy Hercules safely. We had to decline that job.

In Australia, however, we learned of two other possible flying opportunities so we flew to the capital city of Canberra to track them down. The first prospect was hauling trucks from Australia to Katmandu, Nepal, as part of a foreign aid program. We bid for that job but Pacific Western underbid us and we had to cross that one off.

The Australians had originally tried to get some of the trucks to Nepal by surface transport. While the first batch of six trucks was parked at Calcutta overnight, thieves extracted all of the engines, something the surprised drivers learned when they punched the starters the following morning.

Another opportunity was presented to us while visiting British Petroleum offices in Melbourne. John Martin, a BP geologist we had known in Alaska, told us about an aluminum mine being developed at Gove in northwestern Australia. The Swiss mining company, Alusuisse, planned to process the bauxite ore at the mine site, something that would require a massive amount of electric power. Getting the giant turbines from Zurich to Gove by surface means would be far too slow and the risk of pilferage or damage to this costly cargo was too great. It was a job for a Hercules.

We hustled to Zurich and met with Alusuisse officials. Once again, Dot typed up a contract to fly the turbines by Hercules from Zurich to Gove, and Alusuisse approved it. It was our longest haul ever and one requiring several refueling stops along the way. That contract was performed successfully and without incident except for one unscheduled engine change.

International flying jobs that came our way during the four-year delay in getting approval for the Alaska pipeline gradually built up our foreign experience and gave us a sterling performance record. In those four years, our Hercules aircraft operated in 42 different countries. Our emblem was seen at countless airports in North and South America, Europe, Africa and the Middle East, as well as other areas.

The word "Alaska" struck a familiar note with foreigners, especially airline personnel who obviously were confusing us with the larger carrier, Alaska Airlines. We were favored with free or reduced rate transportation virtually wherever we flew on scheduled airlines in Europe and Africa.

Our new global perspective was immeasurably bolstered by the U. S. State Department and by Alaska's Sen. Ted Stevens. Stevens' office arranged for me to meet for several hours with the chief of the State Department's African Section. Here, I was given invaluable information that helped lay the groundwork for our extensive African operations.

Sen. Stevens' office in Washington had called to advise us that there had been a flap in Africa resulting in closure of the border between Zambia and Botswana, as well as part of the Rhodesian border. The normal flow of goods by truck and train was

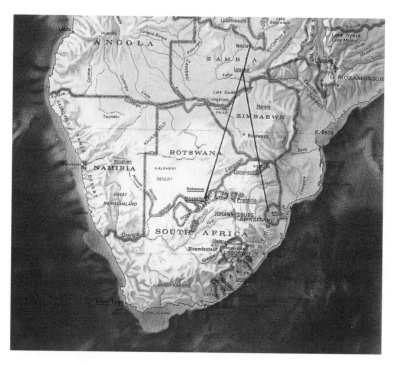

Southern Africa proved to be a golden opportunity for our Hercules operation. Steady flying at good rates continued until we were obliged to return to Alaska to service pipeline construction.

paralyzed. It appeared to Washington, and promptly to us, that there might be a need for an airlift there. We appreciated this help from Sen. Stevens and it wasn't the first or the last.

Once known as Northern Rhodesia, Zambia, a country a little larger than Texas, is mainly a plateau of seemingly endless grasslands out of which brush-covered hills rise occasionally. It is a country rich in resources but, like so many African countries, has had its share of turmoil and conflict.

When I left Washington for Zambia's capital city, Lusaka, I had all kinds of valuable information, including names of people I had to see. I also had a fairly good idea of how to proceed if we were to be successful in concluding a business deal. The tip that proved most valuable was "start at the top." My previous dealings with our federal government had usually not been too pleasant, but I had high praise for the assistance from our State Department.

In Lusaka, I checked into Pan-Am's Intercontinental Hotel, then went to the office of the country's president, a very gracious black man, Kenneth Kaunda. He spoke excellent English and expressed interest in our proposal to carry out air cargo operations in Zambia.

Kaunda's people steered me to the manager of their meat board which was, at the time, wrestling with the problem of the crying need for beef in sections of the country. There were plenty of cattle in Zambia, but cattle owners there were reluctant to slaughter them. In Zambia's culture, cattle represented wealth and status and the owners were reluctant to diminish themselves by cutting down on their herds.

The meat board manager was a Mr. Evenhuis, a Canadian from Manitoba.

"I once spent a couple days in Manitoba," I remarked early in our meeting. "I was there in October 1934 with my dad on a duck-hunting trip. We stayed in Portage LaPrairie and hunted at a farm just north of there. I remember the farmer's name was Lytle."

This startled Evenhuis. "For gosh sakes," he said, "that farm was right next to ours. The farmer's boy, John Lytle, was my best friend all the time I was growing up."

We were off on the right foot, talking about Manitoba, about its grain fields and about its superb goose and duck hunting.

Finally, we discussed the meat situation in Zambia and very shortly came to an agreement on hauling meat from the abattoir at Lobatse, Botswana, to Lusaka.

Before leaving Lusaka, I had to meet with officials of a very loosely organized agency that was the equivalent in most respects to our FAA. It was staffed largely with holdover Britishers who seemed stuffy and imperial at times but warmed up a bit after several meetings and granted us a permit that allowed us to make an unlimited number of flights into Zambia.

One item troubled me. Night flying simply wasn't done in that part of Africa. When I disclosed that ours would be an around-the-clock operation, the aviation officials dug in their heels and gave me a flat "No!"

"Nobody flies at night in our country," one of them said. "They can't! Runways don't have lights and our airports are unattended. It's just impossible!"

"We require very little assistance," I countered. "We'll have our own ground crews and, as we have done in Alaska, we're prepared to install our own runway lights wherever necessary."

After some friendly persuasion, they finally relented and agreed that we could fly at night as well as during the day. Our first Herc brought portable runway lights with it, and from the start we were able to get full utilization out of our airplanes.

My next move was to fly to Botswana to confer with officials of the abattoir at Lobatse and set up a meat supply. This was no problem since, unlike the Zambia situation, cattle owners in Botswana were eager to sell and the abattoir produced a plentiful supply of meat. Having about the same area and climate as Texas, an important part of Botswana's economy has been cattle raising.

In Gabarone, Botswana's capital, I visited the office of Seretse Khama, the country's president.

He called in some of his ministers, several of whom were white. I was surprised to find that Seretse Khama, a black man, was married to a white British lady. They had a whole bunch of kids.

Seretse Khama was a graduate attorney, as was his wife. He spoke excellent English and throughout was a real gentleman. After a few niceties, I was escorted to another office where the appropriate officials began working with me on the details of our meat-haul contract. They agreed they wanted to take advantage of our air transportation capability and I sensed that we were off and running toward a good airlift.

When I left them, it was with the understanding that they would promptly get together with the Zambian officials who approved such things and come up with an agreement on sharing the cost of the airlift.

For several days, I waited around without anything happening. I went back to Zambia and got the same word there; everything was all set to go on the deal, but they just hadn't gotten around to making an agreement.

This didn't sit well with me. Seeing nothing getting done was always frustrating for me. Usually in cases like this, one has to create the push that gets things moving.

I inquired at the Gabarone flying club about renting a small plane, but was informed I couldn't fly in Botswana without first obtaining a Botswana pilot's license. The local aviation inspector, Bill West, rode with me and issued me Botswana Airline Transport Pilot's License No. 1. No other pilot up to that time had ever received an ATR in that country.

Now properly licensed, I was able to rent a Cessna 182 and flew to Lusaka after having obtained the consent of the appropriate Botswanians for a meeting the following afternoon in the Holiday Inn's conference room in Gabarone.

At Lusaka, I picked up three key Zambian government officials and flew them to Gabarone, where the Holiday Inn meeting got under way.

I came armed with a contract that a hotel secretary who took English dictation had typed for me. I included the cost of the flying and, of course, a place for each official in the party to sign.

In less than an hour, I had a signed contract. I have never had more of a hassle bringing two parties together to get a business proposition off dead center. Now I could contact Fairbanks and ask them to send down a Hercules.

I was careful to include in our contract a clause specifying that we would be paid in U.S. dollars by the government of Zambia through the Bank of England. There was no objection to that, and throughout the term of the contract we experienced little difficulty in collecting our money, in substantial amounts, I might add.

When Fairbanks sent the Hercules to Lusaka it was no sooner on the ground there than the word swiftly spread that a giant aircraft was available.

Cargo began showing up from all kinds of different places. It included many things I would never have anticipated — passenger cars, trucks, furniture, and appliances.

So there was plenty of work for us to do, and in the course of our Zambia operations, we set new records in Hercules utilization and per-plane income for our company which, up to then, had been unknown in southern Africa.

The revenue report covering the period from May 1 to May 23, 1974, will illustrate the value of our African operation. Of our seven Hercules, the one performing the Zambian contract excelled in total revenue earning ($370,353.51) in 22 days, and in per-hour revenue ($1,914.80), while the best domestic revenue producer earned only $333,395.32 and only $1,805.06 per hour.

An earlier charter trip for the International Red Cross took our first Hercules to London. The job was transporting ambulances and trucks to Lagos, Nigeria, during a central Africa drought emergency. The trucks were desperately needed to distribute grain and other supplies which relief organizations were rushing to Lagos by air and sea.

That operation, too, was successful, though our flight crews had to endure some uneasy confrontations with drunk and hostile Nigerian soldiers.

During that operation, we got acquainted with a couple of very sharp young transportation brokers in London, Chris Chapman and Mike Freeborn. Their offices were situated at No. 7 Buckingham Gate in London.

Chapman and Freeborn have acted as our overseas contacts ever since. They provided a suitable London headquarters for our company. Through their efforts, we

alaska international air, inc.

REVENUE REPORT | PERIOD FROM MAY 1, 1974 | TO MAY 23, 1974 | DATE MAY 24, 1974

	N-13ST	N-7999S	N-9232R	N-9262R	92INA	N-9259R	N-9265R	TOTALS
REVENUE HOURS:								
LOCAL	184:42	96:26	190:00	125:08	139:35	x 70:27		806:18
CANADA						92:59		92:59
SOUTHERN AFRICA		20:30					193:25	193:25
OVERSEAS OTHER								20:30
TOTAL REVENUE HOURS:	184:42	116:56	190:00	125:08	139:35	163:26	193:25	1113:12
AVERAGE PER DAY	8:01	5:05	8:10	5:26	6:04	7:06	8:24	48:24
NON-REVENUE HOURS:								
PILOT TRAINING	4:01	29:44	2:48	17:16	5:00	x 28:33		58:49
FERRY	5:07	18:42	17:39	7:59	4:37		2:30	85:107
OTHER			:49	3:16				4:05
TOTAL NON-REVENUE HOURS:	9:08	48:26	21:16	28:31	9:37	28:33	2:30	148:01
TOTAL HOURS	193:50	165:22	211:16	153:39	149:12	191:59	195:55	1261:13
AVERAGE PER DAY	8:26	7:11	9:11	6:40	6:29	8:20	8:31	54:50
LOCAL REVENUE	$333,395.32	$157,805.03	$310,958.11	$222,624.26	$225,697.00	$251,554.31		$1,502,034.03
OVERSEAS REVENUE		$ 65,500.00						$ 65,500.00
AFRICAN REVENUE							$370,353.51	$ 370,353.51
TOTAL REVENUE	$333,395.32	$223,305.03	$310,958.11	$222,624.26	$225,697.00	$251,554.31	$370,353.51	$1,937,887.54
AVERAGE PER DAY	$ 14,495.45	$ 9,708.91	$ 13,519.92	$ 9,679.32	$ 9,812.91	$ 10,937.14	$ 16,102.33	$ 84,255.98
AVERAGE PER REV. HR.	$ 1,805.06	$ 1,909.68	$ 1,636.62	$ 1,779.10	$ 1,616.94	$ 1,539.19	$ 1,914.80	$ 1,740.83
AVERAGE PER NON-REV. HR.	$ 1,720.01	$ 1,350.37	$ 1,471.88	$ 1,448.91	$ 1,512.71	$ 1,310.29	$ 1,890.37	$ 1,536.52
NOTES:								

x ACTUAL REVENUE HOURS & FERRY MTC. HOURS FOR PWA. REVENUE NOT ADJUSTED YET!!!!!

The above schedule shows the earnings by seven Hercules. The African revenue was always tops.

Chris Chapman (left) and Mike Freeborn headed the London office. These transportation experts and their staff steered us to profitable flying contracts throughout the free world.

were able to secure many overseas charters and contracts that otherwise wouldn't have come to our attention. These included operations in Europe, South America, the Middle East and other places.

One rewarding job our London contacts steered us to involved flying in hundreds of tons of cement and other material for a runway construction job in Oman, in the Mideast. Neighboring Yemenites were extremely hostile, and we had real concern that as we flew over, they'd be shooting at us. For that reason, we flew many of the Oman flights in hours of darkness. After the flights, we'd inspect the plane carefully looking for bullet holes. We never found any. ✝

CHAPTER 51

Inside Zambia

Reading about Africa in *National Geographic* and personally experiencing it at its rawest are two vastly different things.

Having a spaced-out Zambian soldier jam a bayonet into your gut, for example, leaves a lasting impression.

There were times of terror, there was fear and there was occasional revulsion that made me want to head straight back to Alaska by the fastest means possible.

We had just begun the Zambia meat haul when I got a phone call from Monte Tobin, the chief buyer for one of the largest copper mines in Zambia. At the time, the bitter border dispute was holding up surface transportation of supplies from Johannesburg, South Africa, to the numerous copper mines in Zambia.

Tobin said he urgently needed to meet with me at his office near Ndola.

"I'll pick you up tomorrow morning at 8 in our corporate King-Air at Lusaka's airport. Since our plane won't be available in the afternoon, we'll have a return ticket for you on the scheduled airline."

"Fine," I said. "I'll be there at 8."

Tobin and I had a good meeting which resulted in another cargo job, a sizeable airlift of mining supplies. Afterward, I was driven to the Ndola airport, where I was to board a flight to Lusaka.

An airline employee accepted my ticket in a shack outside the terminal entrance and I soon discovered why.

The terminal was an awful place. The 40- by 16-foot metal warehouse building had no floor, just packed dirt, no plumbing and no chairs, just rough benches along the walls.

I was the only white person among a couple of dozen miserable waiting passengers. The stench inside the building was overpowering. I couldn't breathe.

As I was waiting, a man stood up and urinated on the ground in a corner of the room.

To escape the stench and the blistering heat, I opened a door on the runway side of the building. As I stepped out and gulped the fresh air, a drunken Zambian soldier carrying a rifle with fixed bayonet began running toward me, shouting.

He jammed the point of his bayonet into my stomach. It didn't penetrate enough to wound me, and though I couldn't understand his jabber, I got the message and quickly retreated into that stinking building.

I was afraid he might pull the trigger at any moment. And I expected a bullet in the back as I hustled to the inside of the building, where I buried my face in a handkerchief until the plane for Lusaka arrived.

As we were boarding, I noticed a camouflaged fighter aircraft parked nearby. That soldier had been guarding the plane, though he was thoroughly boozed up. Uncontrolled drinking was rampant among the Zambian troops, and many were reported to have committed all kinds of violence while under the influence.

We found ourselves hauling more mining supplies than meat.

I converted my hotel room into an office. The phone kept ringing off the hook and customers came by at all hours of the day. A phone call from the hotel lobby informed me that two men were enroute to my room to talk flying business. When I responded to a knock on the door I was mildly shocked to see Ian McGregor, the chairman of one of the world's premier mining companies, and a senior company vice president standing there.

We had a short but pleasant meeting in which I agreed that we would fly supplies to their mine at Selebi Phikwe as soon as I could get over to check the safety of their runway. It was okay.

I had brought office materials with me: large and small "daytimer" books, letterheads and the like. I kept paperwork flowing with the help of a hotel secretary who could take dictation in English. I hardly had time to eat, so I had to holler for help.

It took a lot of pressure off me when Chris Chapman flew down from London while Mike Freeborn kept the London office functioning. In a few days, the two switched places.

Both Chris and Mike were sharp, savvy, tireless workers.

I'll never forget one incident involving Chris. A big man with matching appetite and a fussiness about food, Chris wasn't prepared for what can happen in African restaurants.

I had joined Chris for breakfast at a hotel in Nairobi, Kenya, where we had gone on business, when the black waiter approached our table. I pointed to the numbered item on the menu and the waiter nodded. When Chris' turn came, he went on at great length explaining to the waiter just what he wanted to order and precisely how his two eggs had to be prepared and on and on.

My breakfast came and was exactly as it was printed on the menu. Then Chris' breakfast came — two bottles of beer on a plate. The waiter didn't understand a word of English.

Mining companies chose the airport at Francistown, Botswana, as the loading point for their supplies.

Francistown was many miles closer to their mining operations in Zambia, and using that airport would save them money. Also, the runways at Gabarone and Lobatse were nowhere as good as the Francistown strip. Since the border was open between

Botswana and South Africa, our customers could truck their equipment across the border and then up through Botswana to the Francistown base of operations.

There was one hitch concerning use of the Francistown airport. It was a private field owned by a British corporation, and I'd have to get permission to use it.

The Britishers, who lived near the field in a sort of compound, were reluctant to let us use the airport. They said they were afraid the heavy Hercules would tear up their black-topped runway. They finally relented, however, and gave permission to use the field after I presented them with the footprint load of the Hercules tires. Impact on the runway wasn't too great because the Herc has good-sized tandem gear. We set up an efficient loading operation there.

There were problems, of course. I had inspected the runway at Lobatse, Botswana, in the vicinity of the slaughterhouse and found it okay for a Herc except that the north end of the runway abutted the community's golf course and was quite soft.

I informed the Hercules crews to land from north to south, if possible, and avoid the soft area.

However, the captain on the first flight insisted on landing into the wind and landed from south to north. When the aircraft came to a halt, the plane was in the soft area, and on turning to taxi back to the south end where loading was to take place, the tires gouged six-inch-deep ruts in the golf course. That didn't endear us either to the golfers or other citizens. We assured them that never again would we taxi out on that part of the runway.

The meat haul operation proceeded efficiently. The airplane would land, and a truck carrying about 20 workmen would arrive pulling a trailer loaded with more than 40,000 pounds of frozen meat packed in 40-pound boxes. Black youths grabbed the boxes and stacked them swiftly inside the cargo bay of the Hercules. Within a matter of minutes, the entire load of meat was aboard. We would secure the cargo nets over the load and away we'd go.

During the heaviest part of the meat haul to Zambia, we'd occasionally park the airplane overnight at the Lobatse airstrip. When we did, we hired a local black guard who had been recommended to us by officials at the slaughterhouse as being a reliable person.

This man made a habit of guarding the plane by staying right inside it. He brought in a chair and blankets. Though he did a reasonable job of guarding, there was a problem. Our crews began complaining that the Hercules hydraulic system wasn't functioning properly. In checking the system over, our mechanics discovered that the guard had been using the hydraulic tank for a urinal.

The Hercules hydraulic tank is in plain sight inside the airplane. It has a spout protruding out with a cap on it. Apparently our guard thought this was a receptacle to be used. Consequently, our hydraulic fluid became pretty badly diluted. We had to drain out all the hydraulic fluid and put in a new supply. After that, the system functioned normally.

In addition to the beef available to us in Botswana, there was a good supply of meat available in Swaziland as well. This was at an abattoir situated at Matsapha, 50 miles east of the capital city of Mbabane. The Zambian meat board notified us that they could purchase this beef at a very attractive price and wanted to know if we could start flying meat from Swaziland to Zambia.

Aviation officials in Zambia warned me, however, that if we undertook such flights, we'd have to fly around, not over, South Africa.

"There's no way you're going to get permission to fly over South Africa," a Zambian official cautioned me. "The South African military people are very strict."

Flying that circuitous route instead of cutting directly across South Africa wouldn't be economical. I decided to go to the South African capital, Pretoria, and plead my case.

I was granted a meeting with top officers of the South African Air Force. I explained to these officers that we were in a holding position in Alaska waiting for a pipeline permit to be issued. I told them when that happened, we were going to need a lot of airlift capability and perhaps we could lease one or more Hercules from their fleet. They possessed many more Hercs than they needed, so were quite receptive to that idea and began to soften up.

The outcome was that they gave us permission to fly directly across South Africa provided we notified their command ahead of time concerning each trip and the approximate time it would be flying over their territory. This was no problem since we had good radio and phone communications with Pretoria.

When the Alaska pipeline permit was finally issued, we leased two of the SAFAIR Hercules and ultimately bought them.

Flying the "meat flights" into and out of Swaziland presented no major political or regulatory problems, and the flights went well. It was not unusual during this African operation to be offered cargos that we could not accept because of our prior commitment to supply the Zambian government with meat during the emergency. We did, however, transport several loads of cotton and paper from Swaziland to Kenya.

Hauling meat presented no loading and unloading problems — multiple helpers made it quick and easy. Moving mining equipment was a different story. Mining equipment flights required us to assign station managers to Francistown for loading and to Ndola, Zambia, where much of this equipment was off-loaded. Great skill is required for this intricate job. Cargo has to be positioned and secured properly. Weight and balance have to be computed within limits to make it a safe flight operation.

At Francistown, Gary White took over, doing a superb job of organizing the loading crew. He saw to it that cargo was on the loading skids and ready to be moved

Fred Brauch (center), manager of our African operation, is visited by Mr. and Mrs. Mike Stepovich. Mike was a company director and former governor of Alaska.

when the aircraft appeared.

Bill Stephens later replaced Gary White at Francistown. I witnessed first-hand the way Stephens worked. He handled his loading crew with the command of a veteran first sergeant, cracking the whip to the degree necessary to get the airplane loaded as swiftly as possible and thus cut turnaround time to a minimum. Though Stephens was tough, his loading crew liked him.

Spoiled rotten by America's and Europe's luxury hotels, Dot and I saw the other side of the coin when we registered at the Grand Hotel in Francistown. We had been visiting Bill Stephens and his family and decided to risk a night's stay in the community's only hotel. Our room with its two cots was like a miserable jail cell. We felt shut in by the four rough concrete walls. There were no windows. By morning the bedbugs had tattooed a perfect cross on my chest but, for some unknown reason, had stayed away from Dot. Never have we been happier to get out of a hotel room.

One hazard at the Francistown airport was the wild animals. They used the runway as a heating pad. The blacktop runway would heat up during the day, then cool off more slowly during the night than the unpaved ground surrounding it. Wild beasts weighing a ton or more would drift out of the wilderness and settle down on the tarmac. If an airplane had struck them, there would have been one hell of a crash.

We took measures. Just before one of our planes was due to land, we had a driver rush a vehicle up and down the runway honking the horn continuously to make sure the runway was clear of jungle denizens. The same procedure was always carried out just before takeoff. At Gabarone we performed the same maneuver. The hazard there was not animals but flocks of birds that enjoyed the warm tarmac.

With the African operation running smoothly, I was able to return to Alaska. Fred Brauch went down to supervise the overall African job, taking his family with him. He headquartered in Johannesburg which, of course, gave him a comfortable place to live and also made possible good communication with him.

On one trip to Botswana, Dot and I were approached by representatives of British Petroleum to see if we could fly a Hercules to an area where they had a diamond mine prospect. To get to the destination, way in the outback about three-quarters of the way between Gabarone and Maun, we rented a Cessna 172 from the Gabarone flying club.

Though flyable, this Cessna 172's engine was so worn that when I spun the prop by hand, it would turn two or three revolutions before the remaining feeble compression would stop it.

However, I was able to get it off the ground, so we flew it over to look at the proposed diamond-site airport. I found a passable landing spot, set the airplane down and we walked over the area. The ground was much too soft for safe Hercules operations, so I had to turn that proposal down.

We continued on to Maun and spent the night at a local resort there. While there, our attention was attracted by a meat sale going on. The meat market was nothing more than a shack with a counter in front and a door in the back.

The unsupermarket-like operation consisted of leading a steer right up to the back of the store, butchering it right there and cutting it up for immediate distribution to the customers clustered around the counter up front.

Because there was no refrigeration, this lightning-swift method of marketing meat took care of any possible spoilage problem.

While this unique kill-and-sell operation was proceeding, tremendous clouds of flies swarmed around the chunks of bloody, freshly-cut meat. It was not a sight to increase one's appetite.

From Maun, we flew straight across the jungle to the airport at Kazungula not far from Victoria Falls. While we were there, an Aero Commander flew in from Johannesburg. The crew came over to talk to us.

"Where'd you come from?" the pilot asked.

"We flew in from Maun," I told him.

"What route did you take?"

"We came direct," I said.

"You can't do that," the pilot said. "That's against the law down here. The country is too desolate, and if you went down you'd be out of luck. You're required to fly a route that will keep you closer to civilization."

Well, the terrible deed had already been done, against the law or not.

And though much of that route was far from civilization, this kind of shortcut had its advantages. Below, as we moved along, we could see thousands of wild animals. We got unforgettable glimpses of elephants, zebras, wildebeests and a number of animals we couldn't identify. ✛

CHAPTER 52

The Pipeline Permit At Last

Alaska International Air Chairman Jim Magoffin with the "Westwind" corporate jet.

When, at long last, permission came through on Jan. 23, 1974, to go ahead with the Trans-Alaska Pipeline — the most ambitious project ever undertaken by private enterprise anywhere in the world — the economic effect was explosive and overpowering. It was as if a great dam had burst suddenly after years of stagnation, producing a surging flood of activity, growth and development.

Our firm had been waiting in the wings for several long years for this unforgettable moment. Now, the accumulated power of our flying enterprise could take center stage at last.

Everything in Alaska's economy began to move, animated by this powerful development. Oil companies and pipeline builders got caught up in the most intense activity they had ever experienced in their history.

Armies of men and millions of tons of supplies began to converge on Alaska. The pipeline construction project, unique in American history, demanded and received hundreds of trucks, tractors, road-building vehicles and other items of heavy construction equipment.

At strategically located sites along the pipeline right-of-way, work began on the modern camps that would house and feed the ever-growing ranks of engineering and construction personnel. It was something the world had never seen before. This tremendous explosion of activity changed just about everything and everybody in the North.

Now, possessing a fleet of Hercules and other aircraft, we were more than ready to meet this unparalleled challenge. We also had been able to retain intact a group of highly trained pilots with years of experience in arctic and international flying. The proud ranks of these pilots, now set to begin the increasing crescendo of pipeline flying, consisted of the finest pilots in the world. Though I could write volumes about our pilots, I will just point out why they were undoubtedly the world's best.

First, most had come up through the ranks — single-engine bush pilots, then multi-engine co-pilots and finally airline captains.

Second, they could not only perform usual airline operations into controlled airports with good runways, they could fly over a marginal airstrip in the wilderness and judge its suitability for landing. They could also determine the amount of snow or ice on the runway, the strength of the crosswind, the hazards of fog or blowing snow and many other factors that demand judgment and brainwork as well as simple piloting. And last, they had experience flying in climates ranging from the North Pole to southern Africa and the Middle East, while most airline pilots fly the same routes day after day and year after year.

Everything that had happened to us before — our Sagwon development, our profitable international flying, our hiring of highly efficient pilots and mechanics — all seemed to fall into place now.

We rolled up our sleeves.

We searched for and found ways to bring greater efficiency to our Hercules operation. Inside our main hangar, we built a unique maintenance structure that allowed us to keep to an absolute minimum the amount of time these huge planes remained on the ground. The structure was designed in such a manner that as soon as a Hercules was towed into position, all four engines immediately became accessible to teams of mechanics comfortably positioned to perform instant maintenance and repair on these big whales of the sky.

The Hercules kept flying around the clock, giving a major boost to our aircraft utilization and our burgeoning company income.

We had to hire and train additional pilots, mechanics and support personnel as the tempo of pipeline construction kept increasing.

During one hectic flying period, we were assessed a hefty fine by the FAA on the grounds that our pilots had exceeded the allowable flying time. They also found that we were allowing them to fly without providing them with sufficient rest periods according to their regulations.

Our flying activity had expanded so dramatically that we enjoyed sufficient cash flow to allow us, without any sweat, to order an additional Hercules from Lockheed. That order brought us some tense moments.

Just before the scheduled delivery date, an aircraft broker called to ask us to sell him the aircraft, offering a substantial profit. We agreed to the deal but subsequently got a mild scare when we learned that the transaction was causing international reverberations and was being investigated by the U.S. State Department.

It turned out that the ultimate purchaser of the aircraft we had relinquished had been the highly unsavory Uganda dictator and tyrant, Idi Amin.

Partly because of Amin's atrocities and his generally obnoxious international behavior, U.S. law prohibited the sale of any item of military value to Uganda. Dealing through a broker, the crafty Amin was able to obtain the Hercules he wanted as his own private airplane. It was the plane he used later when he was finally forced to flee his country.

We did not know that the plane was going to Amin and were fully cleared of any wrong-doing. We had taken no part in the deal hatched between Amin and the broker.

It was during this explosive period of aviation growth that our company goofed badly in our unfortunate purchase of the Weaver Brothers truck line. We should have known better or, stated more properly, I should have known better.

Jim O'Sullivan (left), vice president of administration, and Robert C. "Bud" Marquiss, vice president and general manager of Weaver Bros.

Our purchase of Weaver Brothers was a prime example of how to fail in business: get into something you know absolutely nothing about, and in which you lack experience.

At first, however, it didn't look like such a bad idea. It was prompted by an original and innovative concept and we had a highly efficient gentleman to run the operation, Bud Marquiss. Our plan was to use a steady stream of Weaver Brothers trucks to haul heavy loads to the slope over the ice road. When unloaded, we planned to drive the trucks into the cargo holds of our empty, southbound Hercules aircraft. The trucks would be back in Fairbanks in just a little more than an hour, all ready to be loaded once again. In addition, this would spare the drivers the kidney-shattering two-day drive to Fairbanks over the rough, sometimes treacherous road. We would benefit by the substantial savings we made in drivers' pay and the wear and tear on our trucks.

It didn't work out that way at all. Although Bud Marquiss and his people did an outstanding job and the trucks did produce good revenue for a while, the purchase of Weaver Brothers turned out to be a classic business boner.

The plan that was supposed to speed up cargo movement and drastically cut our payroll costs gave us, instead, a whole series of horrendous headaches. At virtually every turn, we were thwarted by the Teamsters, who perhaps may have wanted to pay us back for their union's previous unsuccessful assault on our business.

Teamster drivers demanded a full day's pay for their one-hour flight back to Fairbanks. A bitter and potentially work-threatening squabble broke out between officials of the Anchorage and the Fairbanks offices of the union about which of the union's members were going to drive the trucks between the two cities.

Lon McDermott, president of Alaska International Construction, with sockeye salmon at Saltery Lake on Kodiak Island, Alaska.

The huge trucking operation spawned another nagging problem. It generated friction and hard feelings among some of our best flying customers, poisoning relationships that up until then had been positive and friendly.

Ron Bergt, a vice president, was given the job of straightening out the truck line mess. The job just about drove Ron and many of us crazy, swallowing up an absurd amount of executive time. It was like that from the start; problem after problem, headache after headache.

The Teamsters had us hogtied, and the whole thing kept festering until we put in motion what was unquestionably the best solution to this terrible mess. We got rid of the truck line lock, stock and barrel and were delighted to kiss the Teamsters goodbye.

Now, with that awful albatross removed from around our necks, we were able to move forward with fresh resolve, doing what we should have restricted ourselves to doing in the first place — *flying* cargo.

Jim Magoffin Jr., sons Brent and David, and Steve Rittenhouse have all they can lift. Halibut taken at Saltery Lake Lodge, Kodiak, Island.

Additional salt in the truck line wounds was the result of our leasing more land from the state, paving the entire area and constructing a modern truck operations and maintenance terminal. That hefty expenditure was money wasted, as was our premature attempt to computerize our accounting. At that time computers were bulky, heavy and required a dust-free, air-conditioned room. However, a bigger problem was obtaining and keeping competent operators. Why should they suffer the rigors of Fairbanks winters when they were in great demand in warmer climates? Though the computer material that was produced was timely and useful, our prudent decision was to return to conventional accounting. The computer experiment resulted in another wad of money down the drain.

I might add that, in sharp contrast to the ill-fated Weaver Brothers transaction, a somewhat similar purchase we made during this era worked out beautifully. In terms of the lasting benefits we enjoyed from it, it was probably one of the wisest business decisions we ever made.

We decided to purchase the Alaska Construction Division of the Alaska Interstate Co. of Texas. This brought us trucks, tractors and a whole array of heavy equipment. Lon McDermot, an experienced construction executive, headed our Alaska International construction division. What turned out to be the most rewarding item on the inventory of assets we acquired in that purchase was a parcel of 20 acres of patented land on Kodiak Island which, at first glance, seemed a peripheral, insignificant part of the purchase.

To get a look at what we had acquired on Kodiak Island, Jim O'Sullivan, assistant to the president, and I flew a Grumman Widgeon to the property. We landed on a beautiful fresh-water lake a little more than a mile long. It was situated about 100 feet above sea level and only a mile inland from the ocean.

The picturesque 20 acres we now owned were nestled along the southeast shore of the lake. The property included a lodge building, three cabins, a generator building and a boat with trailer. There was no other habitation on the lake.

The lodge building was in rough shape, its roof leaking badly from the onslaught of many seasons of rains so common in the Kodiak area.

But what was most delightful and intriguing about this beautiful, primitive Alaskan "Walden Pond," now that it was ours, was the hunting and fishing potential it offered.

A proliferation of deer tracks dappled stretches of the beach on our property. The fishing, we soon discovered, was superb in the sparkling clear lake, its beautiful inlets and the one large outlet flowing the short distance to the ocean. The lodge was previously named Saltery Lake Lodge by two big game guides who conducted hunting and fishing trips from that headquarters. They had been forced to sell the property when they encountered financial problems.

We continued to use the name: Saltery Lake Lodge. The outlet stream entered the Pacific Ocean at Saltery Cove, so named years earlier by the Russians who operated a fish salting plant at that location.

From the moment we laid eyes on it, this pristine, insulated-from-civilization outdoor paradise stole both my heart and Dot's.

In the years that followed, we improved the property substantially and found constant use for it. We used the lodge to entertain customers and business associates and to make possible memorable free vacations for our company's personnel. Our guests at the lodge included some of our directors, as well as friends from Flying Tigers, Alaska Airlines and officials of numerous oil companies and banks.

When a decision was made to sell the property, Dot and I elected to buy it from the company. To avoid possible criticism and to take into account the substantial improvements we had made, we paid double the value quoted on the original inventory.

Eventually, however, the responsibility of caring for Saltery became too big a burden for us. We leased the property to a group of Kodiak businessmen who now operate it commercially. It remains one of Alaska's most beautiful places, a perfect headquarters for hunters, fishermen and naturalists.

As I indicated earlier, unlike the terrible truck line fiasco, this was a purchase we never regretted.

It was a period during which we had far less time than we would have liked to enjoy Saltery. Our main concern was to keep our business humming. In this regard, our search for permanent operating authority remained an on-going project.

Buoyed by our growing cash flow both from the successful overseas operations and the stimulating effect of the recent issuance of the pipeline permit, we turned our attention to a move we felt might ensure our longevity. We thought a merger with Reeve Aleutian Airways just might be in the cards and felt it would be highly beneficial to both firms. At a time when we were showing handsome profits, Reeve possessed a priceless asset we lacked: a permanent federal certificate. Clearly the time had come to explore the possibility of merging the two companies for the good of both.

I met with Bob Reeve on Aug. 29, 1974, in his downtown Anchorage office, a meeting I continue to recall with some sadness.

I hadn't seen Bob in more than a year, and it was somewhat of a shock to see him in deteriorating health. Having experienced heart problems and practically blind in one eye, his former vigor and sharpness were diminished. I was sorry to find the exceptionally tough former glacier pilot, who pioneered Aleutian flying, now looking pale and much older.

The Reeve legend lived, however. He was still a very impressive person and a remarkable Alaskan. Tempered by many years of hard struggle, Reeve remained a man of rare courage and unquenchable determination. That was why I found it so painful to witness what happened next.

We had barely started our discussion when Reeve's No. 2 man, Bob Hanson, burst into the office. Hanson was terribly upset. He and Reeve clashed immediately and tangled in a shouting, heated argument as if I were not present. Both displayed unbridled anger. For me, this confrontation was terribly embarrassing. They were still at it hammer and tong as I quickly excused myself and departed.

I have thought often about the significance of that sad, emotional episode. The conclusion I reached was that Reeve probably had been trying to hang on too long.

The unpleasant episode in Reeve's office, oddly enough, had some very positive fallout for me. It got me thinking about my own situation in our firm and the possibility for deteriorating relationships if I hung around too long.

I saw the clash in Reeve's office as a kind of warning and came to the conclusion that I ought to arrange things so that nothing of the kind could happen in our firm. I

Bob Reeve, founder of Reeve Aleutian Airways, Inc. The pilot (and man) I admired above all others in Alaska. A true friend for more than 30 years.

now resolved that if the situation in our company would permit it, I would retire for good no later than age 65.

So I found myself thanking Bob Reeve once again. Even though our meeting, such as it was, to arrange a merger failed, it helped put me on the right path with regard to my own relationships with my company.

Bob Reeve gave Alaska a still-thriving airline serving Alaskans over a route nobody but Bob wanted in the early days of Alaskan aviation because it was so desolate and treacherous. The favors he bestowed and the support he gave our company over the years will always live in my memory.

So there was special sadness for me when Bob Reeve died in his sleep in Anchorage on Aug. 25, 1980 , at the age of 78. ✝

CHAPTER 53

To Africa Again

In the spring of 1977, I was contacted by Bob Weed, a good friend when we were students at Michigan Tech. After completing his mining engineering education, he compiled an impressive record as an officer in the U.S. Army Corps of Engineers, about which he wrote an interesting and revealing book, "In Time of War," describing his experiences in North Africa and other areas.

At the time of his phone call to me, he was the retired manager of Anaconda's copper mine at Cananea, Sonora in Mexico and was now doing consulting work as a mining engineer. In this phase of his career, a Japanese company hired him to check into their uranium prospect in Niger, a large, remote African territory with jungles, savannas and deserts.

Having worked with the Japanese engineers for quite some time, Weed concluded that the uranium mining operation was feasible. He told me that, to get it going, a large airlift would be required and wanted to know if we would be interested.

By that time, the heavy demand for airlift had subsided in Alaska and we had extra Hercules time available for such a project. Weed invited me down to discuss the details.

He met me in Tucson, and we set out by car for his hacienda at Cananea. When we crossed the border at Naco, Arizona, Weed nodded to the Mexican customs officer, jabbering with him in Spanish, and the officer waved us through immediately. This informal entry into a foreign country had me concerned because I had come prepared with the proper documents to be admitted into Mexico legally.

"Don't bother with that," Weed said.

At Cananea, Weed took me to his office, where he had maps of Niger and northern Africa spread out on tables. He explained in detail the proposed uranium operation and the problems confronting the Japanese.

"They're going to need a lot of machinery to get down to where the ore is," he said. "Once mining begins, they're going to have to fly the concentrated ore, a uranium oxide we call 'yellow cake', back out to its final refining destination. This concentrate is extremely valuable stuff, and they're going to want it moved just as fast as possible."

After I ran out of questions, Bob said, "Now, let's go hunting!"

"Gosh, Bob," I told him. "I don't have any hunting clothes with me. And what are we going to hunt?"

"We're going to hunt wild turkeys. I'll lend you some clothes and a gun."

He provided me with a 16-gauge Winchester Pump-Model 12 shotgun, some cowboy pants and a jacket. The boots were a different matter. Bob's foot size is 10 and mine is 12. It happened that another friend of his had been down hunting deer earlier and left his hunting boots, which fit me perfectly.

Weed's wife, Lydia, went along with us as we drove out to the mountains and set up our camp. Lydia did the cooking while Bob and I went out to bag some wild turkeys. We weren't successful in getting one on that trip, but while we were up in the mountains sweating away and trying to locate a gobbler, one waddled through the camp where Lydia was cooking, gobbling its head off. She could have shot the bird easily, but we were miles away with the only guns.

On our way back to Cananea, I asked Bob about the hunting season.

"Oh, hunting season is closed," he said.

"You mean to tell me we've been hunting out of season?"

"Yep."

"Well, who owns the land we were hunting on?"

"The Mexican government. This whole place is a federal game refuge."

That shook me. Here I was, an illegal alien, hunting out of season without a hunting license on a federal game refuge!

"If I'd been caught, they probably would have pitched me in jail and thrown away the key," I complained.

"Don't worry about it," he said, smiling. "When you know the ropes down here, you can manage those things okay."

Bob gave me the names of the American companies involved in the Niger uranium play. The largest of those interested were Standard Oil and Conoco. I figured that while I lined up this Japanese business, I might as well see what was available from the oil companies and subsequently met with them in their offices.

The Conoco manager in Denver briefed me thoroughly on that firm's plans. "We're not only going to mine uranium, we're going to farm flowers," he said. "One of our biggest underground problems at the mining site will be an incredible amount of water. We plan to pump millions of barrels of it from beneath the desert so we can proceed with mining. Instead of discarding all that water, we're going to use it for irrigation in a farm operation we're going to set up."

I was told that they would need several flights a week from Niger to London and Paris, as well as other points where the flowers could be sold. They had already surveyed the markets and received assurances they could sell all the flowers they produced.

The prospect for flying machinery, ore and flowers seemed excellent. To look into the matter further, I flew to Niger aboard a DC-10 operated by the French flying

company, UTA. During the flight, the crew
invited me up front. They made the flight enjoyable for me by explaining in good English
the operation of the aircraft and a lot about
their African routes.

Niger is a French-speaking country. I had
studied French in both high school and college and could understand it quite well, but
my conversing in French left a lot to be desired. In fact, my French instructor at VMI
told me several times I was the worst student
he had ever tried to teach to speak understand-
able French.

*Jim Magoffin with Japanese clients in Niger
testing the desert for Hercules operations.*

Hot, dry and dusty Niger in the northern part of Africa is a former French colony
larger than Texas and California combined.
Much of the country's territory is taken up by the Sahara Desert.

I was not impressed with the capital city of Niamey, where the only place I could
get a hotel room initially was at the horrible Moustache Hotel, a miserable dive. On
that sweltering hot night, I got up to my room to find that there was no air condition-
ing and the one window was closed. When I opened the window, there was no screen.

The next morning I observed that the walls were lined with blood-filled mosquitoes, and there was no question whose blood they were bloated with.

That day, I conferred with the U.S. Consul in Niamey, an intelligent, friendly
black man who phoned around and got me a room at the Grand Hotel, a more comfortable place to stay, though the food seemed terrible to a badly spoiled American.

Later, I met with officials of the Japanese mining company who arranged a flight
to take me and one of their engineers out to their mining prospect several hundred
miles away near a town named Arlit.

The French had been operating a producing uranium mine at Arlit for several
years. The Japanese concession was several miles south of the Arlit mines, as were the
concessions controlled by the American companies.

My main interest in conferring with the Japanese was to determine a location
where we could land a Hercules safely. Finding a long enough flat area was no problem because most of the country around there was flat. I had been concerned about
the ability of the ground to support the weight of a Hercules.

I was pleasantly surprised to discover that the Niger desert wasn't really desert as
I had envisioned it — all soft sand. Actually, the sand had small gravel and clay mixed

with it. Vehicles could run on top of it and hardly make a track.

I was driven to various places in a Toyota, and we dug test holes at several points. After the testing, there was no doubt in my mind that we could operate a Hercules safely very close to the area where they planned to mine.

On getting back to Niamey, I met with the people representing Conoco and Standard Oil and discussed the air operation with them.

Every aspect of the job seemed to be developing quite favorably. However, just two days later, Standard Oil phoned me and said that their home office had notified them of a sudden change of plans.

When I visited their office, I found they were packing up their office materials, preparing to move out of Niger.

It was explained to me that the change was prompted by discoveries of high-grade uranium ore in Canada. After studies, the home office had concluded that they could purchase Canadian uranium ore cheaper than they could mine it in Africa. The same situation applied to Conoco, so that part of the African operation did not materialize. As for the Japanese, while they didn't pull out immediately, their whole operation was put on hold.

I had been in Niger only a couple of days when I woke up one morning to find my pillow soaked with blood issuing from my nose. Getting medical help became a problem because the resident American medical technician in Niamey had gone back to the states on vacation, and the American consulate warned me against seeking medical help at the local hospital.

Though the problem with my nose was worrisome, there were things I had to do should the Japanese go ahead with their development of a mine. I had to find out where we could take on incoming cargo and off-load outgoing sealift cargo without flying all the way to Europe. I traveled to Togo, a hot tropical country in west Africa, and to Ghana, a country formerly known as the Gold Coast, to inspect airport and seaport facilities there.

While in Lome, Togo's capital, I located a nurse's aide at the U.S. Consulate. She examined me and informed me that the inner part of my nose had been attacked by a parasite that invades the upper lining of the nostrils. She advised me to get to a doctor as soon as possible.

After completing my work in Togo and Ghana, I returned to Anchorage, where Bob Heath, our vice president of finance, set up an appointment for me with his favorite doctor. Pills and a nose spray solved the problem.

When I was weighed in Anchorage, the scales showed I weighed 153 pounds. My normal weight is around 165. It was all part of the price one pays for traveling in the Dark Continent. ✝

CHAPTER 54

The Joys Of Deregulation

Company officers and directors: (from the left) Kenneth Weaver, chairman of the board, Weaver Bros., Inc.; John C. Sackett; Neil G. Bergt; James S. Magoffin; Roy L. Isackson; George M. Sullivan; Jerry L. Church; Mike Stepovich. Dick Roberts and Bob Heath are not pictured.

Though years overdue, deregulation of the U.S. airline industry in 1978 was an exceedingly welcome development for our closely regulated company.

At last we had the authority that we had struggled to obtain for years. Under the new, less stringent national policy, we were provided with sufficient authority to do pretty much what we wished.

At about the time we were beginning to enjoy the fruits of deregulation, Wien Airlines, a pioneering firm rooted deep in Alaska's aviation history, was having serious labor and financial problems.

These difficulties proved too pervasive and the firm ultimately had to suspend operations. Fortunately, our good friend and former employee, Ralph Brumbaugh, had recently retired as Wien's vice president of operations and maintenance. He agreed to come back to work for our company and was soon named president and chief operating officer.

Ralph was unusually well qualified to fill this position as he had gained much experience during the many years he worked for both Interior Airways and for Wien.

He knew the routes, the equipment that was needed and the caliber of the personnel in both companies. He did his usual efficient job of setting up an operation for us that would include both scheduled passenger and cargo services.

Although the demise of Wien Airlines offered a tempting opportunity, I was not enthusiastic about returning to the passenger-carrying business. I felt far more comfortable with cargo operation after the many years we'd devoted to it.

There are aspects of flying passengers that are far more complex than an exclusively cargo business, including the number and variety of employees, the many services required and the increased liability. Our concentration on cargo in the past had given us special know-how and a firm command of tasks associated with air cargo on a global basis. And finally, we had the requisite equipment to be able to take advantage of cargo airlift opportunities virtually anywhere in the world. There continue to be many such opportunities in Africa and other troubled areas.

Even so, the opportunity to jump into the passenger airline business in the fresh atmosphere of deregulation offered a new challenge. The company sold some Hercules, acquired some Boeing 737 jets and initiated passenger service while continuing limited cargo operations.

Deregulation brought the assurance that our 30-year battle for existence was over at last. No longer were there continuing annual crises. No longer were we subject to the unprovoked onslaughts by the "fuz" and the "blue ribbon" inspection teams. In the bracing new environment it was possible, at last, to plan on a long-range basis instead of year to year. And deregulation made it easier for bankers to look with more favor when credit was needed by aviation people.

The new environment gave refreshing solidity to scheduled air operations in Alaska. No longer was it necessary for us to solicit flying contracts in distant parts of the globe. And no longer was there a crying need for me to further neglect my health and my family.

All in all, deregulation has been a boon to Alaska. And what a difference it would have made to us if it had taken place during those years when we were struggling so desperately to survive and ran into bureaucratic roadblocks at every turn. ✝

CHAPTER 55

Accidents, Thrills And Observations

I have been asked, "What was your most terrifying experience?" The answer is easy and has nothing to do with spectacular crashes in the Alaskan wilderness or bush pilot adventures. My most frightening experience by far was on the Los Angeles freeway. Nothing that ever happened to me in the air rivals it.

To set the stage for that nightmarish event, Texaco was planning to dispatch, in the early '60s, two geology parties to conduct studies on the North Slope. They asked me to come to Los Angeles to negotiate a contract for air support. They needed to have two Grumman Widgeons available to fly mail and supplies to their people and to bring back rock samples for air shipment to Los Angeles.

My meeting with the Texaco people in downtown L.A. was fairly routine, though it involved one incident that few aircraft operators experience.

After operational aspects of the job were thoroughly discussed, the actual written agreement that I had drafted was turned over to one of Texaco's contract specialists, a Mr. Gilbert.

As Gilbert reviewed the contract, he came to the clause quoting our normal charter rate. What he said then was the kind of statement I had never before heard in contract discussions.

"You're quoting a reasonable rate," he told me, "and it's certainly acceptable. However, on this job we're going to require *special* air service. We'll add $10 per hour to the charter rate you quote, providing you give our Texaco crews priority service over your other customers."

I was delighted, of course, and we provided Texaco with super-service on that job.

All in all it was a very pleasant and rewarding meeting. What was terrifying was getting there.

When I got to the L.A. airport on that trip, a Texaco geologist was waiting for me and proceeded to drive me to their downtown headquarters in a tiny Volkswagen.

As we proceeded along the traffic-choked, multi-laned freeway, for one of the few times in my life I felt the paralysis of fear.

Alongside us, so close I could touch them, were the huge whirling tires of a giant truck barreling down the freeway at a ridiculously high rate of speed. I was petrified. A single swerve, a moment's inattention on the part of the truck driver, and we'd be crushed in an instant under those fast-spinning wheels. The terror I felt then was never

Fontana Aviation's "Cardinal." Designed by Glenn Curtis, manufactured by St. Louis Aircraft Co. Shown here with engine cowling in place.

matched by anything I'd ever felt while flying an aircraft. I suppose people who drive the L.A. freeways in Volkswagens get used to this kind of menace. I don't think a safety-minded bush pilot ever would.

Nevertheless, my flying experience did include a few momentary thrills, but no serious fright. One memorable event occurred on a cold fall day when I was following the Mississippi River beneath a blanket of treetop-high stratus clouds. I was on a trip from Brainerd to Rochester, Minnesota, flying a Waco RNF biplane and was carefully making every turn of the river. Suddenly, the air just in front of the plane was peppered with more than 30 pairs of flapping wings. I had run smack into a flock of migrating Canada geese moving along at my altitude. Neither I nor the geese had time to turn. Some seemed to disperse between the wings. Luckily, none of them smashed into the windshield, the prop or the flying wires, but I've never forgotten those geese.

Another time, I was landing a Meyers OTW at LaCrosse, Wisconsin, after dark. The airport then was just a north-south grass strip intersecting an east-west grass strip. There were no lights and no terminal, of course, just an old barn off the runway intersection.

I'd arrived later than I should have and darkness had set in. The faint outlines of the grass strips were still visible but that was about all I could see.

I managed to land okay and rolled to a stop near the runway intersection. As I

Fontana's Meyers OTW, used for advanced training.

turned the plane sideways so I could see where to taxi, I spotted a horse standing less than 100 feet in front of me. That gave me a chill. If the plane had rolled just a little farther after landing, there would have been one bashed-up airplane and one dead horse.

Startling things can happen to spoil your whole flying day. On one black night I was northbound to Milwaukee flying a Cardinal, a plane manufactured by the St. Louis Aircraft Co. I'd followed the lighted airway from Chicago. This was my first night flight in the Cardinal, and it provided me with a surprise on landing.

The plane's 85-horsepower Lebonde radial engine had no exhaust collector ring, and the aesthetic cowling had been removed, exposing the short stacks protruding from the cylinder heads. In daylight, the plane's exhaust was invisible. With cruise power at night, however, a short blue flame was produced.

When I closed the throttle on final approach, the spouting blue flame turned a dazzling orange, shooting out about a foot and practically blinding me. I had to feel gingerly for the ground on that landing but managed to make it okay.

Accidents are the bane of all operators of moving equipment. Our experience has shown that about 5 percent of our pilots caused 95 percent of the accidents. Aside from possible loss of life or serious injury, accidents can seriously disrupt a business. They destroy badly needed equipment, send insurance rates soaring and the expense

The Waco RNF, owned by Mario Fontana. We used this plane for aerobatics and cross-country training. 1939-40.

of salvage and repair can be devastating. A safe airline operation may be profitable even when business is slack, but a few mishaps can start the red ink flowing.

The most painful accident is the one you see taking place but can do absolutely nothing to prevent. This happened to Ralph Brumbaugh and me one day while flying over the North Slope.

We had just finished unloading our DC-3 at Oliktok and were climbing southbound to return to Fairbanks.

We were at 5,000 feet on a beautiful, clear March day when we witnessed an accident about to happen. We observed one of our C-46s circling Lake Edna (so named by Lloyd Logan, the party chief for Western Geophysical) for a landing. Except on rare occasions, the Alaska Arctic Coast wind is either from the northeast or the southwest. The newly arrived seismic company's bulldozer operator was apparently unaware of this crucial fact. He had dozed a northwest-southeast runway, making it exactly cross-wind. When apprised of his mistake, he dozed out a proper runway, aligning it with the prevailing wind. The first strip was allowed to fill in with snowdrifts up to four feet high.

Brumbaugh and I watched with dread as the Interior Airways C-46 flew over the good strip from southwest to northeast, then circled to the left. Instead of making a wide, 360-degree turn, the pilot cut it short at 270 degrees and began approaching the unusable southeast strip. Both of us hollered into our microphones: "Don't land there!" There was no response.

We watched in disbelief as the heavily loaded plane settled down and began plowing into the deep drifts. Swallow-tails of hard-packed snow began spouting along both sides of the fuselage and over the tail surfaces. When the snow settled, we were relieved to see that the plane was right-side up and standing on all three landing gears.

We descended quickly, landed and surveyed the damage. It was minor and, after removal of a damaged elevator skin, the plane was flown back to Fairbanks where the elevators and dented flaps could be replaced and the plane could be thoroughly inspected. Few airplanes other than the rugged C-46 could withstand such treatment and live to fly again.

I couldn't believe the terrible "slopover" I had just witnessed. How a qualified airline captain could do such a thing is still a mystery to me.

A few days later, the same pilot was involved in another mishap at Bud Helmericks' airstrip at the mouth of the Colville River. The poor guy was miserable after the Colville River mishap.

"Damn it," he said, feeling real anguish, "It looks like I'm the one that's involved in every accident this company has! I feel I should resign!"

I talked him out of it since he had joined us at a time we were desperate for pilots during the Teamster strike, had done much good work for the company and was popular with our customers. I thought he had earned another chance.

Now as we fly to many parts of Alaska, Canada and the lower United States, we enjoy a wealth of good communications and navigational aids that make for safe air travel. Our airways are blessed with a network of VORs, ILS, radar and other boons to the pilot. Weather reporting is vastly improved, and good, modern airports are the rule rather than the exception.

In the cockpit, the pilot is assisted by an array of electronic servants: ADF, OMNI, LORAN, DME (distance measuring equipment) and Global Positioning Receivers.

Other products of modern science have made flying much safer and far more enjoyable than in the past. We don't miss the old directional radio ranges and the lighted airways that we depended on 50 years ago, or the helmets, goggles and gosports that were a nuisance. The "good old days" are fine to remember, but the "good new days" are profoundly better.

The modern flying environment is one that opens great, new vistas to pilots. Beautiful areas of Alaska and the Canadian North still remain to be visited by us and we intend to see them.

We're going to be up there enjoying modern flying so long as we can pass the flight tests and the physical exams.

It has been a real privilege for us to be witness to those matchless years of growth and development in Alaska. We have experienced some hungry times and one major setback, but feel proud of the fact that we never conceded defeat.

Much of what was accomplished seems incredible now. It seems inconceivable that a business that began in 1946 with one 65-horsepower, piston-engine aircraft capable of carrying only one passenger, 12 gallons of fuel and restricted to a range of 300 miles could have blossomed so spectacularly over the tumultuous years.

That horse-and-buggy kind of operation developed gradually into one of the world's finest aviation enterprises. Our one miserable little aircraft was transformed by the years into a mighty fleet almost unimaginable in its power and capacity. Millions of tons of cargo were carried in our giant Hercules aircraft powered by four 4,508-horsepower turbine engines, having a fuel capacity of 9,667 gallons, a range of 4,550 nautical miles and a payload of 50,861 pounds. What a change a half-century makes!

Our pilot group expanded from a single pilot in 1946 to 62 in 1977, with an accompanying increase in support personnel. To this day, the company founded on a dream and one little ancient aircraft continues to grow.

It is a business that has contributed directly to Alaska's growth and development. It was one of the strong right arms that helped bring a new source of oil to America and the world. It continues to be a major business employing hundreds of people throughout Alaska and the lower United States.

Scheduled operations and the use of planes equipped with the latest in electronics and a fine network of navigational aids on the ground have helped reduce accidents. It also helps that our pilots are no longer using river bars, ocean beaches and barren hilltops as airports — at least not to the same degree as in the past.

Despite all this, accidents still occur. An example is the foolish loss of a valuable Boeing 737 in June of 1990 because the pilot failed to execute the prescribed approach at Unalakleet. However, considering the hours and miles flown, the accident rate has diminished and should continue to show improvement. ☩

CHAPTER 56

Retirement

Alabama turkeys are big — and unbelievably smart.

Retirement in 1982 at age 65 didn't include holding down a couple of easy chairs. Still very active pilots, we have continued to enjoy Alaska, Canada and the lower states.

We appreciate the beauty of Kodiak Island in the summer with its fabulous fishing and hunting and, of course, spending time near our family in Fairbanks where we maintain our home.

But in the fall, a flock of geese heading south might be accompanied by a small twin-engine flying boat, the Widgeon. That has always been my favorite airplane of more than 60 different types and models I have flown.

We've made it a habit to fly the Grumman Widgeon south every year during the fall migration of ducks and geese, and when they head north in the spring, we're also in the same flight pattern.

The flight south includes stops at Grande Prairie and Brooks, Alberta. Here we spend a few days visiting with the Hutterites and farm families in the area where we hunt ducks and geese. These friendly and hospitable people have become our true and valued friends.

A social and hunting stop at Aberdeen, South Dakota, is also an annual ritual. We greatly appreciate the kindness shown us by these enterprising, hard-working, farm-belt friends, some of whom have favored us with visits to Alaska. Our brief hunts in the Aberdeen area never fail to add a few pheasants and grouse to our winter menus.

Alaska is still our home and always will be, but the severe winter weather has forced us to seek a warmer climate elsewhere.

Much of the winter is spent in Ashland, Alabama, where Dot grew up. We find that the sporting opportunities the state has to offer are incentives to stay active forever.

Alabama is a beautiful state with rugged hills and huge lakes. It has an abundance of deer, wild turkeys and fish.

Further, we have developed a whole new cadre of friends —different from

Alaska is fine in the summer, but Alabama is our wintertime choice. Dot with Lulu and Mixie in Alabama, March 1992.

Alaskans only to the extent dictated by warmer climate and geography. Most are basically honest, helpful country folks. They have accepted us in their way of life and have been most generous in teaching us how to hunt the unbelievably elusive wild turkeys. They have included us in their recreational activities and provided the needed "tips" on locating the schools of delicious bass, bream and crappies in the many Alabama lakes.

New activities for Dot include watercolor painting, clogging and golfing on golf courses with real grass greens instead of the rolled sand ones we struggled with in Fairbanks.

Now our time is not consumed by commercial piloting, executive travel and meetings with employees, customers, attorneys and accountants. We are able to share our many years of good luck with others who have been less fortunate. Charitable activities, formerly neglected because we were too busy to become involved, can now be pursued.

Had we given in to the Civil Aeronautics Board's order to "cease and desist" 46 years ago, there would have been no Interior Enterprises, Inc., Alaska International Industries, Interior Airways, Alaska International Air or MarkAir. The names may change, but the history remains the same.

We're glad we didn't give up.

Would we attempt to do it all over again?

No! Next time we might not be so lucky. ⊥

Index

The Perfect Gift For

Pilots-Sportsmen-Businessmen

"TRIUMPH OVER TURBULENCE"

AUTHOR: Jim Magoffin

ALASKA'S LUCKIEST BUSH PILOT

ORDER FROM: BOOKWORLD SERVICES, INC.
1933 WHITFIELD LOOP
SARASOTA, FLORIDA 34243

PHONE: 800-444-2524 Ext. 416
FAX: 800-777-2525

Price: $29.95 U.S. plus $3.95 shipping